The Power of Transformation

The Power of Transformation

Re-imagining the Parables of Jesus

Nélida Naveros Córdova, CDP

Paulist Press
New York / Mahwah, NJ

Scripture quotations are from New Revised Standard Version of the Bible, copyright © 1989 Division of Christian Education of the National Council of the Churches of Christ in the United States of America. Used by permission. All rights reserved worldwide.

Cover image by Barbaradin / Dreamstime.com
Cover design by Sharyn Banks
Book design by Lynn Else

Copyright © 2024 by Nélida Naveros Córdova

All rights reserved. No part of this publication may be reproduced, stored in a retrieval system, or transmitted in any form or by any means, electronic, mechanical, photocopying, recording, scanning, or otherwise, without either the prior written permission of the Publisher, or authorization through payment of the appropriate per-copy fee to the Copyright Clearance Center, Inc., www.copyright.com. Requests to the Publisher for permission should be addressed to the Permissions Department, Paulist Press, permissions@paulistpress.com.

Library of Congress Cataloging-in-Publication Data
Names: Córdova, Nélida Naveros, author.
Title: The power of transformation: re-imagining the parables of Jesus / Nélida Naveros Córdova, CDP.
Description: New York, Mahwah, NJ: Paulist Press, [2024] | Includes bibliographical references. | Summary: "This book uses the virtue ethics of ancient Greek philosophers and the Greek rhetorical tools of the progymnasmata, or preliminary exercises for prose composition, to read and interpret selected parables of Jesus by elucidating the vivid language and the virtues reflected in each parable"—Provided by publisher.
Identifiers: LCCN 2023049404 (print) | LCCN 2023049405 (ebook) | ISBN 9780809156399 (paperback) | ISBN 9780809188024 (ebook)
Subjects: LCSH: Jesus—Parables.
Classification: LCC BT375.3 .C65 2024 (print) | LCC BT375.3 (ebook) | DDC 226.8/06—dc23/eng/20240321
LC record available at https://lccn.loc.gov/2023049404
LC ebook record available at https://lccn.loc.gov/2023049405

ISBN 978-0-8091-5639-9 (paperback)
ISBN 978-0-8091-8802-4 (e-book)

Published by Paulist Press
997 Macarthur Boulevard
Mahwah, New Jersey 07430
www.paulistpress.com

Printed and bound in the
United States of America

To Sister Myra Rodgers and Sister Inesita Vélez
In gratitude for their unconditional support in my
religious vocation and scholarly career

Contents

Abbreviations ix

Introduction: The Quest for Happiness 1

Chapter 1. Knowing and Understanding Jesus's Parables 9

Chapter 2. Internalizing Jesus's Message in the Parables 34

Chapter 3. Wrestling within the Human Heart: Growth in Virtue 66

Chapter 4. Transformation and Happiness in Virtue 99

Chapter 5. Conclusion 129

Notes 135

Glossary 163

Bibliography 165

Abbreviations

Aphthonius
    Prog.   *Progymnasmata*
Aristotle
    Eth. eud.   *Ethica eudemia* (Eudemian Ethics)
    Eth. nic.   *Ethica nicomachea* (Nicomachean Ethics)
    Poet.   *Poetics*
    Rhet.   *Rhetorica* (Rhetoric)
BCE   Before Common Era
Bib   *Biblica*
BibInt   *Biblical Interpretation*
BR   *Biblical Research*
CBQ   *Catholic Biblical Quarterly*
CBQMS   Catholic Biblical Quarterly Monograph Series
CE   Common Era
Cicero
    Part. or.   *Partitiones oratoriae*
    Inv.   *De inventione rhetorica*
    Verr.   *In Verrem*
CTR   *Criswell Theological Review*
CurTM   *Currents in Theology and Mission*
Demetrius
    Eloc.   *De elocutione* (Style)
Demosthenes
    Fals. leg.   *De falsa legatione* (False Embassy)
Hermogenes
    Prog.   *Progymnasmata*
HvTSt   *Hervormde Teologiese Studies*
Int   *Interpretation*
JBL   *Journal of Biblical Literature*

JETS	*Journal of the Evangelical Theological Society*
Josephus	
A. J.	*Antiquitates judaicae* (Jewish Antiquities)
War	*Jewish War*
JP	*Journal for Preachers*
JRH	*Journal of Religious History*
JSNT	*Journal for the Study of the New Testament*
Longinus	
Subl.	*De sublimitate* (On the Sublime)
LXX	Septuagint, the Greek Jewish Scripture
m. B. Bat	Mishnah Baba Batra (Bava Batra)
m. Bek.	Mishnah Bekorot (Bekhorot)
Nicolaus	
Prog.	*Progymnasmata*
NovT	*Novum Testamentum*
NT	New Testament
NTS	*New Testament Studies*
OT	Old Testament
Ovid	
Metam.	*Metamorphoses*
Philostratus	
Vit. Apoll.	*Vita Apollonii*
Plato	
Apol.	*Apologia* (Apology of Socrates)
Euthyphr.	*Euthyphro*
Leg.	*Leges* (Laws)
Min.	*Minos* (Meno)
Prot.	*Protagoras*
Resp.	*Respublica* (Republic)
Theaet.	*Theaetetus*
Plutarch	
Art.	*Artaxerxes*
Mor.	*Moralia*
Virt. mor.	*De virtute moralia*
Fort.	*De fortuna*
PRSt	*Perspectives in Religious Studies*
Quintilian	
Inst.	*Institutio oratoria*

Abbreviations

ResQ	*Restoration Quarterly*
RevExp	*Review and Expositor*
Stobaeus	
Ecl.	*Eclogae*
SVF	*Stoicorum veterum fragmenta*
Theon	
Prog.	*Progymnasmata*
USQR	*Union Seminary Quarterly Review*
WUNT	Wissenschaftliche Untersuchungen zum Neuen Testament
y. Ber.	Babylonian Talmud Berakhot

INTRODUCTION

THE QUEST FOR HAPPINESS

As human beings we strive for happiness. It is the goal (*telos*) inherent in our human nature. But how do we answer the question, what is happiness? The ancient Greek philosopher Plato (ca. 429 BCE–347 BCE) provides a definition of happiness (*eudaimonia*) by stating that to achieve happiness is ultimately to "become like to God" or "likeness to God" (*homoiōsis theō*).[1] In his ethical system, the practice of virtues, particularly the four cardinal virtues—prudence, justice, courage, and temperance[2]—motivates human beings to have high moral standards in order to live freely from all hindrances and vices.[3] Plato's way of defining happiness can enlighten our understanding of the ethical values of Jesus's parables. Furthermore, studying the parables of Jesus within the understanding of the virtues in ancient Greek philosophical systems and ancient Greek rhetoric can give Jesus's messages in the parables greater clarity.

This present work takes a fresh literary approach that elucidates the vivid language and the virtues reflected in each of the selected parables of Jesus.[4] In this way, the parables speak for themselves and guide modern readers to a greater understanding of Jesus's parables. While the book is sophisticated enough to entice professional biblical scholars, I also want to make the parables comprehensible to a more general, educated audience and to lead them to appreciate the parables as an invitation to a higher ethical stance.

This book illustrates how Jesus's parables can incite a transformative experience in the modern reader through a provocative interpretation. Jesus's parables when assimilated as lessons and/or experiences inspire change or cause a shift in the human point of view. Reading Jesus's parables, then, is the beginning of a *transformative* encounter with the self. This new approach in the traditions of both Greek philosophical ethical systems and Greek rhetoric has as its goal the persuasion of speech, inducing the reader to practice virtues and avoid vices. From the Christian locus, however, this would go in line with the search for holiness on the way toward the kingdom of God or salvation. Biblical scholars have rightly pointed out that Jesus used parables as his teaching device; from the Synoptic Gospels (Mark, Matthew, and Luke) we know that he taught about God and the kingdom of God in parables.[5]

The evangelists used Jesus's parables for their own purposes. For Mark, the parables had an eschatological significance in a community that lived between the resurrection and Jesus's return. For Matthew, the parables were a form of exhortation that challenged Christians to live ethically; for Luke, the parables depicted the everyday lives of ordinary people at the time when they were adapting their lives to the challenges and demands of Christian life.[6]

In this book, I present the parables of Jesus as a spiritual guide for readers to cultivate spiritual development. In the Gospel parables, readers can learn the basic teachings to achieve holiness; yet they are also able to obtain fundamental knowledge of God and the qualities of virtue that God possesses in God's divine nature, and the reciprocal relationship between God and human beings as well as human beings with one another. In Jesus's parables, human beings encounter *a higher, virtuous level of understanding of Jesus's teachings*. While Lohfink defines the parables as "diamonds,"[7] I say they are a "bubbling fountain" of virtues from which the best lessons about human life in its various relationships derive. Jesus's parables point us on the path to the cultivation of virtues and the experience of true happiness—a greater likeness to God. In our time and at all levels of encounters and experiences—personal, at home with family, at work with colleagues, at church with parishioners, and the like—the parables of Jesus still speak powerfully. They help us strive for a deeper and longer-lasting spiritual transformation in the way we are called to live and practice virtue. During his public ministry, Jesus taught his followers and disciples with parables. In the scholarly world of New Testament study, pivotal questions remain regarding Jesus's parables, such as the number of parables in the canonical Gospels, the literary nature of some of the parables, and the originality of the parables. Different opinions among biblical scholars have led to a plethora of definitions of the term *parable* and to various interpretations of Jesus's parables. Although these are important topics, this book does not intend to engage in these controversial issues; the views and interpretations of most biblical scholars will be respectfully reflected throughout this book. Therefore, as a way of introducing this book and preparing the reader for the coming chapters, I will provide the definition(s) of the word *parable* in the context of the canonical Gospels, enumerate the major turning points in the study of Jesus's parables, and briefly describe the Greek rhetorical techniques employed in this book.

Defining a Parable

The best definition of Jesus's parables, apropos of this study, comes from Klyne R. Snodgrass. In his extensive research in *Stories with Intent: A Comprehensive Guide to the Parables of Jesus*, Snodgrass defines a *parable* as "an expanded analogy used to convince and persuade."[8] The English word itself derives from the Greek word *parabolē*, which means "comparison." It is rendered *mashal* in the Hebrew Scripture.[9] Scholars have pointed out various meanings of *mashal*, such as riddle, fable, mocking by word, allegory, parallelism, oracle, proverb, wise saying, maxim, figurative speech, simile, similitude, metaphor, taunt, example story, and parable.[10] The Hebrew word *mashal* could also be translated as "synonym" or "comparative word,"[11] which leads us to the definition of "expanded analogy."[12] This definition is seen clearly when looking at a parable as a figure of speech in which a comparison is made (e.g., "it is like," "may be compared to," "to what shall I compare?") between God's affairs and something real or imagined in the world.[13] In the rabbinic tradition, parables had a two-fold structure: the narrative part or the *mashal* proper, and the instruction or the *nimshal*.[14] The *mashal* is the *comparison*, often identified as an ordinary account with a simple plot, using archetypal figures and situations in life, and artificially constructed. The *nimshal* is the *object* of the parable, usually introduced by the phrase "in a similar way" and often containing a biblical quotation and/or rabbinical expression to give an authoritative explanation of the Torah.[15]

A Brief History of Research on Jesus's Parables

The variety of translations of the Hebrew word *mashal* and the Greek word *parabolē* have led modern biblical scholars to offer a wide range of different approaches and interpretations of Jesus's parables.[16]

The scholar who is considered the pioneer in modern studies of Jesus's parables is the German Adolf Jülicher (1899).[17] Although most of his arguments today have been challenged, his valuable contribution became a turning point. Jülicher opened a new era of research; he raised and addressed the question, what is to be interpreted in Jesus's parables? As the pioneer of historical approaches, Jülicher rejected the allegorical elements in the parables of Jesus, arguing that allegory was too complex for Jesus. The German scholar claimed that Jesus's parables illuminate a single point: a rule, an idea, an experience that is "valid on the spiritual as on the secular level."[18] In other words, Jesus's parables "were simple stories of comparisons, which were self-evident and *did not need interpretation*" (italics original).[19]

The major scholars who have dominated the interpretation of the parables of Jesus since Jülicher have focused on different areas of studies. For example, A. T. Cadoux studied the original setting and meaning of Jesus's parables in the context of his *public ministry*.[20] Similarly, C. H. Dodd emphasized the intention of the parables in the historical context and interpreted the parables as simple metaphors or similes drawn from nature and common life, engaging the audience with their vividness. Dodd, who substantially advanced the study of parables, believed that he could rediscover the original meaning of the parables by reconstructing their original "setting in life" or *Sitz im Leben*.[21] Since the 1950s and 1960s, biblical scholars have particularly investigated three aspects of Jesus's use of parables. First, they have reconstructed the likely version of the parables as Jesus told his audience; scholars have been influenced by the different needs of the early Christian communities for whom the evangelists were writing—instructive, apologetic, and polemic. Second, these scholars have reconstructed the likely setting in which Jesus told the parables by building on insights and drawing from tradition criticism as well as redaction criticism. Third, they have paid particular attention to the presentation of Jesus's parables, both their style and meaning, by focusing on the parables as metaphors and narratives. This approach has served to stimulate the audience's imagination in order to draw them into the parable's situation, causing hearers to reflect on the parable's experience and their own situations.[22] Joachim Jeremias further developed Dodd's approach and intended to recover Jesus's original meaning by studying the parables in the setting of the life of Jesus.[23] Interestingly, Jeremias claimed that Jesus was the first Jewish teacher to use parables, thus causing a polarization between the rabbinic parables and the parabolic teaching of Jesus.[24] Jeremias also argued that the parables of Jesus must be understood in connection with his message about the imminent eschatological crisis presented in his public ministry.[25]

Other scholars have studied the parables in light of the sociocultural setting within their political function. Two major contributions in this area are William R. Herzog II and Luise Schottroff.[26] Herzog's analysis focused on the framework of a sociohistorical and sociological analysis of the parables' context. He asked a key question: "How do the social scenes and social scripts of the parables disclose and explore the larger social, political, economic, and ideological systems of Palestine during the time of Jesus?"[27] According to Herzog, the parables are designed to communicate primarily social analysis and to expose the contradictions between the actual situation of its hearers and the Torah of God's justice.[28] Along the same line, Schottroff explored the "eschatological interpretation," which disclosed the liberating message of Jesus, a message that reflected the real-life circumstances of its hearers and that had the power to change the hearers.[29]

Robert W. Funk and Dan Otto Via applied a literary approach to Jesus's parables.[30] Funk, who was followed by John Dominic Crossan and Norman Perrin, who interpreted the parables as poetic metaphor,[31] studied the parables as metaphors and argued that the parables lay "bare the structure of human existence that is masked by convention, custom, consensus, [to] expose the 'world'" in which a person is enmeshed.[32] Warren Carter and John Paul Heil noted the emphasis in Jesus's parables is on what they *do* to his audience.[33] Funk examined the parables as poetic forms where a deep appreciation of metaphor opened the way to new understandings of the literary and theological importance.[34] Along the same line, Via focused on the aesthetic objects in the parables (e.g., exaggerations, surprises, twists, numbers, contrasts, open-ended stories, and unexpected endings) in light of the historical-literary criticism, literary-existential analysis, and existential-theological interpretation. His approach challenged previous understandings by creating new possibilities to explore Jesus's parables.[35] Scholars such as Jack D. Kingsbury, John Drury, and John R. Donahue tackled the understanding of the parables as they appear in each of the Gospels.[36] They argued—against Funk, Via, and Crossan—that to go behind the books (Gospels) is always speculative, and to recreate an original setting within the public ministry of Jesus and an original form of a parable is always hypothetical. In their arguments they emphasized the parables within the texts at hand, as they have come to readers today, and the analysis of them in their canonical texts is more surefooted than alternatives.[37]

Rhetorical Tools Used in This Study

In ancient Greece, rhetoric was the art of a public speaker, or rhetor. Handbooks of rhetoric were studied by those who aspired to a public career to affect beliefs, actions, and/or emotions of an audience through techniques of persuasion. George A. Kennedy, the influential scholar in classical rhetoric, argued that the New Testament books were written in Greek by and for speakers of Greek, many of whom were familiar with forms of public address in Greek or who had been educated in Greek schools.[38] Ruth Webb also pointed out that early Christian authors reflected techniques of argumentation, especially "descriptive speech" (*ekphrasis*), that belong to the "preliminary exercises" in composition and rhetoric called the *progymnasmata*.[39] Mikeal C. Parsons and Michael Wade Martin attempted to bridge the studies of classical rhetoric and biblical studies. They claimed that biblical studies can be better studied against the backdrop of compositional skills first learned in the *progymnasmata*.[40] As a result, a new subarea, rhetorical criticism, developed in form criticism, an approach that focuses on the text itself (the world of the text) in New Testament study.[41] My aim is to explore how the parables of Jesus might have functioned persuasively for the audiences to whom they were directed and to show the importance of rhetorical criticism in the understanding of Jesus's parables as spiritual guides for today's readers.

Within the tradition of the *progymnasmata*, important features of "descriptive speech" (*ekphrasis*) will be considered in the analysis of Jesus's parables. The first and most important is "vividness" (*enargeia*; Latin, *evidentia*), a rhetorical device used to represent a "vivid description" that brings the story or object "vividly before the eyes" of the hearer.[42] In other words, *enargeia* is the power of the text "to create visual images" in the mind in order to turn the hearers into observers in the story.[43] The second rhetorical feature is "clarity" (*saphēneia*), employed often in narratives, so that the hearer visualizes imaginatively the things reported.[44] The third tool is "conciseness" (*suntomia*), which allows the hearer to imagine the vivid description and therefore display in the mind's eye what is described.[45] The fourth feature is "style" (*lexis*), used to enhance vividness to further increase the *ekphrastic* effect by evoking the imagination of the hearer in order to create good feelings.[46]

The fifth element is "verisimilitude" (*pithanotēs*). This *ekphrastic* tool strengthens the persuasive character of the story. For a story to be persuasive and readily imaginable, the author must provide a sense of believability. The sixth element is "imagination" (*phantasia*; Latin, *vision*), the best way of representing a vision to see what is being described.[47] In order to effect "vividness" (*enargeia*) two important rhetorical elements are used: "repetition" (*anaphora*) to achieve an emotional impact, and "amplification" (*auxēsis*) to contribute to the credibility and plausibility of the narrative.[48] Other features learned in the *progymnasmata* are "proverb" (*gnōmē*), "comparison" (*synkrisis*), and "encomium" (*enkōmion*). The goal of vivid descriptive speech is to arouse an emotional response in its readers and hearers. In classical rhetoric, this technique was a powerful tool for persuasion, something that the authors of the New Testament used wisely by presenting vivid rhetorical descriptions to emotionally affect and transform their readers' and hearers' worldviews and actions.

As the parables are explored within the larger Greco-Roman intellectual perspectives represented in rhetorical methods, I want to make clear that I do not argue or presume that Jesus was familiar with the techniques of the *progymnasmata* and was consciously using them in his parables. I aim to highlight features of the rhetorical-poetic techniques in the parables, considering that the evangelists, who were familiar with these techniques, *retold* rhetorically the stories that Jesus *told* his audiences. In this context, I draw out important virtues and apply them to develop a clearer understanding of the parables that goes beyond the traditional historical-critical approaches already well-known. In this book, therefore, we shall see how Jesus's parables vividly bring before the readers' eyes what is described, transporting them into the story, thus creating spiritual transformation.

Parables Lead to Happiness

This book interprets selected parables of Jesus employing the rhetorical techniques of persuasion as found in the *progymnasmata* within the context of virtues in the Greek philosophical ethical systems. An innovative aspect of this book is the omission of the familiar names or titles given by scholars to the parables being analyzed. Indeed, my intention is to purposely avoid the use of the parables' names known to modern readers in order to leave the readers' minds and imaginations open, and as much as possible, less manipulated. In other words, I want to let the reader decide how to interpret each parable. I will also provide basic rhetorical tools that readers, on their own initiative, may extrapolate and apply to other parables in the Gospels. I invite readers to encounter the stories as if they were reading each parable for the first time. Only at the end of the analysis of each of the selected parables will I give the parable an appropriate name based on the virtues and rhetorical features highlighted.

Chapter 1 shows readers how to *know and understand* Jesus's parables in a new light. The short parables in the triple tradition—Mark 4:26–29, 30–32 // Matt 13:31–33 // Luke 13:18–21—are key to introducing readers to Jesus's parables. In chapter 2, readers not only gain knowledge and reflection but also *internalize* the essence of Jesus's message. The parables found in the double tradition, Matt 25:14–30 and Luke 19:12–27, transport readers into the scene that Jesus voices in these parables through vivid description and key elements from ancient Greek rhetorical-poetic techniques. In chapter 3, the analysis of the parables in Luke 16:19–31, Matt 20:1–16, and Luke 16:1–13 challenges readers to discover the true message of Jesus in his parables and how this can generate an internal wrestling between good and evil (virtue and vice) within the human heart/mind. Chapter 4 centers on virtues and the experience of transformation derived from a right hearing and right understanding of the parables. Through the rhetorical-poetic description of the parables in Luke 15:11–32, Luke 18:1–8, and Matt 18:23–35, two important virtuous qualities find harmony in the human heart/mind: moral transformation and "happiness" (*eudaimonia*), qualities that lead to the Christian ideal of becoming perfect like our Father is perfect (Matt 5:48).

1

Knowing and Understanding Jesus's Parables

"Welcome" might have been a word often pronounced by Jesus to his followers and hearers in the first century CE as he began telling them parables. Two thousand years later, Jesus still welcomes us to the parables cherished and saved by early believers in the canonical Gospels. While Jesus's parables might have been unique or *sui generis* for his first-century audience—although this is argued by some scholars—this is not the case for us.[1] Christians, even non-Christians, around the world have encountered at least pieces of the wise teachings in Jesus's parables; common examples are the Good Samaritan and the Lost Son, both found in the Gospel of Luke. Church experts and biblical scholars have interpreted Jesus's parables in a manner that speaks to us today and provides applicable messages that lead us to have more meaningful lives. In this chapter, readers are invited to perceive Jesus's parables as a rich and "bubbling fountain" of wisdom. Through his parables, Jesus as the Sage and Wisdom Teacher *comes to us*, *speaks with us*, *reveals to us* his most intimate feelings and desires, and *shows us* who he is and his unique relation to God our Father. In one sentence: if we want to know Jesus, his parables are the best source.

In this chapter, Jesus is introduced as the Wisdom Teacher who possesses virtues and wants us to like him, who himself is the Image of God (2 Cor 4:4; Col 1:15–17; cf. John 5:19). Therefore, to begin I will introduce the parables that will train us how to *know and understand*

Jesus and what he offers to us in his parables by using the parables in Matt 13:31–33; Mark 4:26–29, 30–32; and Luke 13:18–21. These stories are considered part of the triple tradition since they derive from one source (Mark) and are found in all three Synoptic Gospels with a little variation. Scholars have called these stories "parables of the kingdom." I avoid this designation because I want Jesus's words in these parables to speak for themselves through the vivid descriptions and the rhetorical techniques employed by the evangelists. This organic approach to the interpretation of Jesus's parables is unique in modern interpretations and exegesis. As we come to encounter Jesus through three memorable parables, we are led to know and understand Jesus's parables.

Another important aspect of this chapter is that readers will start to become familiar with the basic tools from the ancient Greek rhetorical and poetic techniques. This is how we will imaginatively enter into the first-century world of Jesus (Jesus's *Sitz im Leben*). Three points are important to keep in mind here and throughout the other chapters: (1) Knowledge and understanding are two key virtues. (2) In order to know and understand how the parables can bring both transformation and virtuousness requires effort and struggle. (3) Through struggles and perseverance, readers can attain happiness through the experience of a powerful transformation. This is a moment of enlightenment, when readers will truly come to know and understand the message in the parables of Matt 13:31–33, Mark 4:26–29, 30–32, and Luke 13:18–21.

Mark 4:26–29: The Nature of God's Heavenly Realm

To attain happiness, first we must be introduced to God's world and affairs, that is, we must come to know and understand what God's heavenly kingdom is and what it entails. With the help of Jesus's parables in Mark 4:26–29 and 30–32, Matt 13:31–33, and Luke 13:18–21, we will be able to accomplish this important task. The analysis of these parables will highlight and answer three crucial questions: (1) What is Jesus about to reveal? (2) How is the invisible realm present in the simplest aspects of life? And (3) how are we to understand Jesus's parables? At the end of the analysis of each parable, we will give a proper name to the story. To begin our journey into the parables pronounced by Jesus,

Knowing and Understanding Jesus's Parables

we will look at Mark 4:26–29, which is a unique Markan parable, followed by a parable found in the triple tradition, Matt 13:31–32 // Mark 4:30–32 // Luke 13:18–19; finally, we will look at a parable that derives hypothetically from the Q document, that is Matt 13:33 // Luke 13:20–21.[2] During his later Galilean ministry (3:13–6:29), the Markan Jesus told the following parable to his audience, particularly to those outside who were not given the mystery of the kingdom of God:

> [26]He [Jesus] also said, "The kingdom of God is *as if* a man would scatter seed on the *ground*, [27]and would sleep and rise night and day, and the seed would sprout and grow, [*as if*] he does not know how. [28]The *earth* produces of itself, first the stalk, then the head, then the full grain in the head. [29]But when the grain is ripe, at once he goes in with his sickle, because the harvest has come.

This short yet powerful and revelatory parable forms part of the collection of parables in 4:1–34 and is placed between 3:20–35, Jesus's teachings in Capernaum, and 4:35–41, Jesus's miracle of the calming of the sea in Galilee. The Markan Jesus, addressing the larger Galilean audience (4:26; cf. 4:1–9), returns to the growth process as a metaphor of the "kingdom." As a whole, Mark 4:26–29 contrasts small beginnings (the seed) and a great conclusion (the harvest).[3] In other words, in the parable Jesus reveals that *something* is happening in the present (the process of growth) and that *something* is mysterious to human beings (the seed growing "of itself," *automatē*).[4] Interestingly, the only action that the person does in the story is that of scattering the seed, revealing that the sower is not at all involved in the growth of the seed.[5]

Now, looking through the lens of the *progymnasmata,* or "preliminary exercises" in classical composition, we see that in this short parable the Markan Jesus depicts for his audience's eyes how, like a seed, the kingdom of God germinates in mysterious fashion by divine guidance or providence (God's care). Jesus tells his audience that the sower "knows not how" (4:27) the seed grows, and they understand that the seed on the ground has power independent of human endeavor and effort because it mysteriously "produces of itself" (4:28). For the hearers, the message is clear: proper response to the kingdom is to be ready when the harvest is announced (4:29; cf. 1:14–15; Joel 3:13).[6] The kingdom comes in "power" (*dunamis*),[7] enters the individual's heart, and mysteriously enlightens his or her mind to know and understand Jesus's message about God's heavenly realm.

Within the context of ancient classical rhetoric, the modern reader notices that in only four verses the Markan Jesus provides "vivid descriptive speech" to explain to his hearers the nature of God's heavenly realm in *parabolē*, meaning "comparison." George A. Kennedy noted that among the ten exercises practiced in *progymnasmatic* exercises in grammar or rhetorical schools was "comparison" (*synkrisis*).[8] The parable's main topic is clearly God's divine dwelling, the heavenly realm; however, Mark expresses it in terms of "the kingdom of God" (v. 26).[9] Within the larger context of the Greco-Roman world, the Greek philosopher Plato, Middle Platonists (80 BCE–220 CE), and the Jewish philosopher Philo of Alexandria (20 BCE–50 CE), for example, would refer to it as the "intelligible world" (*kosmos noētos*) or heavenly world.[10] This perfect world is the pattern for the "sensible world" (*kosmos aisthētos*) and is also in opposition to the sensible, earthly world. Language related to the kingdom of God appears often throughout Mark's Gospel; in fact, the phrase "the kingdom of God" is explicitly mentioned twenty times.[11] Unlike the other two Synoptic Gospels (Matthew and Luke), in Mark the kingdom of God is a major theme that reflects God's rule or God's reign.

The Markan Jesus speaks more of the kingdom of God than he does about anything else.[12] Mark's emphasis on the kingdom of God serves the author as the metaphor to speak about "God's will being done" and does not refer to earthly (human) kingdoms—a territory or a specific geographical place. In the Gospel of John, Jesus answers Pontius Pilate, saying, "My kingdom is not from this world" (John 18:36). The kingdom that is heavenly and of God in Mark comes when God's "will is done," and it is accomplished *in Jesus*. Jesus himself brings about the accomplishment of God's will through his crucifixion or death on a cross.[13] Readers must keep in mind that Mark understands God's kingdom as the will of God being accomplished through Jesus's sacrifice in the most virtuous and perfect manner. Jesus's exemplary life must also be reflected in the lives of his followers. The kingdom that the Markan Jesus speaks of possesses qualities that belong to the heavenly realm; it is divine, immaterial, eternal, incorrupt, perfect, invisible, and incorporeal, similar to the Platonic idea of the intelligible world, the *kosmos noētos*. In contrast, the inferior sensible world—*kosmos aisthētos*—is characterized by being material, corrupt, visible, finite, imperfect, and corporeal. The Markan Jesus prioritizes the heavenly kingdom of God over the earthly world or kingdoms (3:24) and introduces for the first time that the kingdom "has come near" (1:15). That God's kingdom is *at hand* renders an ethical transformation that requires the adoption of a new way of life.[14] For Mark, the attainment of the heavenly kingdom, then, calls for the practice of virtues and the avoidance of vices.

Mark, as a "radical Christian rhetor,"[15] introduces his main topic: God's divine realm. For the evangelist, a simple rational explanation is not enough to successfully reveal the mystery of the nature of the kingdom of God. Therefore, in his parable in 4:26–29 he employs some *ekphrastic* techniques, which would have been well-known or at least familiar to his hearers; hence, they would have understood Jesus's parable. Mark provides details, so that the comparison he is about to make owes its vividness to the fact that key accompanying circumstances in the seed's growing are mentioned and nothing is omitted.[16] The introductory phrase "he also said" (lit. "he was saying") is Mark's stylistic device used to link previous sayings in 4:3–9 with the ones to come in 4:26–32. Immediately, he introduces his main topic regarding the kingdom of God, and then he reveals the nature of the kingdom of God by making a comparison between it and the parabolic imagery to follow.[17] This is the first of the two times that the evangelist explicitly identifies the saying as a kingdom parable with the introductory formula, "*thus* the kingdom of God is *as if*" (vv. 26 and 30). Interestingly, this occurs nowhere else, and no other parable starts with "thus…as if." This rhetorical style often occurs at the end of parables in the explanation, or the *nimshal*, sometimes referring to what preceded it but not to what follows it (e.g., Matt 7:17; 13:40, 49).[18]

According to the conventions of classical Greek, one should expect the phrase "as if" (*ean hōs*) rather than the simple "as" (*hōs*) to introduce the comparative clause.[19] However, Mark's simple use of "as" is enhanced by his use of five subjunctive verbs ("would scatter," "would sleep," "would rise," "would sprout," "would grow"). Thus, it demands that the adverb "as" (*hōs*) equals "as if" (*ean hōs*).[20] To make his comparative parable about the nature of God's heavenly realm *ekphrastic*, in v. 26 Mark vividly describes a common practice of first-century agrarian society that includes someone (literally "a man"),[21] the seed, and the ground (literally "earth"). These three important elements allow the evangelist to portray a known and common activity understood by the Markan Jesus's hearers. The ordinary activity of "scattering seed on the ground" captures the hearers' interest, so that the activity is placed into the hearers' imagination. The vivid representation is meant to create a sense of truth or reality since hearers imagine that they themselves "would scatter seed on the ground." What is key in this Markan parable is that the hearers be the ones who perform *the act of planting the seed on the ground*; thus, the parable that speaks about the nature of God's kingdom becomes a reality in the mind of the hearers.[22]

As the hearers participate in the revelation of the nature of God's heavenly kingdom, the evangelist reinforces the *enargetic* character of the parable by placing before the hearers the consecutive actions of the sower and the seed. As Mark writes, "and [he] would sleep and rise night and day, and the seed would sprout and grow" (4:27ab). The man's activity in sowing and his action of sleeping and getting up, together with the seed's process of sprouting and growing, are represented in "a rhythmic and lulling pattern."[23] The subjunctive action verbs in reference to the sower and the seed enhance the vivid picture of the actions of the man and the process of the seed's natural growth. The five uses of the conjunction "and" linked with the subjunctive verbs ("would scatter," "would sleep," "would rise," "would sprout," "would grow") clearly reflect Mark's strategy to ensure clarity and verisimilitude, as a good orator does. His use of repetition, which is an important rhetorical device of *enargeia* (vividness), enhances the effect of vividness more than just providing a plain narration of a parable. These powerful rhetorical techniques are meant to capture the imagination of the orator's audience and offer an organic description of the nature of God's heavenly realm in a language familiar to the hearers.

That Mark's unique parable helps Jesus's audience feel as if they were actually eyewitnesses to the story is reinforced by his words "night and day" in 4:27.[24] The order, first "night," then "day," reflects the Jewish custom; night precedes day because the day was regarded as beginning with sundown.[25] The evangelist skillfully stresses the ordinary practice of the sower's action—sleeping and rising *night and day*—in order to amplify evidence of what follows in 4:27c (the seed would sprout and would grow). The sower had to wait. He sleeps and rises "night and day." As Gerhard Lohfink notes, this language invokes a long series of nights and days.[26] The rhetorical element of amplification, an aspect of vividness, seeks to enhance the attention on the seed's growing process, a metaphor (of the kingdom) contrasted with the sower's activity in scattering the seed on the ground.

In his vivid description, Mark applies familiar agricultural activity with two techniques of vividness: metaphor and amplification. Both become the basis for Mark's clarity and distinction between the activity of the sower and the activity of the seed during the growing process.[27] As Cicero points out, metaphor and amplification are ways to "set the fact before the eyes (*paene ante oculos*)."[28] The repetitive subjunctive verbs—"sprout" and "grow" (literally "lengthen")—create a sense of the unhurried passage of time to emphasize the divine power reflected in the seed growing by itself (*automatē*).[29]

Likewise, the repetition of the adverb "as if" (*hōs*) is applied to direct the attention of the hearers away from the sower's ordinary and familiar activity (scattering seed) to the sense of mystery at the end of 4:27c: "he does not know." While Mark disconnects the seed's growing process from the sower's activity, he continues his emphasis on the sower (literally "a man," *anthrōpos*). Indeed, the evangelist in v. 27c stresses the noninterference of the sower. The hearers clearly understand that the sower "does not do anything for the growing seed"; the sower *knows* nothing about how the seed grows or what causes the seed to grow. Mark's rhetorical technique of vividness reflects not the sower's lack of interest in the seed; in fact, it is not that the sower "does not seem to care," as Hendrickx argued.[30] Rather, Mark creates a vivid description with the purpose of challenging the hearers to become like the sower and acknowledge that the sower does *not know* the nature of the kingdom of God, or the heavenly realm of God. This is supported by Mark's following progressive representation of the seed's growth on the ground: "The earth produces of itself, first the stalk, then the head, then the full grain in the head" (4:28). Hultgren rightly notes that "the sequence of the development of stalk, head, and grain gives the hearer and reader a vivid and moving picture of the development."[31]

While Mark gives a progressive representation of the seed's development in four stages, from seed to maturity, the use of the repetition of the words "earth," "on the earth," and "the earth" (vv. 26b, 28a) heightens the mysterious transformation that the seed goes through *on the ground*. Such emphasis on the unknown to reveal the unknown creates a sense of wonder in the mind of the hearer and reader. For Mark, it is crucial that his audience knows and understands both the seed's growth without human effort and the divine power to produce or bear fruit.[32] In this way, Mark shows it is God's will for human beings to know the mysteries of the nature of God's heavenly kingdom and to understand what is entailed to attain it. Mark's use of ancient classical rhetorical techniques purposely serves him to redirect his hearers' conception of the divine. Significantly, to provide clarity to his vivid description, Mark appeals to the authority of Jewish Scripture as a reference to evoke appropriately the image of the harvest, which has come (4:29).[33] Indeed, the expression "he goes in with his sickle," when the grain is ripe, reflects the prophet Joel's command, "put in the sickle, for the harvest is ripe" (Joel 3:13).[34]

Mark uses scriptural authority in reference to "harvest" as a rhetorical tool required by the detailed stages of the seed's growth. As Snodgrass states, "it would be strange to list the stages and stop short of the harvest";[35] thus, there is no objective reason to omit the language of going "in with his sickle" to offer a convincing case for virtuous living. While it is true that v. 29 has overtones of eschatological urgency and points toward final judgment (e.g., Matt 9:37–38; Luke 10:2; John 4:35), as scholars have argued,[36] in Mark's parable, v. 29 is used as a rhetorical device to give authority to Jesus's message: how through a simple action familiar to first-century people, *Jesus reveals the unknown, the nature of God's heavenly realm*, vividly described by Mark as "the kingdom of God." Therefore, the added scriptural element prepares the hearer and reader to distinguish imaginatively the passive behavior of the sower (literally a man) toward the seed's growing process (4:27c) from the direct action upon the grain, which is "ripe," at harvest time (4:29). Indeed, the rhetorical function of the adverb *euthus*, "immediately," Mark's favorite word,[37] heightens the man's action of *going* "in with his sickle, *because* the harvest has come."

It is evident that the Markan Jesus presents the sower in two ways: at the beginning and at the end of the parable, the "man" (*anthrōpos*) is directly engaged with the seed—he scatters the seed on the ground (4:26b), and he goes to the field to harvest the grain (4:29b). In the middle of the parable, the man neither works nor knows how the stalk develops from the seed to the ripeness of the grain (4:27–29a). Although the man's inactivity during the growth of the seed is emphasized, he still is the center of the story. Thus, it is the activity of the man on the ground or field that the Markan Jesus vividly describes as the best representation of the nature of God's heavenly realm. The metaphorical nuance of the sudden "harvest time," with its eschatological overtones, stresses the mysterious power of God, yet it also creates in the hearers' minds an awareness that the harvest comes with the man's crucial assistance: *scattering and harvesting*. Mark hopes that his hearers perceive that the presence of the invisible realm can be found in the simplicity of life; that the mystery of God's kingdom is revealed through divine intervention and human participation. He also hopes that his hearers understand that the sower's activity highlights the virtue of simplicity and that his inactivity also emphasizes the important virtues of patience, confidence, endurance, and faith. These important virtues are highlighted by the rhetorical techniques Mark has used. Now, it is time to give a title to this short yet revealing story: The Parable of the Trustful Man. In order to know the heavenly realm, the kingdom of God, the element of trust (in God) is required.

Matt 13:31–32 // Mark 4:30–32 // Luke 13:18–19: What Is Like the Heavenly Realm?

What example could Jesus use to show *what is like* something that is beyond human language (or comprehension), beyond the earthly realm? Jesus uses similitude to explain the nature of God's heavenly kingdom.[38] Remarkably, he does it concisely and in the simplest way, using examples from the natural and animal worlds, as we will see in the next parable, found in the triple tradition.[39]

In Matthew, this is the third of seven parables in the collection of parables called by scholars the "Parable Discourse" (Matt 13). Within this context, the Matthean Jesus addresses this parable to the crowds.[40] In Luke, the parable appears within the context of the so-called Travel Narrative (9:51–19:27). It follows the healing of a crippled woman on the Sabbath in a synagogue (13:10–17) and precedes Jesus's teachings on salvation and the mystery of rejection as he makes his way to Jerusalem (13:22–30).[41] In Mark, it follows Mark's Parable of the Trustful Man, where Jesus, addressing the crowds in the presence of the disciples (4:33–34), reveals the nature of the heavenly realm. This parable also concludes the parable sermon in Mark 4. The comparisons of these parables in the Synoptics often focus on the internal elements of the parable, especially on the linguistic level.[42] Strikingly, while both Mark and Luke explain the nature of the heavenly realm in terms of the *kingdom of God*,[43] Matthew explains it in terms of the *kingdom of heaven*.[44]

Table 1.1. Matt 13:31-32 // Mark 4:30-32 // Luke 13:18-19

Matt 13:31-32	Mark 4:30-32*	Luke 13:18-19
[31]He put before them another parable: "The kingdom of heaven is like a mustard seed that a man took and sowed in his field; [32]it is the smallest of all the seeds, but when it has grown it is the greatest of shrubs and becomes a tree, so that the birds of the air come and make nests in its branches."	[30]He also said, "With what can we compare the kingdom of God, or what parable will we use for it? [31]It is as a mustard seed, which, when it is sown upon the ground, is the smallest of all the seeds on earth; [32]yet when it is sown it grows up and becomes the greatest of all shrubs, and puts forth large branches, so that the birds of the air can make nests in its shade."	[18]He said therefore, "What is the kingdom of God like? And to what should I compare it? [19]It is like a mustard seed that a man took and casted into his garden; it grew and became a tree, and the birds of the air made nests in its branches."

* Cf. Gospel of Thomas, Logion 20: "The disciples said to Jesus, 'tell us what the kingdom of heaven is like.' Jesus said to them, 'it is like a mustard seed, smaller than all seeds. But when it falls on prepared soil, it produces a large branch and becomes a shelter for the birds of the sky.'" Robert J. Miller, ed. and trans., *The Complete Gospels: Annotated Scholars Version* (Santa Rosa, CA: Polebridge Press, 1994), 309.

To explain rhetorically *what is like* the nature of God's heavenly realm, the three evangelists use the similitude of a "mustard seed" (*kokkō sinapeōs*). The mustard seed does not provide an analogy of the kingdom, as Snodgrass and others have argued (although it can be interpreted this way).[45] The description of the mustard seed vividly textualizes images of farming in order to increase the hearers' own representational understanding of God's heavenly realm. Through the simplest examples from the natural world—the mustard seed—and the animal world—the birds of the air—the three evangelists provide in their own words the most evocative representation of the kingdom of God/of heaven. While at first glance the three parables may appear to be the same, each author uses different *ekphrastic* rhetorical elements and devices. Indeed, the power of the rhetorical words emphasized in each parable, as outlined in the *progymnasmata*, inevitably heightens the *enargeia*.

The Five Parts of the Parables

Mark, Matthew, and Luke each use rhetorical representations in their parables to help their audiences understand God's heavenly realm or kingdom. To present their effectiveness, we will concentrate our attention on five parts of the parables: (1) the introduction; (2) the sowing of the mustard seed; (3) the description of the seed; (4) the growth of the seed; and (5) the conclusion. Studying the three accounts in parallel will allow readers to engage with the three stories more effectively. In each of the five parts, we will give close attention to the features of descriptive speech (vividness, clarity, conciseness, style, verisimilitude, and imagination) as well as to the two major features of vividness—repetition and amplification.

INTRODUCTION (MATT 13:31A // MARK 4:30 // LUKE 13:18)

Rhetorically speaking, in the *introductory* part of the parable we find specific *ekphrastic* features that vary from one author to another. Mark's introduction, which according to Hendrickx is the original version of the parable,[46] contains two rhetorical questions. Mark writes: "He [Jesus] also said, 'With what can we compare the kingdom of God, or what parable will we use for it?'" (4:30). Literarily speaking, both rhetorical questions are used as a "hook." As a good orator would do to create a sense of reflection in the story he is about to describe, Mark puts himself in the audience as one more among the hearers. His rhetorical style reinforces the *ekphrastic* technique by stressing two repeated components in the parable: "can we compare" (*homoiōsōmen*, lit. "shall we liken") and "can we compare" (*parabolē*, lit. "shall we place it in parable"). This technique of putting together two words would demand a comparison that would require similitude (what? a mustard seed). But Mark goes one step further when he highlights his two rhetorical questions with the third person plural—"with what can *we* compare…" and "what…will *we* use…"—to invite his hearers to participate in deciphering *what is like* God's kingdom. In this way, Mark's similitude that follows would not be his own but also the hearers'.

Quite similarly, though with a different emphasis, Luke captures the attention of his audience with two rhetorical questions: "He said therefore, 'What is the kingdom of God like? And to what should I compare it?'"

(13:18). The *enargetic* feature of repetition is used: the first is the word "like" (*homoios*) in its adjectival form (*homoia*, lit. "like") and verbal form (*homoiōsō*, lit. "shall I liken"), and the second is the interrogative indefinite pronoun "to what" (*tini*) preceding the adjectival and verbal forms. Notably, unlike Mark, Luke does not put himself in the audience as a spectator (*theōros*); rather, the evangelist remains the orator who would offer to his audience a concise parable. Rhetorically speaking, however, Luke captures the imagination of his hearers and achieves vividness using repetition (*homoios* and *tini*).[47] Both Mark, amply, and Luke, concisely, play on rhetorical techniques of descriptive speech and vividness with the same rhetorical goal of putting before their hearers a parable that will teach them *what is like* God's kingdom, the heavenly world.

Although for the modern reader Matthew may sound unique or perhaps be considered an outlier in the manner he introduces his parable, within the context of the *progymnasmata* the evangelist knows how to bring the story before his audience's eyes. Although he omits the use of rhetorical questions, his rhetorical style in telling Jesus's parable shows conciseness and clarity. Matthew's introduction, "He [Jesus] put before them [hearers] another parable" (13:31a), reflects two important rhetorical skills:[48] his emphasis on the word "parable" (*parabolē*), which Jesus is about to tell his disciples, and his use of the verb "put before" (*paratithēmi*) immediately after the word "parable." "Parable" is deployed as a hook to capture interest on the part of the hearers, and "put before" reinforces the vivid description. So, Matthew convincingly says that Jesus *put before* his disciples' *eyes* another *parable*. The Greek verb *paratithēmi* also has other meanings besides "to put before," for example, "to entrust to," "to quote as evidence," or "to bring forward" something trustful.[49] In terms of the conceptual wording, each evangelist stands alone; however, rhetorically, the three authors seek to accomplish the same goal through the use of their own *ekphrastic* techniques: that is, to *bring before the eyes* of their hearers or readers *what is like* the nature of God's kingdom.

Sowing the Mustard Seed (Matt 13:31b // Mark 4:31ab // Luke 13:19a)

When we turn to the *sowing of the mustard seed* itself, we find characteristic features that belong to the art of ancient rhetorical practices outlined in the preliminary exercises. As Mark begins the *what-is-like* explication, he opts for an example of a similitude that will sound familiar to his hearers, "a mustard seed" (4:31a). In the Galilean milieu of the first century CE, Zimmermann notes, "mustard was a well-known plant that was often cultivated but also grew as a weed."[50] While mustard seeds were not the smallest seeds in the literal sense, they were known for their small size in both Hellenistic and Jewish contexts and often used proverbially.[51] Mark introduces the mustard seed with the repetition of the adverbial "as" (*hōs*), which he used before in 4:26b (the Parable of the Trustful Man). His repetition is clearly intentional, for he wants to connect the topic of the kingdom of God in 4:26–29 with his explanation regarding the nature of the kingdom in 4:30–32. Moreover, Mark's particular choice of the mustard seed among other small seeds (for example, orchid or cypress seeds were smaller) to vividly compare it with the heavenly realm shows his skillful way of connecting what is common, familiar, and ordinary with what is unknown, mysterious, and outside this earthly world. Mark finds in one of the simplest examples from nature (the mustard seed) an extraordinary way to capture his hearers' imagination to achieve vividness.

Mark further emphasizes the centrality of the mustard seed by using repetition to increase vividness. This is noted in two ways: first, he omits any reference to "a man" or "someone" who would scatter the seed, as done in the Parable of the Trustful Man (4:26–29), where it is explicitly stated that "a man would scatter seed" (4:26b). In fact, in this second parable the evangelist writes: "when it is sown" (4:31b). While in 4:26b "as if" (*hōs*) is stylistically placed together with "a man" (*anthrōpos*), here in 4:31, Mark places "as" (*hōs*) together with "a mustard seed" (*kokkō sinapeōs*); the former is meant to highlight the man, while the latter highlights the seed. In this parable the Markan Jesus reveals not only what the nature of the heavenly realm is but also *what* its nature *is like*. Second, it is paramount, rhetorically speaking, that Mark's vivid description conveys an appealing impact when the literal repeated phrase "upon the ground" (*epi tēs gēs*), found in 4:26b and 4:31b—both preceded by the same repeated verb "to sow" (*speirō*)—highly increases the vividness of the central role of the mustard seed similitude. In Mark's thought, it is a mustard seed *in the ground* that will reveal and explain *what is like* the nature of the kingdom of God.

In the case of Matthew and Luke, their vivid descriptions are basically similar, though with a few variations. For instance, Matthew has "the kingdom of heaven," and Luke, like Mark, opts for "kingdom of God" in 13:18b. Luke's conciseness is highly stylistic, which not only gives clarity but also points directly to its central rhetorical element, the mustard seed similitude accompanied by the man's action (13:19). Both Matthew and Luke explain the nature of the heavenly realm using the rhetorical tool of "like" (*homoios*) to represent the comparison between the kingdom of heaven/God and the mustard seed (Matt 13:31b and Luke 13:19). While both evangelists emphasize the two subjects of the seed and the man, providing details of the sower's actions of taking and sowing the seed in the soil, the vivid representation of the man's engagement in the planting of the mustard seed is described using different words. Matthew explains that "a man took and sowed into his field" (13:31b), but Luke states that "a man took and casted into his garden" (13:19a). While the action of the parable appears identical, Matthew emphasizes the aorist active indicative verb "to sow" (*espeirein*), and Luke reinforces his descriptive parable with the use of the aorist active indicative verb "to cast" (*ballein*), which is a repetition of Mark's verb in 4:26c (the Parable of the Trustful Man), where "a man scattered seed on the ground."

In both Matthew and Luke, the man's action is clearly highlighted; it is *a man* who takes the role of planting the mustard seed (Matt 13:31b // Luke 13:19a). Yet what is distinctive and significant between both evangelists is that neither of them follows Mark's emphasis on the "ground" (*gē*) in 4:26c and 4:28a. Matthew and Luke emphasize the man's act of sowing the seed, but the man in Matthew sows the seed *on his field*, and in Luke the man casts the seed *on his garden*. As Snodgrass noted, outside Luke 13:19, the word "garden" is mentioned in the New Testament only in John 18:1, 26; and 19:41 (twice).[52] From the agricultural context we know that first-century Jews grew mustard in their gardens. According to the rhetorical handbooks and/or *progymnasmata*, part of the technique to achieve vividness—to place the story before the eyes of the orator's audience—is to describe the circumstances of the action.[53] So, both evangelists provide the vivid detail of the field (Matthew) and garden (Luke), which both belong to the man, thus creating a sense of belonging, an intimate connection between the mustard seed and the place (field/garden) into which the seed is planted. It also expands the emphasis on the theme of the natural world (seed, ground, field, garden). Cicero defines this technique as "amplification," often used to evoke in the audience's imagination the scene being described,[54] so that

Knowing and Understanding Jesus's Parables

the readers themselves can picture the action of sowing or casting the mustard seed.

DESCRIPTION OF THE SEED (MATT 13:32A // MARK 4:31C)

The *description of the seed* in Mark (4:31c) and Matthew (13:32a) is omitted by Luke. We have seen (above) that mustard seeds are *not* the smallest seeds, but they were proverbially known for their small size (cf. Luke 17:6).[55] In both Mark and Matthew, the centrality of the mustard seed is once more heightened when the authors vividly provide a detail of the seed's qualities: that it is the *smallest of all the seeds* (Matt 13:32a // Mark 4:31c).[56] Offering a pictorial image of the mustard seed creates a stronger impact in the parable, particularly in the sense of comparing the mustard seed with other seeds. The central image of the mustard seed serves Mark and Matthew to persuasively represent the reality of *what is like* God's heavenly realm. In its original state, the mustard seed is vividly described as the "smallest" (*mikroteron*) seed in the natural world, and to increase its privileged nature, the evangelists amplify it with the extra detail "of all the seeds" to increase vividness.

GROWING PROCESS (MATT 13:32B // MARK 4:32A // LUKE 13:19B)

The dynamics of vividness in the *growing process* of the mustard seed are noteworthy. Focusing on the rhetorical techniques of vivid description, Mark and Matthew alike bring the seed's growth before "their hearers' eyes" to achieve vividness. Mark gives more details about the seed's process of growing in the present tense; he writes: "yet when it is sown it grows up and becomes the greatest of all shrubs, and puts forth large branches." First, the evangelist combines a conjunction ("when"), a subjunctive verb ("it is sown"), and present active (passive/middle) verbs ("it grows up" and "it becomes") to enhance the emphasis on the adjectival or superlative "greatest" (*meizon*, lit. "greater"). Second, he uses again the *enargetic* device of repetition by highlighting the act of sowing and the distinctive quality "of all" in v. 32a (see v. 31b). Third, the adjectival or superlative "greatest" is preceded by two verbs ("grow" and "become") not only to provide extra details but also to offer clar- what Mark wants to convey. Mark develops the comparison in a

The Power of Transformation

superlative form in this way: the "smallest" seed becomes the "greatest" of all shrubs and puts forth large branches. His hearers would imagine how the smallest seed (v. 31c) has now become the greatest of all (v. 32a) that is able to put forth not just branches but *large* branches (v. 32b).[57]

Clearly, Mark intentionally employs the figurative speech of hyperbole in his rhetorical representation of the seed's process of growing. Snodgrass explains the seed's growing development: the "seed germinates within five days and grows quickly to a height of about ten feet and has large leaves, especially at its base."[58] Mark heightens the credibility of the parable by referring to the seed's becoming a "shrub," which also adds verisimilitude, because he is more precise in referring to the plant as a shrub with large branches than as a tree. Indeed, the mustard plant does not become a tree, as Matthew and Luke say (Matt 13:32b; Luke 13:19b). Mark intends to create realism in his vivid description, and he does it by representing similitude in a comparative form stylistically. Donahue is right when he claims that "the parables of Jesus are characterized by realism...arresting the hearer by its vividness or strangeness."[59] The evangelist's vivid representation amplifies all in reference to the mustard seed in order to show clarity, an *ekphrastic* quality, to strongly highlight the mustard seed's superiority in the natural world. In contrast, Matthew states, "but when it has grown it is the greatest of shrubs and becomes a tree" (13:32b). He emphasizes the growth process, "when it has grown," in order to connect with his previous description in 13:31b, "and sowed." Also, the evangelist focuses on the superior quality of the mustard plant when he describes it as "the greatest of shrubs" (13:32b). The Matthean phrase "becomes a tree" is added to describe the amplitude of the tree.

Matthew combines a realistic description (shrubs) with an unrealistic fact (becomes a tree), omitting the adjectival "of all" to simplify his statement, perhaps attempting to capture his readers' and hearers' attention. By employing the description of the "greatest of shrubs," Matthew makes his description vivid to his audience, who would get a picture of the seed growing and becoming a tree. Unlike Mark and Matthew, Luke is simpler but is close to Matthew in saying "it grew and became a tree" (13:19b).[60] In this case, Luke's focus is only on the development of the mustard seed that grew and rapidly became a tree (13:19b). That the mustard seed "became a tree" (unlike Matthew's active present verb "becomes") is Luke's way of relying on scriptural support, since the phrase "became a tree" is a common Hebraism and frequently used in the Septuagint (LXX, the Greek Jewish Scripture).[61] Significantly, Luke does not mention either the smallness of the seed or the greatness of the tree. However, he develops the growing process in a straight line without interruption to put before his readers' and hearers' eyes the *mysterious growth*. For him, the seed has already become a tree.[62] His way of evoking vividness is through a series of aorist verbs—"took," "sowed," "grew," and "became." As an adept Greek writer, it is not surprising to see Luke polishing his source by omitting details that would distract the readers' attention. The evangelist opts for two *ekphrastic* devices—conciseness and simplicity—that would involve a method of representing the circumstances of sudden growth of the mustard seed. Luke achieves vividness through his use of selective verbs rather than the employment of two adjectives in superlative forms.

Conclusion (Matt 13:32c // Mark 4:32b // Luke 13:19c)

The climactic moment, in which the three evangelists put before the eyes of their readers and/or hearers *what is like* the nature of the heavenly realm, is represented at the *conclusion* of the parable. Mark is unique in the final part of his parable. He writes, "so that the birds of the air can make nests in its shade" (4:32b). The conjunction "so that" (*hōste*) serves as a literary technique to bring together the true message of the parable, which will help the hearer understand *what is like* the nature of the heavenly realm, or in Mark's words, the kingdom of God. To evoke the concept of it in their imagination and make more real the accessibility of the presence of the kingdom of God, Mark appeals once more to the natural world. He opts for what is familiar to his audience, the "birds of the air," in order to put before the eyes (and understanding) *what is like* God's kingdom. The birds, which according to Matthew and Luke are naturally and providentially taken care of by our Providential God (Matt 6:26–27 // Luke 12:24), convey the grandeur of God's heavenly realm. As Mark skillfully shows how a seed with an insignificant beginning (the smallest of all) grows to a mighty magnitude (the greatest of all), he is likewise able to *ekphrastically* explain how simple and insignificant creatures from the animal world (birds) could represent in his audience's minds the best image of *what is like* the nature of God's kingdom. The mustard seed, which became a shrub, attracts the birds to its large branches for shelter, protection, and food.[63]

The Power of Transformation

For his Jewish audience, Mark reinforces his rhetorical presentation of the parable with a familiar scriptural allusion to Ezekiel 17:23 that would help the hearer and reader to imagine the extent of *what is like* God's kingdom. The prophet writes, "On the mountain height of Israel I will plant it, in order that it may produce boughs and bear fruit, and become a noble cedar. Under it every kind of bird will live; in the shade of its branches will nest winged creatures of every kind."[64] The images of fruit, birds, branches, and nest reinforce the similitude, which would best provide an analogy to the heavenly realm. Mark's climactic ending of the comparison reveals that, *like the mustard seed*, the nature of the heavenly realm starts as something small and insignificant but unexpectedly and mysteriously becomes something quite large.[65] Through the familiar examples of nature from the created world, like the mustard seed, shrubs, birds, branches, nests, and ground, Mark has successfully conveyed to his readers what he has intended in his Parable of the Trustful Man (4:26–29). The evangelist hopes that they now know and understand the heavenly realm as mysterious yet present and visible in the simplicity of nature. The *ekphrastic* techniques employed in his parable (4:30–32) create vivid scenes before their eyes, giving a full revelation of the grand benefits of God's heavenly kingdom.

Matthew's and Luke's descriptive language is virtually identical in the conclusion of the parable. Matthew's version says, "so that the birds of the air come and make nests in its branches" (13:32c), and Luke writes, "and the birds of the air made nests in its branches" (13:19c). Both evangelists have the birds dwelling in the branches of the plant, unlike Mark who describes the birds as able to make nests in its branches (Mark 4:32b). The differences are that Matthew has the conjunction "so that" (*hōste*, like Mark), and two verbs "come" and "make" conjoined with the conjunction "and" (*kai*). Luke, however, shows his rhetorical style and highlights the *ekphrastic* techniques of conciseness and simplicity by narrowing down to one verb, "made" (*kateskēnōsen*), used in the aorist tense to agree with the previous verbs. As said above, Luke tends to edit his sources and eliminate elements not necessary to his narrative. Instead of focusing on the shade produced by the large branches (Mark), both Matthew and Luke emphasize the branches of the mustard plant, as they write, "in *its* branches" (Matt 13:32c // Luke 13:19c). Thus, even though both authors provide less details in comparison to Mark, their strong emphasis on the seed similitude—focusing on the branches, not the shade—produces the same effects of vividness. Therefore, despite the variation in their use of descriptive speech and vividness, Matthew and Luke, like Mark, have provided the readers and hearers visual experiences of the nature of the heavenly realm, or kingdom of God.

The rhetorical features employed in the parable function as effective techniques for the authors to achieve vividness. The mustard seed similitude serves the evangelists as the central point of comparison or analogy to create a sense of knowledge and understanding of their main topic of discussion, God's heavenly realm. Their *ekphrastic* technique is animated by vividness, clarity, style, amplification, and repetition, in the case of Luke also conciseness, and in the case of Mark verisimilitude too. These ancient rhetorical features serve the imagination, an imagination that is believed to be a rhetorical weapon to get around the censor of the intellect (or mind) and persuade the audience to adopt the rhetor's point of view. In the three versions of the parable (Matt 13:31–32 // Mark 4:30–32 // Luke 13:18–19) we have seen that the use of "vividness" (*enargeia*) creates powerful mental images clearly and distinctly in order to elicit not only an emotional response but also beneficial results. Their compelling representation has the power of transporting the audience into participants in the act of sowing and into observers of the mustard plant's mysterious growth and the service and protection it naturally provides to the birds of the air.

The power of words convincingly persuades the readers and hearers; they come to the realization that knowing and understanding are two important virtues intrinsically connected with the heavenly realm. Thus, in order to know and understand God's kingdom, modern readers, too, must recognize the sower's actions toward the seed as his or her own effort in participating in the mystery of God's power. Also, readers must realize that the heavenly realm, God's kingdom, is accessible to those who know and understand as well as participate in it with trust and patience. Likewise, readers come to see an essential element in their spiritual journeys: to achieve God's kingdom requires personal transformation like the mustard seed. This parable, then, opens our eyes for the first time and exhorts us to a change, first internally and then externally, like the mustard seed. Jesus's parables are meant to effect personal growth; thus, knowing and understanding the power of God's mysteries are a path to transformation. As we conclude the rhetorical analysis of this parable, it is time to give it a name: The Parable of the Silent Sower.

Matt 13:33 // Luke 13:20–21: Restatement of What Is Like God's Heavenly Realm

It may seem that to know and understand *what is like* the nature of the heavenly realm for Matthew's and Luke's audiences, the previous Parable of the Silent Sower (Matt 13:31–32 // Luke 13:18–19) was not sufficient. The evangelists see the need to immediately present another short parable.

Table 1.2. Another View of the Kingdom	
Matt 13:33	Luke 13:20–21
[33]He told them another parable: "The kingdom of heaven is like leaven that a woman took and mixed in with three measures of flour until all of it was leavened."	[20]And again he said, "To what should I compare the kingdom of God? [21]It is like leaven that a woman took and mixed in with three measures of flour until all of it was leavened."

In Matthew and Luke this parable follows the Parable of the Silent Sower. Except for the introductory material, the wording of the two accounts is virtually identical (Matt 13:33a // Luke 13:20a). For this reason, most biblical scholars believe that this parable derives from the hypothetical Q document, the source that both evangelists used. Focusing on the rhetorical techniques of each introduction, we find in Matthew the repetition of the phrase "another parable" (13:31a; see also 13:3, 24) as a literary technique to help the reader focus on the central topic, the nature of the kingdom of God. Matthew explicitly states that he is about to describe a *parabolē*; hence, he creates a connection between the previous parable in 13:31–32 (the Parable of the Silent Sower) and this one (13:33). Interestingly, Matthew's direct words in 13:33a, "He told them another parable," is linked with his statement, "he put before them another parable," in the preceding parable (13:31a). This repetition, an *ekphrastic* device used to achieve *enargeia*, would put his audience, who seem to be the same people, into a state of concentration and readiness to imagine Jesus's message.

When we turn to Luke, his rhetorical technique remains concise, as he writes, "and again he said" (13:20a). His use of the word "again" (*palin*) rather than "parable" (*parabolē*) rhetorically joins together this parable with the previous one in 13:18–19 (the Parable of the Silent

Sower) to have the same effect as Matthew's parable. In this way, he keeps his audience's attention and mindfulness on the nature of God's heavenly kingdom. As is common in Matthew, the centrality of God's heavenly realm is referred to as the "kingdom of heaven" (13:33b), while Luke maintains the traditional expression of the "kingdom of God" (13:20b). Stylistically, Luke introduces his parable with a repetition of a rhetorical question pertaining to the central topic: "To what should I compare the kingdom of God?" (13:20b). Keeping his audience's eyes on the target object (the kingdom of God), Luke's rhetorical question creates a sense of mystery around the parable or comparison itself. This important stylistic trait not only enhances his vivid description but also reinforces his role as rhetor or orator, who will reveal to his audience *what is like* the nature of God's kingdom.

As in the Parable of the Silent Sower (Matt 13:31–32 // Luke 13:18–19), both evangelists use the word *homoios* (like), Matthew uses its adjectival form (*homoia*) and Luke its verbal form (*homoiōsō*, lit. "I shall liken") in close connection with God's heavenly realm, or the kingdom of heaven/God. When coming to the parable itself, we find again a parable in which the heavenly realm is compared to something familiar from the natural world: leaven (Matt 13:33b; Luke 13:21a). The leaven similitude plays the same role as the mustard seed similitude,[66] although this role is not now in relation to a "man" (*anthrōpos*) but to a "woman" (*gunē*). Adding a parable that reflects the same comparison or similitude leads modern readers to wonder (and appreciate) whether both Matthew and Luke intend to seek inclusivity between male and female genders. Knowing and understanding the nature of God's heavenly realm is then such an important, and inclusive, element in the spiritual journey, growth, and transformation that the evangelists may have opted to direct a parable to each gender (Matt 13:31–33 // Luke 13:18–21). These two parables (Matt 13:31–32 // Luke 13:18–19 and Matt 13:33 // Luke 13:20–21) can be seen as "twin parables."[67] The kingdom of heaven/God is likened to two elements from the natural world, mustard seed and leaven, where a man (sower) and a woman (who makes bread) are engaged in the process of revealing the nature of God's heavenly realm.

The example of "leaven" (*zumē*) used as a similitude is quite unexpected, thus surprising. In the Jewish tradition, leaven was viewed negatively because of Passover and the necessity of eating unleavened bread for seven days.[68] Mixing leaven with flour (to make bread) was a common activity for women in their households. Snodgrass points out that leaven is not the same as yeast, the small substance we use to cause leavening.[69] It is important to note that yeast is a leavening agent, but not all leaven is yeast. For example, today a leavening yeast could be purchased in refrigerated cubes or as a dried substance in a package. In antiquity, however, leaven consisted of fermenting dough. When baking, therefore, women used to save some of the fermented dough to ferment the next batch. According to the Mishnah, the task of baking was one of the seven duties women do for their husbands,[70] an ordinary and everyday practice among women of ancient times. So, in both Matthew (13:33b) and Luke (13:21), the explication that the nature of God's heavenly realm "is *like leaven that a woman took and mixed in with three measures of flour until all of it was leavened*" offers powerful visual imageries to evoke vividness. Like the "seed" in the Parable of the Trustful Man (Mark 4:26–29) and a "mustard seed" in the Parable of the Silent Sower (Matt 13:31–32 // Mark 4:30–32 // Luke 13:18–19) are associated with a man—the sower—in this parable (Matt 13:31 // Luke 13:20) the leaven similitude (Matt 13:33b // Luke 13:21) is presented in connection with a woman.

The rhetorical techniques employed in this short parable (Matt 13:33 // Luke 13:20–21) are clarity, conciseness, style, verisimilitude, and, of course, vividness. These features generate an image of the woman's activity that is both vivid and real to the audience's own experiences. The visual presence of the leaven and the woman is heightened using two action (aorist) verbs, "took" and "mixed"; this visual language further helps the readers and hearers to imagine they are present at the actual event. To create realism, thus verisimilitude, both evangelists use the *enargetic* technique of amplification by describing the exact amount of flour, as they say, "three measures of flour." Culturally, three measures (*sata*) of flour would be about a bushel of flour and would be about all one woman could knead. As Hultgren notes, that amount would weigh about forty pounds, which is immense.[71] It would obviously make a lot of bread, enough to feed 100 to 150 people, if the measurements have been understood correctly. The amount of leaven required to ferment that quantity of flour is estimated as three or four pounds. The large amount suggests that the woman might have been kneading dough for her neighborhood group. Baking was often done in courtyards; since the houses were small, it was probably a communal act.[72] Rhetorically, Matthew and Luke turn their audiences into spectators and "place before their eyes" a detailed process of baking—taking and mixing in leaven and flour until all of it is leavened.

Using the rhetorical technique of *ekphrasis* and its elements, Matthew and Luke reinforce the same explication about *what is like* the heavenly realm as in the previous Parable of the Silent Sower. The virtues emphasized are also the same, those of knowledge and understanding, and the focus is on the woman's action of preparing the dough to bake bread. Beginning small, the leaven, through the woman's work ("taking and mixing in"), mysteriously grows until the dough becomes completely leavened. The repeated element in the leaven similitude is, like the mustard seed, the inward growth and the outward growth, which expresses the hidden power of God and His kingdom. With the help of the rhetorical techniques of the *progymnasmata*, the evangelists use rhetorical hyperbole not only to convey information but also to penetrate into the audience's mind/heart to provoke an emotional reaction.[73] Once more, Matthew and Luke explain the parable *ekphrastically* in order to explicate their views of *what is like*, according to Jesus, the heavenly realm. At this point, the authors assume that their readers were able to *see* what the nature of the heavenly realm *is like*. Their use of *enargeia* or vividness clearly contributes to knowing and understanding Jesus's parables, but most importantly for modern readers, it brings about the realization that to attain God's heavenly kingdom requires disposition and transformation. This parable, which emphasizes the woman and the leaven to teach effectively about God's kingdom, deserves to be called the Parable of the Industrious Woman.

Conclusion

The rhetorical analysis of the parables in this chapter has highlighted important elements in a personal spiritual journey toward God. The descriptive speech and vividness in each parable—the Trustful Man (Mark 4:26–29), the Silent Sower (Matt 13:31–32 // Mark 4:30–32 // Luke 13:18–19), and the Industrious Woman (Matt 13:33 // Luke 13:20–21)—heighten the individual's actions and expose his or her own disposition and trust in God's invitation to participate in His divine world. Using a powerful rhetorical device—the kingdom of God (Mark and Luke) or the kingdom of heaven (Matthew)—the evangelists' Jesus reveals to his disciples how to know and understand his parables. In the simplicity of an ordinary human activity, like sowing seed in the Parable of the Trustful Man (Mark 4:26–29), the nature of God's heavenly realm becomes known to and understood by human beings. The Markan Jesus provides the best explanation of God's heavenly realm and a clear revelation of a person's *active role in sowing the seed* and perceiving its growth as God's mysterious ways of acting. Likewise, in the simplicity of a mustard seed in the Parable of the Silent Sower (Matt 13:31–32 // Mark 4:30–32 // Luke 13:18–19), the evangelists' use of rhetorical devices emphasizes their explication of *what is like* the nature of God's heavenly realm through the *sower's action and quiet disposition* to see God's power. Furthermore, using the simplicity of leaven, both Matthew (13:33) and Luke (13:20–21) in the Parable of the Industrious Woman clearly represent the individual's role in knowing and understanding *what is like* the nature of God's heavenly realm. It is not only a revelation of God's heavenly world; it is a revelation of an individual and active participation in attaining God's divine realm.

    The evangelists' effective ways of using rhetorical techniques of the *progymnasmata*, such as descriptive speech and vividness, help their audiences, and us as readers, to gain the virtues of knowledge and understanding. Significantly, the Parables of the Trustful Man, the Silent Sower, and the Industrious Woman have revealed two essential points: the focus is *not* on the kingdom of heaven/God—this is a theme used as a rhetorical device—but on both the "man's" and the "woman's" ordinary activities, either active or passive, and on their responses to the implications of knowing and understanding God's heavenly realm. Hearers are invited to make the male sowers' and the woman's activities *their own activities and responses*; in these parables we know and understand the true message: our role is *participation,* and we are called to *participate.* The rhetorical features of vividness emphasized the positive attitudes of the sowers and the woman expressed in two action verbs and a passive one: an ordinary, simple action of *sowing*; a trustful, patient, and silent *awaiting* (Mark 4:26–29; Matt 13:31–32 // Mark 4:30–32 // Luke 13:18–19), and an industrious participation in a familiar and daily task of *leavening* (Matt 13:33 // Luke 13:20–21).

    These three parables have placed before the readers' and hearers' eyes, first, how something small can become something great, and second, how human activity and attitude can foster the practice of virtues. We see that knowledge and understanding in connection to Jesus's parables can be a simple, insignificant beginning that with a good disposition can lead to something great. Knowledge and understanding are the beginning of becoming active participants and of having a positive attitude, which in return will elicit a series of other virtues: for example, being trustful and silent will bring forth the virtues of humility, reliance, faith, and patience; being active and industrious will bring forward the virtues of confidence, service, and trust. These virtues are essential to begin our spiritual journey toward genuine happiness and holiness, which means the attainment of God's heavenly realm. Therefore, the features of power, mystery, and surprise associated with God's divine nature should not leave modern readers in distress. Rather, the virtues of trust and patience as well as faith/faithfulness should encourage readers, as it did to Jesus's audience, to embark on a spiritual journey in the quest for human transformation.

2
INTERNALIZING JESUS'S MESSAGE IN THE PARABLES

After coming to know and understand Jesus's parables (chapter 1), we will examine two beautiful parables, Matt 25:14–30 and Luke 19:11–27, to help us internalize Jesus's message as we continue our spiritual journey toward *eudaimonia*, "happiness," and spiritual transformation.[1] As mentioned before, the analysis of the rhetorical character of each parable will help us to identify a suitable name for them at the conclusion of our discussion. Throughout the rhetorical analysis of these two parables, we will again highlight the components outlined in the "preliminary exercises" or the *progymnasmata*, which provided Matthew and Luke with a store of practical techniques of presentation and argumentation, in particular, "descriptive speech" (*ekphrasis*), which helped them to structure their parables to provide their messages more effectively.

The rhetorical analysis of the parables in Matt 25:14–30 and Luke 19:11–27 encourages us to internalize the parable's true message. Indeed, when reading Matthew's and Luke's parables within the *ekphrastic* context, modern readers get a sense of belonging that allows Jesus's parables to become personal experiences for them. Thus, the story becomes not about someone *then* (two thousand years ago) but about the hearer or reader *now*. Our study of these two parables focuses primarily on the *individual* as Jesus puts before our eyes the attitude and response of two servants. The rhetorical analysis answers two questions: What is the *message* of Jesus in these parables in light of the parables studied in chapter 1? And how do we achieve happiness, thus attaining God's heavenly kingdom?

Internalizing Jesus's Message in the Parables

Jesus's Parables: The Way toward God

According to Plato, the Stoics, and Aristotle, the practice of virtues is key to gaining human happiness, which ultimately has the goal of "becoming like to God." However, these Greek thinkers believed that one single virtue was necessary in order to possess any of the others—"prudence" or "practical wisdom" (*phronēsis*).[2] Having this powerful virtue meant to have or to possess all the other virtues. In other words, among the four cardinal virtues (prudence, justice, courage, and temperance) and all the other virtues, the virtue of prudence secures the individual's likeness to God.[3] In this context, Plato's Socrates spoke of the unity of virtue and argued that "virtue is one."[4] Similar to ancient Greek philosophers, Hellenistic Jewish authors, particularly Philo of Alexandria and Paul of Tarsus (contemporaries in the first century CE), also perceived the possession of virtues as the benefit flowing from one particular virtue. Philo believed that the virtue of "piety" (*eusebeia*) is the key virtue that not only holds the other virtues but also leads the human soul to attain perfection. For Philo, the person who possesses piety also possesses all the other virtues.[5] For Paul, the combination of possessing the Spirit (of God) and practicing the virtue of "love" (*agapē*) elicits virtues. In Galatians, Paul introduces the framework of his ethics where the "Spirit" (*pneuma*) is the fountain or source of virtues (Gal 5:1–6:10). The Spirit of God/Christ received in baptism empowers the believer to be holy and righteous before God through the possession of virtues. Indeed, Paul claims that the one who is guided by, or lives by, the Spirit has the "fruit" of the Spirit: love, joy, peace, patience, kindness, generosity, faithfulness, gentleness, and self-control (Gal 5:16, 18, 22–25).[6] In Paul's list of virtues, love holds the primary place, but not until his letter to the Corinthians does Paul privilege the virtue of love as the queen of virtues (greater than faith and hope, 1 Cor 13) and attribute to it the other virtues.

One of the goals of examining the use of rhetorical techniques of descriptive speech and vividness in this chapter, then, is to bring to the surface and highlight the virtues and vices that are reflected in, or possessed by, the major characters in each of the two parables—the servants. This new and fresh take on the parables of Jesus heightens the importance of the practice of virtues and the avoidance of vices, ethically speaking, essential to holiness and to living a life pleasing to God.

The Power of Transformation

Matthew 25:14–30: Virtuous Attitudes in Business

This parable appears in the "Eschatological Discourse" of Matt 24—25. It is third in a list of parables concerning the events of the *parousia*, or second coming of Christ. During the interim period in which the early believers were living, Matthew saw the urgency to tell believers in his community to be faithful and watchful because no one knew when Jesus would return. Matthew writes the following parable.

Table 2.1. Matt 25:14-30
Business Language: [14]For it is as if a man, going on a journey, summoned his servants and entrusted his property to them; [15]to one he gave five talents, to another two, to another one, to each according to his ability. Then he went away. [16]The one who had received the five talents went off at once and traded with them, and made five more talents. [17]In the same way, the one who had the two talents made two more talents. [18]But the one who had received the one talent went off and dug a hole in the ground and hid his master's money.
Expected Response: [19]After a long time the master of those servants came and settled accounts with them. [20]Then the one who had received the five talents came forward, bringing five more talents, saying, "Master, you handed over to me five talents; see, I have made five more talents." [21]His master said to him, "Well done, good and trustworthy servant; you have been trustworthy in a few things, I will put you in charge of many things; enter into the joy of your master." [22]And the one with the two talents also came forward, saying, "Master, you handed over to me two talents; see, I have made two more talents." [23]His master said to him, "Well done, good and trustworthy servant; you have been trustworthy in a few things, I will put you in charge of many things; enter into the joy of your master."
Negative Response: [24]Then the one who had received the one talent also came forward, saying, "Master, I knew that you were a harsh man, reaping where you did not sow, and gathering where you did not scatter seed; [25]so I was afraid, and I went and hid your talent in the ground. Here you have what is yours." [26]But his master replied, "You wicked and lazy servant! You knew, did you, that I reap where I did not sow, and gather where I did not scatter? [27]Then you ought to have invested my money with the bankers, and on my return I would have received what was my own with interest. [28]So take the talent from him, and give it to the one with the ten talents.
Teaching Moment: [29]For to all those who have, more will be given, and they will have an abundance; but from those who have nothing, even what they have will be taken away. [30]As for this worthless servant, throw him into the outer darkness, where there will be weeping and gnashing of teeth."

Internalizing Jesus's Message in the Parables

This Matthean parable is, together with Luke's parable in 19:11–27, among the longer narrative parables, and it is clearly important for the evangelist.[7] It has been argued that Matthew's version is a "fairly straightforward double indirect narrative parable without a *nimshal*," that is, without a lesson.[8] Biblical scholars link this parable with the two parables in Matt 24:45–51 and 25:1–13 and the Matthean theme of the coming of the Messiah on judgment day.[9] As Harrington notes, Matthew gives special attention to the Markan theme of constant watchfulness (Mark 13:35). Indeed, this parable contributes to the picture of what constitutes responsible behavior in preparation for Jesus's second coming.[10] Although the eschatological horizon is an important theme in the parable, our rhetorical analysis will focus on the proper behavior and attitude required to attain the heavenly realm (or heaven).

To help us internalize Jesus's message in this parable, I intend to highlight the techniques used in *ekphrasis* or descriptive language—vividness, clarity, conciseness, style, verisimilitude, and imagination—as well as the features of *enargeia* or vividness—amplification and repetition. For the purpose of clarity and effectivity, the parable in Matt 25:14–30 is divided into four parts: (1) the business deal, vv.14–18; (2) the expected response, vv.19–23; (3) the negative attitude, vv. 24–28; and (4) the teaching moment, vv. 29–30.[11] We will focus on the major character in the story—the servant—and the dynamic relationship between the servant and the master (or lord) in regard to the talents. Rhetorically "servant" refers to the major character in the story and represents one person with three different responses. We are invited to see ourselves faced with three different responses and attitudes to choose and follow.

The Business Deal (25:14–18)

Once more the Matthean Jesus delivers a parable using a familiar practice in the milieu of the Judean and Galilean first century CE. This example comes from the economic world—the proper way of *doing business*. Business loans between those with resources and workers were common in the ancient world; these are attested by several parables and various other sources.[12] However, any discussion of interest loans in ancient Palestine, including Galilee, is complicated. It might have been that no prohibition on business loans was in effect in the first century CE.[13] According to the view of a Mediterranean peasant, seeking more was always morally wrong, because the pie (of all good and goods) was both limited and already distributed. In the economic system of the Mediterranean world, the standard of doing business involved the belief that an increase in the share of one person automatically meant a loss for someone else.[14] The hearers, who knew the intricacies of the honor-and-shame society as well as what it meant to live in a "Palestinian primitive" community or village, expected servants to cooperate with their masters. Ancient Mediterranean cities (e.g., Sepphoris and Tiberias, both Herod Antipas's capital cities) were characterized by political rule and economic control, which inevitably affected small villages and towns. Within this context, social elites in cities exerted economic control over Galilee.[15] In other words, servants would not have the power for commercial enterprise; the master had absolute control over both economic transactions and the servants' future.[16]

The archaeological evidence for Galilean business affairs estimates the impact on international trade based on urban architecture and population size.[17] Public architecture in the first century CE increased interregional trade. Colonnaded market areas with paved streets and water channels were introduced to Galilee. These Roman-style features facilitated the transportation of resources, goods, and money in interregional trade and business.[18] Galilean demographics show population growth, which created a shift not only in agricultural but also in economic patterns across Galilee. In Galilean society, villagers and rural peasants were familiar with the increased agricultural production fostered under centralized Herodian authority. On the one hand, Judean and Galilean villagers and peasants were aware that the practice of doing business (or trading) required a higher demand for taxes to support a growing administrative apparatus, a manufacturing sector, and construction crews.[19] On the other hand, wealthy villagers, urban landowners, or members of the ruling apparatus were solicited as magnanimous patrons. They were the largest landowners and provided seasonal work, allowing peasants to stay on their land and work it. Members of the ruling apparatus could sometimes ease individuals' tax burdens in exchange for service and honor.[20]

In 25:14–18, the Matthean Jesus employs the language of business as a "hook" to capture his listeners' attention. The story begins with a peculiar introduction already familiar to his audience, "for it is as if a man" (25:14a). Two rhetorical elements produce the vividness of the introduction; first is the adverbial word "as if" (*hōsper*), which tells us that the author is about to present a *similitude*, a type of parable. Second, with the conjunction "for" (*gar*), Matthew creates a bridge between the previous comparison in Matt 25:1–13 (a parable about ten bridesmaids) and this similitude in Matt 25:14–30. The rhetorician Quintilian claims that in vivid illustration or representation, it is a great gift to be able to set forth the facts in a way that appeals to the listeners.²¹ In order to evoke a sense of connection with the parable, to put the story or subject before the readers' and hearers' eyes, Matthew applies the technique of repetition, an important device of "vividness" (*enargeia*). In the Parable of the Silent Sower in Matt 13:31–32 (see chapter 1), the evangelist used the word "a man" (*anthrōpos*, v. 31c); now he repeats the same word (25:14a) to create *continuity* between what we already know and understand about Jesus's parables (in close connection with what is like the nature of God's heavenly realm) and the internalization of Jesus's message in his parables. Thus, Matthew's short yet rhetorically powerful introduction shows his acquaintance with essential techniques learned in basic composition to effectively convey information and persuade his audience.²²

The form in which Matthew elaborates his narrative contains advanced features of vivid representation, such as "amplification" (*auxēsis*), "clarity" (*saphēneia*), "repetition" (*anaphora*), "verisimilitude" (*pithanotēs*), and "imagination" (*phantasia*). Matthew uses amplification in key points in his narrative. The first device of amplification appears immediately after the indefinite noun "a man" in 25:14b: "going on a journey." This puts before our eyes the object, a man who is preparing to leave (see Mark 13:34). At this point (25:14c–15c) the evangelist presents two of the three central features: "the servants" (*douloi*) and the "talents" (*talanta*). The scenario that depicts *a man* who "summoned his servants and entrusted his property to them" (v. 14c) shows that the man is very rich, and the servants are simple villagers or peasants. The Matthean Jesus presents to his audience a common practice of Galilean and Judean economic affairs. Whether the increase of economic wealth was viewed as *just* (a view from the perspective of the elite) or *unjust* (a view from the perspective of the peasants), the business deal—entrusting his property—that "a man" arranges with his servants represents a tangible experience for many of Jesus's audience.

Then, with the vivid language, "entrusting his property," Matthew helps the listeners to imagine the business deal that follows in v. 15. They create in their "imagination" (*phantasia*) a picture of a rich man going on a trip and leaving his property with his servants.²³ This economic transaction involving talents (the man's property) is brought before the eyes and not just the ears.[24] As Matthew narrates, "to one he gave five talents, to another two, to another one, to each according to his ability" (25:15). We see the evangelist's style used in defining realistically, according to the first-century period, *how many talents* each servant receives. Likewise, his statement "to each according to his ability" not only justifies but *amplifies* his presentation of the number of talents that each servant receives. This extra, yet important, information functions as an *enargetic* device to elicit an emotional response, to be developed further in parts 2 (vv. 19–23) and 3 (vv. 24–28).

Each description creates a sense of clarity and verisimilitude to contribute to the plausibility of the story.[25] Matthew's use of "five talents" given to the first servant represents a rhetorical hyperbole, since this was a great deal of money. Indeed, one talent in the ancient world was a monetary weight of approximately sixty to ninety pounds,[26] or about six thousand denarii. Therefore, the value of a talent was equivalent to six thousand day's wages (denarii), roughly twenty years of work![27] This hyperbolic detail is meant to elicit surprise, in which we would also imaginatively connect it with the mustard seed's hyperbolic description of "greatest" in Matt 13:31–32.[28] The addition in v. 15d of "then he [the man] went away," reinforces the *enargetic* device of repetition, which highlights the expression previously stated in v. 14a, "a man going on a journey." Thus, the author creates an *inclusio*; indeed, in both statements Matthew uses the same verb "to go away/abroad" (*apodēmeō*). The repetition of a "man going on a journey" prepares for the narrative section in part 3 (vv. 24–28) and part 4 (vv. 29–30).

Within the backdrop of the economic system in the Mediterranean world—where doing business involved the servants' cooperation with the increase of their masters' wealth—Matthew elaborates symmetrically rhetorical techniques in 25:16–18. This short section (three verses only) helps us visualize the three actions of "a servant," who is engaged in business; two actions are the same, and one is odd. The statement "a servant" is part of the rhetorical techniques of "descriptive speech" (*ekphrasis*). Matthew gives to this servant a particular emphasis to effect "vividness" (*enargeia*); this allows us to see ourselves as the "servant." The descriptive statements in vv. 16–18 use the element of repetition, heightening the significance of the "servant" and the "number of talents" received. Matthew quickly and vividly presents three actions of an imagined "servant," yet he does not provide details (or time) of the servant's engagement in the commercial enterprise or trade.

In an orderly and repeated pattern (see the language in v. 15 and vv. 16, 17), Matthew describes the servant's business transactions as vividly as possible to "bring it before the eyes" of his listeners. He describes that the "one who had received the five talents went off at once and traded with them, and made five more talents" (v. 16). Matthew strategically repeats twice what he said in v. 15 ("five talents"), a powerful rhetorical sign for his hearers and readers to "imagine" (*phantasia*) that they themselves are the "servant" who received "five talents" (30,000 denarii, equivalent to one hundred years' wages!) and produced "five more talents" (for a total of 60,000 denarii!) in doing business. That the servant "went off at once and traded with them [talents]" (v. 16) presents pictorially the servant's engagement in a successful "interregional business" or trade. The verb "went off" (*poreuomai*) has the meaning of "travel," "journey," or "go."[29] Thus, it implies that the servant traveled some distance to do business with the five talents.[30] Furthermore, the aorist verb *ērgasato* (translated here as "traded") reinforces the servant's action, providing the specific information that the servant engaged in trading, but not specifying what kind of business the servant was doing (the same would be true for the servant in v. 17).

Within the context of the *progymnasmata*, Matthew's omission of the kind of business in which the servant engages facilitates our ability to put ourselves in the servant's place, which helps Matthew's desire to persuade us. His ambiguous statement leaves open for the audience the various possibilities in the business world, so that we can imagine the business type we are most familiar with. In this way, we can easily see ourselves working with the available talents and *doing business*.[31] The technique of amplification in v. 17 ("in the same way") reinforces the amplifications previously seen in v. 14 ("going on a journey"), v. 15 ("to each according to his ability"), and later in v. 19 ("after a long time"). It also alerts us that the business deal of the second servant will follow the same action. Indeed, we can now transport ourselves into the scene to see that the servant "who had received two talents" traveled away to do business, engaged in interregional trade, and successfully made two more talents. The adjective "more" (*alla*) is a rhetorical touch that glosses the element of excitement expected from the servant (and us). ⁿur imagination, we can see ourselves doubling the huge amount of ʳeceived from the rich man (12,000 denarii, equivalent to forty years' wages, doubled to 24,000 denarii!). The use of hyperbole helps us engage with the story as if we are doing the same action, that is, "imitating" (*mimesis*) the trading.

Matthew now turns to another action in his highly structured parable. At the end of the first section (25:18) he switches to the servant who received "one talent." Matthew writes: "But the one who had received the one talent went off and dug a hole in the ground and hid his master's money." The conjunction "but" (*de*) creates a sense of contrast between the previous two actions of the "servant" in vv. 16 and 17. Matthew's technique of repetition, such as "one talent" (vv. 15, 18), and "went off" (vv. 16, 18; here *apelthōn*, lit. going away, or departing), reflects again the stylistic technique of clarity to enhance our imagination. His descriptive language relates the different action of the third servant as he buried his master's money. The evangelist's vivid description provides a lifelike picture of the servant digging "a hole *in the ground*" to bring before our eyes the action. His representation of the scene is enhanced by the repetition "in the ground" (*gē*, lit. "earth") to create connection, thus continuity, with the actions of the Silent Sower, who sows mustard seed "upon the ground" (Matt 13:31b). Hiding money in the ground was a common practice as attested in Jewish literature (e.g., the Qumran Copper Scroll 3Q15 is a list of hidden treasures),[32] and this gives credibility to Matthew's story and "brings before the eyes" the scene of the servant's action. As Hultgren points out, to place money into the ground for safekeeping was not unusual in the world of Jesus (e.g., Matt 13:44, the treasure hidden in the field).[33]

Matthew's narrative style generates a vivid visual presence by changing two words. "A man" (*anthrōpos*) in 25:14a becomes a more specific character, the "master" or "lord" (*kyrios*) in 25:18. This stylistic feature confirms two things that we may have already imagined; the "man" is indeed very rich, a "master" or "lord," who has employed peasants or villagers in his commercial business. Second, the "talents" are "money," the master's property.

To further enhance the vividness (*enargeia*) of his story, Matthew uses two tools—repetition and amplification. In the first part of his parable, vv. 14–18, Matthew uses a series of symmetrical repetitions— "servant," "talent," "five," "two," "one," "another," "more." The evangelist combines his technique of repetition with the device of amplification in specific locations—"going on a journey" (v. 14), "Then he went away," "to each according to his ability" (v. 15), and "in the same way" (v. 17).

Internalizing Jesus's Message in the Parables

These two elements help Matthew prepare the minds of the hearers and readers for what follows in the parable. At the same time, Matthew creates a sense of continuity with the Parable of the Silent Sower by using two repeated words: "man" and "in the ground." The author's emphasis on the "money" reveals the expected action of increasing the master's wealth (or fortune) by trading his money in business. All the servant's "three actions" could be anticipated given the great amounts in the outcomes of the parables of the Silent Sower and the Industrious Woman. Even *hiding money* was a normal practice.

THE POSITIVE RESPONSE (25:19–23)

Matthew now moves beyond the rationalization and knowledge of Jesus's parable toward an eschatological context. Matthew's goal in writing the parables is to have his readers or hearers *internalize* Jesus's messages. He knows that his audience needs help doing this, which Matthew gives with rhetorical and allegorical interpretative systems about the last judgment. In four verses, vv. 19–23, Matthew seeks to turn readers into spectators, thus, providing a vicarious visual experience for them.[34] He believes that the effects of "vividness" (*enargeia*) will stir the emotions necessary to internalize Jesus's message in the journey to true happiness.[35] In this section, the rhetorical "style" (*lexis*) influences the evangelist's choice of words, metaphors, images, narrative, and arrangement. These important rhetorical skills combine with the element of surprise—the unexpected response—that the readers or hearers may find difficult to understand. Here Matthew emphasizes not the "action" but the "response."

Matthew's rhetorical narrative in these four verses (vv. 19–23) is quite remarkable. It contains both repetition (more than any other section in the parable) to achieve vividness and business language *enargetically* framed in dialogue between the servant and the master. Matthew begins by alluding to the delay of the *parousia*, "after a long time" (v. 19a), to capture his audience's attention. The coming of the last judgment is a major and familiar topic for the believers in the Matthean community (see 24:45–51; 25:1–13), so the evangelist skillfully includes this central motif in his narrative to amplify his vivid description. The master, who entrusted money (talents) to his servants, returns to settle accounts with them (v. 19b). The first-century audience would know that the master expects a huge increase of his wealth (or property) through the business deals done by the servants. They have received money according to their own "ability," and the master expects *proper behavior* and a *proper response*.

The vivid representation in 25:20–23 is filled with repetition, which for Matthew is key not only for understanding but also for internalizing Jesus's message. To evoke a sense of realism in the audience's imagination, the evangelist creates an identical and well-structured dialogue between the servants and the master.

> [20]Then the one who had received the five talents came forward, bringing five more talents, saying, "Master, you handed over to me five talents; see, I have made five more talents."
>
> [21] His master said to him, "Well done, good and trustworthy servant; you have been trustworthy in a few things, I will put you in charge of many things; enter into the joy of your master."
>
> [22]And the one with the two talents also came forward, saying, "Master, you handed over to me two talents; see, I have made two more talents."
>
> [23]His master said to him, "Well done, good and trustworthy servant; you have been trustworthy in a few things, I will put you in charge of many things; enter into the joy of your master."

Matthew emphasizes the eagerness and the faithfulness of the first and second servants. Both servants do what is expected by the master ("see, I have made…more talents"), and both servants show their effectiveness and loyalty as servants ("Well done, good and trustworthy servant").[36] The evangelist develops the vividness of the business dialogue between the master and the servants by making the second dialogue the same as the first. Initially, the identical repetition (with the exception of the number of talents, v. 20bc and v. 22bc) appears unnecessary, or maybe too repetitious. However, in the context of the techniques of "descriptive speech" (*ekphrasis*), Matthew's skillful use of "vividness" (*enargeia*) as his rhetorical tool allows the audience to *see* the scene of the business deal between the master and each of the servants.

First, we internalize Matthew's repetitions—"the one," "talents," "came forward," "saying, 'Master, you handed over to me…talents,'" "see, I have made…more talents,'" "His master said to him, 'Well done, good and trustworthy servant; you have been trustworthy in a few things, I will put you in charge of many things; enter into the joy of your master." The repetitions unify the business dialogue in vv. 20–23 between the master and his servants. Secondly, the repetitions enhance the vivid images of the behavior of the two principal characters, the master and the servant. The business dialogue is presented graphically to our minds, not the action itself. The servant's response to his master is what Matthew highlights through repetition. In the first response, the servant says, "Master, you handed over to me five talents; see, I have made five more talents" (25:20bc), and the second servant responds likewise saying, "Master, you handed over to me two talents; see, I have made two more talents" (25:22bc).

In the context of the *progymnasmata*, two points in the responses of the servant in both v. 20bc and v. 22bc are worth mentioning. First, the strong connection between Matthew's style, vividness, repetition, and clarity makes it difficult to separate the servants' responses.[37] That is, the visual language helps us to see in our mind's eye *two same responses* of *a* servant, not two servants. Interestingly, the servant's responses in both cases are not only the *same* (the servant doubled the amount of talents) but are both surprising and challenging. From a first-century-CE worldview, especially from a peasant point of view, the servant's responses of increasing the master's huge wealth would have been viewed as simply unacceptable. However, the process of internalizing the message of Jesus's parables provokes a challenging reaction! Peasants would have viewed the servant as a robber who had cooperated with the evil master in extortionist schemes designed to steal the resources of others.[38] With this picture in mind, the Matthean Jesus challenges his audience to look beyond what is expected; in fact, the servant's responses (vv. 20, 22) show the correct behavior (vv. 21, 23)! The master entrusted his property to his servant, which comes to its fulfillment with the positive responses; indeed, the hyperbolic enormous amount (first *ten* talents and then *four* talents) vividly demonstrates the expected responses.

Secondly, Matthew alludes to the sense of sight in order to help his readers use their imagination and *see* with their mind's eye.[39] Twice the evangelist writes the word "see" (v. 20c and v. 22c), in each case vividly emphasizing the servant's expected response. We are able to visualize the good behavior, which is repeated twice, so that we internalize the behavior expected of the servants. Matthew knows that in rhetorical-poetic representation, what is vivid appeals to the senses, particularly to sight.[40]

Matthew's technique of repetition and his emphasis on the sense of sight bring before the eyes of his audience the importance of the practice of virtues. The positive response reveals that each servant received talents according to his *own ability* (see 25:15c). This indicates that by doubling the number of talents received, the servant made good use of his ability. In the process of internalization, we do not imagine whether the servant's response is contrary to the socially expected behavior from the peasants' viewpoint. Rather, Matthew's vivid description brings to light virtues, first, the servant's *faithfulness* and the master's *trust*. Other virtues are reflected in the business dialogue when the master twice commends (repetition) the servant's positive response: "Well done, good and trustworthy servant" (25:21, 23). To add clarity—a quality of amplification—to his vivid description, he appeals to the authority of Jewish-Christian tradition by alluding to the Messianic banquet in vv. 21 and 23: "enter into the joy of your master."[41] This *ekphrastic* technique focuses on revealing key virtues in the master's commendation, which speaks of the virtues of responsibility, goodness, trustworthiness, and joy. These virtues lead the master to put this faithful and trustworthy servant in charge of "many things." For the servant (and for us), his virtues become the "source" for internalizing Jesus's message.

When we remain in the stage of just knowing and understanding Jesus's parables (chapter 1), the message is understood only on the surface. In other words, the hearer or reader believes that the servant's response is just like the master's response, a response that is rapacious and shameless, and judges the master as a thief, and arrogantly inhumane. Therefore, the wrong belief is that honorable people should not try to get more; otherwise, this servant would be considered a thief.[42] Negatively judging the servant's response of increasing the master's wealth at the expense of others is clearly wrong. What reveals the true meaning and message is the vivid description reflected in the business dialogue. The *ekphrastic* devices, which produce graphic pictures of the scenes in the human mind, help to reorient us to the true message of Jesus's parables. Therefore, the master's praise contains a sense of mystery, which is highlighted in the vivid presentation of the servant's reward: "enter into the joy of your master" (25:23). Matthew's powerful language within the context of the Messianic banquet shows that the servant's successful handling of responsibility is a vivid expression of

Internalizing Jesus's Message in the Parables

his virtuous character. Thus, the vivid metaphor of the final judgment rhetorically suggests the positive qualities of the servant.

The internalization of Jesus's message leads us to two important reflections about the servant: first, his positive *response* demonstrates the servant's ability to perform "other things" successfully; second, the reward given to the servant involves the *practice of virtues*. Indeed, the servant possesses virtues, especially the virtue of "joy" (*chara*). The emphasis on the virtue of joy is essential in the process of internalization. Surprisingly, Matthew does not use the language of the "kingdom of heaven/God" in this parable. Vividly he brings before his audience's eyes God's heavenly realm in the virtue of joy. Matthew expresses the joy and true happiness of God's heavenly realm as he states, *"enter* into the *joy* of your master" (25:23). Thus, the virtue of joy is used as a synonym of (or an indirect allusion to) the kingdom of heaven, and the role of the master is a vivid metaphor for God. In a person's journey toward happiness, the internalization of Jesus's message comes to a turning point expressed in virtues, and joy is singled out to represent the final goal of one's spiritual journey. The virtues of trust, faithfulness (these two were already reflected in the sowers' and the woman's actions in chapter 1), responsibility, goodness, trustworthiness, and joy are the virtues necessary to move on to the next stage of spiritual growth (chapter 3) and are the foundation of achieving happiness (see chapter 4).

THE NEGATIVE RESPONSE (25:24–28)

In the second part of the dialogue between the master and the servant,[43] Matthew uses dramatic language involving repetition, style, and amplification.[44] The business dialogue again exhorts the importance of the practice of virtues in opposition to vices. In this section, Matthew's repetition connects back to the language of farming seen in the parable of chapter 1 as the basis of the persuasion attributed to Jesus. In addition, the evangelist vividly presents the master's harsh language before the audience's eyes.

Matthew uses the conjunction "then" (*de*) to transport us into a new scene in the parable. He writes, "Then the one who had received the one talent also came forward, saying, 'Master, I knew that you were a harsh man, reaping where you did not sow, and gathering where you did not scatter seed; so I was afraid, and I went and hid your talent in the ground. Here you have what is yours'" (25:24–25). This servant's

The Power of Transformation

response radically differs from the two previous examples in 25:20–23. As Matthew described in 25:18, the servant received one talent, a huge amount of money (6,000 denarii). Using the technique of repetition in 25:24–25—"received," "one talent," "also," "came forward," "master"— Matthew rhetorically connects this dialogue with the two previous sections in the parable (vv. 14–18 and vv. 19–23). Also, the addition of the servant's repeated farming language—"reaping," "sow," "gathering," "scatter," "seed," and "in the ground"—skillfully creates a link between this parable and the Parable of the Silent Sower. These techniques offer clarity and enhance the vividness of the narrative by arousing our "imagination" (*phantasia*). The surprising element in the servant's words is that he did not engage in business with the one talent that his master entrusted to him.

Matthew also uses the amplification device, "I knew you were a harsh man" (25:24b), to provide the rationale behind the servant's omission of doing the expected business. His reaction is odd because he describes his master's character as "harsh," a qualification not described in 25:14. He likewise connects the master's harsh attitude with a series of repetitions related to farming actions familiar to Matthew's audience (see chapter 1). While the rational, cognitive narrative highlights the master's character in his doing business with his servant and portrays him as a bad master who takes advantage of his servant, the rhetorical-poetic description highlights the servant's negative response, his failure to act opportunely. The rhetorical techniques of repetition and amplification emphasize the importance of engaging with the object (e.g., seed, leaven, or talent) in the person's possession.

We have seen ourselves imaginatively in the action, sowing the mustard seed or leavening the flour, and have understood the importance of *action*. Now, through the repeated words (especially the farming language), Matthew urges remembrance of the appropriate behavior. So, in this parable the Matthean Jesus challenges his audience by revealing a key element in the journey toward happiness: the unexpected behavior becomes the expected behavior. From the first-century-peasant viewpoint, the expected behavior was to secure the talent by hiding it; indeed, this was considered the honorable thing to do. At first glance, the servant appears to be acting in a morally responsible way.[45] For the audience, this servant acted honorably because he refused to participate in the rapacious schemes of the master. This view is supported by scripture; based on Old Testament law, charging interest to other Israelites was prohibited (e.g., Exod 22:25; Lev 25:35–37; Deut 23:19–20).[46]

We must view the response in 25:24–28 through the lens of rhetoric and go deeper into the significance of Jesus's message. The servant hides the "one talent" he was entrusted with because he is "afraid" (25:25a), and he accuses his master of illicit gains, reaping where he did not sow and harvesting where he did not scatter (25:24b). The servant fails to act because of "fear" (*phobos*), one of the four passions the Stoics believed should be eliminated.[47] He lacks confidence and the virtues that would enable him to do something with his one talent, except to secure it by burying it *in the ground*. In the servant's words to his master in vv. 24–25, nothing good and worthy is revealed. Both the *ekphrastic* and *enargetic* features bring before our eyes the negative character of the servant—his insecurity, his judgmentalism toward his master, his laziness, his irresponsibility, his hypocrisy, his low self-esteem, and his inability to respond appropriately. The amplification of "here you have what is yours" (25:25b) shows the servant's proud and arrogant behavior and demonstrates that his choice was out of fear. He will find out soon that his choice of returning the one talent to his master was wrong.

In the dialogue of 25:26–28, the master's answer to his servant strongly reflects the wrongdoing of his servant:

> [26]But his master replied, "You wicked and lazy servant! You knew, did you, that I reap where I did not sow, and gather where I did not scatter? [27]Then you ought to have invested my money with the bankers, and on my return I would have received what was my own with interest. [28]So take the talent from him, and give it to the one with the ten talents.

Again through repetition, the Matthean Jesus uses the negative response of the servant to convince his audience that they *should not* repeat the servant's wrongdoing. The rhetorical language with its vivid picture expresses the master's disappointment, for the servant *ought* to have used his *ability* and engaged in a business transaction. The master's harsh language against the servant vividly highlights the servant's vices of wickedness, laziness, and disobedience. Sadly, the servant does not display a single virtue; his response reflects only vices and the perception that he does not know his responsibility and obligation toward his master. Matthew's stylistic narrative uses a play on words: "You knew, did you" (25:26c), which rhetorically plays an important role in his art of persuasion. The Matthean Jesus directly confronts and challenges us using the repetition of the phrase "I reap where I did not sow, and gather where I did not scatter" (25:26c; see 25:24b), clarifying the fact that the servant *should have known* his obligation and responsibility. Using the same words as the servant, the evangelist makes the master discredit the servant's wrong argument with the sharp response, "Then you ought to have invested my money with the bankers, and on my return I would have received what was my own with interest" (25:27).

Jesus's audience can imagine the possibility of opting for the servant's choice, which is not taking even the minimal risk of investing the talent with bankers.[48] The harsh condemnation he receives at the hands of the master is just what peasants have learned to expect in the real world; the rich take care of their own.[49] However, Matthew has tried to vividly present before his audience's eyes the reverse, that the servant ought to do business with the money according to his own ability. The servant's negative response has negative consequences; the master gives orders to "take the talent from him [the servant]" and "give it to the one with the ten talents" (25:28). Matthew develops his rhetorical description to teach that the servant loses the talent because *he lacks essential virtues*. He had wrong expectations thinking that by "hiding the talent in the ground" he was practicing the virtue of prudence. Unlike the servant who received five talents and made five talents more, this third servant does not display or practice virtues but rather has shown only vices through his response: unfaithfulness, pride, fear, laziness, wickedness, selfishness, disobedience, irresponsibility, distrust, and infidelity.

Rewards are given to the servants who cooperate, those who practice virtues and avoid vices. But it is not sufficient for the servant to show his potential and ability expressed in virtues. In 25:24–28, Matthew teaches his audience that the practice of virtues and the avoidance of vices are required in order to internalize the message of Jesus's parables. His vivid presentation, which helps to bring the servants' responses before the eyes of his audience, creates a sense of reality in their minds, that the message of Jesus's parables is a message of virtues expressed through the individual's own character and ability. Thus, internalizing Jesus's message means going beyond the social and economic norms and challenging the expected with the unexpected response.

Internalizing Jesus's Message in the Parables

THE TEACHING MOMENT (25:29–30)

Matthew concludes his parable with a short, clear message.[50] Before the Matthean Jesus finishes his parable, he provides a vivid moral exhortation, so that his audience clearly visualizes both the reward and the harsh condemnation. Matthew writes, "For to all those who have, more will be given, and they will have an abundance; but from those who have nothing, even what they have will be taken away. As for this worthless servant, throw him into the outer darkness, where there will be weeping and gnashing of teeth" (25:29–30). Although the saying seems difficult to fathom and appears to be unfair from a rational point of view, the rhetorical features employed heighten the persuasive quality of the parable's lesson. Once again Matthew relies on the Jewish-Christian tradition of the eschatological expectation to give authority to Jesus's teaching moment. This technique strengthens the audience's attention in order to bring before their eyes the scenes of the story, thus fixing in their minds the central idea of the parable. According to Jesus's teaching, the person who has been trustworthy in small matters can be trusted with larger ones.[51] Jesus says, "to those who have, more will be given" (25:29a); "more" will be *given* to those who *respond positively* to the message of Jesus's parables.

The servants who received five and two talents, according to their ability, responded positively to the master's abundant generosity. However, when internalizing the message of Jesus's parable, we must realize that it is not about having material possessions or wealth (talents) but having virtues and displaying them in good and trustworthy action. Thus, the person who practices virtues—responsibility, goodness, trustworthiness, faithfulness, trust, generosity—will have "an abundance," that is "joy" (*chara*). Having or possessing joy, a primary virtue, means having all the other virtues. The practice of virtues is essential in the journey toward happiness, which is an important virtue akin to the virtue of joy. Within the context of the Greek philosophical understanding of virtue ethics, joy is *the* foundational virtue (equivalent to the virtue of prudence in philosophical ethical systems) and truly a representation of God's heavenly realm or divine kingdom.[52] We internalize Jesus's message in this way: joy is happiness, and happiness is *to attain holiness*.

In 25:29b Matthew shifts the attention to those who do not display or practice virtues. With the conjunction "but" (*de*), the evangelist redirects the audience's focus by vividly describing the harsh condemnation of those who respond negatively. He writes, "but from those who have nothing, even what they have will be taken away" (25:29b). The punishment reflects the opposite of the reward that comes through the practice of virtues. Matthew reinforces his emphasis on the lack of virtues; the description "those who *have nothing*" reveals clarity and style used as rhetorical devices to show the seriousness of not responding according to one's ability. A negative response to generosity leads to the practice of vices and to the absence of virtues. Therefore, Matthew's expression "even what they *have* will be taken away" highlights the inability to act, which places the person in a position of despair, completely isolated from joy and happiness and incapable of achieving God's heavenly realm.

The evangelist ends the parable by vividly presenting the frustration of the servant who lacks virtues and practices vices, who finds himself in "the outer darkness, where there will be weeping and gnashing of teeth" (25:30).[53] We internalize the consequences of having vices and lacking virtues by visualizing the darkness outside the boundaries of joy and happiness. The vivid metaphor enhances the pictorial images of a life of vices, excluded from the master's joy; it is a life represented as "weeping and gnashing of teeth." As we internalize the true message of Jesus's parable, we see that this parable teaches us how to behave and practice virtues and avoid vices in order to have a positive response to God's invitation to enter the heavenly realm, where the experience is genuine joy. Thus, the proper name for this story is the Parable of Joy.

Luke 19:11–27: Finding Meaning in the Ordinary

At first glance, we notice striking linguistic similarities between this Lukan parable and Matthew's Parable of Joy. Both parables contain about fifty identical words, and ten more are the same word in different forms or a cognate. For this reason, some biblical scholars argue that both parables derive from the same source, the Q document.[54] Others claim that the two are sufficiently different in detail as to suggest that they derive from the special Matthean (M) and Lukan (L) traditions, respectively.[55] Luke places the parable (19:11–27) after the Zacchaeus story (19:1–10) and before the triumphal entry into Jerusalem (19:28–44)

Internalizing Jesus's Message in the Parables

at the end of his Travel Narrative (9:51–19:27).[56] In his last days in Jerusalem, the holy city, the Lukan Jesus tells his followers this parable.

Table 2.2. Luke 19:11–27
Introduction: [11]As they were listening to this, he went on to tell a parable, because he was near Jerusalem, and because they supposed that the kingdom of God was to appear immediately.
Business Language: [12]So he said, "A nobleman went to a distant country to get royal power for himself and then return. [13]He summoned ten of his slaves, and gave them ten pounds, and said to them, 'Do business with these until I come back.' [14]But the citizens of his country hated him and sent a delegation after him, saying, 'We do not want this man to rule over us.'
Expected Response: [15]When he returned, having received royal power, he ordered these slaves, to whom he had given the money, to be summoned so that he might find out what they had gained by trading. [16]The first came forward and said, 'Lord, your pound has made ten more pounds.' [17]He said to him, 'Well done, good slave! Because you have been trustworthy in a very small thing, take charge of ten cities.' [18]Then the second came, saying, 'Lord, your pound has made five pounds.' [19]He said to him, 'And you, rule over five cities.'
Negative Response: [20]Then the other came, saying, 'Lord, here is your pound. I wrapped it up in a piece of cloth, [21]for I was afraid of you, because you are a harsh man; you take what you did not deposit, and reap what you did not sow.' [22]He said to him, 'I will judge you by your own words, you wicked slave! You knew, did you, that I was a harsh man, taking what I did not deposit and reaping what I did not sow? [23]Why then did you not put my money into the bank? Then when I returned, I could have collected it with interest.' [24]He said to the bystanders, 'Take the pound from him and give it to the one who has ten pounds.' [25](And they said to him, 'Lord, he has ten pounds!')
Teaching Moment: [26]'I tell you, to all those who have, more will be given; but from those who have nothing, even what they have will be taken away. [27]But as for these enemies of mine who did not want me to be king over them—bring them here and slaughter them in my presence.'"

The Lukan parable is divided into five parts (v. 11; vv. 12–14; vv. 15–19; vv. 20–25; vv. 26–27) and follows an internal structure similar to the Matthean Parable of Joy.[57] As Luke Timothy Johnson points out, the parable is a story about a king who goes to get a kingdom, gets it despite opposition, and returns to establish his rule by killing his rivals and placing in positions of authority the servants who have shown themselves trustworthy. Johnson argues that in the eschatological context, the parable is about the successful establishment of a kingdom.[58]

The Power of Transformation

However, looking at Luke's parable within the context of the Parable of Joy in Matthew, we see that the teaching of Jesus also concerns the internalization of his message.[59] By examining the rhetorical character of the parable, we can bring to the surface Luke's personal *ekphrastic* and *enargetic* emphases, keys to deepening the personal response and internalization of Jesus's message. We shall see that Luke's unique rhetorical approach teaches the same lesson as Matthew's Parable of Joy.

INTRODUCTION (19:11)

As is common in Luke's narrative, the evangelist adds historical context at the beginning of his parable. In this case, Luke writes, "As they were listening to this, he went on to tell a parable, because he was near Jerusalem, and because they supposed that the kingdom of God was to appear immediately" (19:11). As Luke leads his audience into the story, he clearly states that the story is a parable (*parabolē*). Following his narrative style of arousing imagination through clarity, Luke repeats a major theme in his Travel Narrative: Jesus is on his way toward Jerusalem. This narrative detail maintains an important fact in the providential destiny of Jesus's life: that Jesus, like other Jewish prophets, will die in Jerusalem. In 19:11, Luke brings before his audience's eyes the close connection between the parable he is about to present and Jesus's suffering, death, resurrection, and ascension. The Lukan parable becomes more dramatic rhetorically by being described in the context of Jesus approaching the holy city where he will fulfill God's salvific plan.[60]

Placed close to Jerusalem and the climactic events of Jesus's life, this parable also addresses the Jewish-Christian belief in the coming of God's kingdom. Indeed, Luke amplifies his introduction with the statement, "because they supposed that the kingdom of God was to appear immediately" (19:11b). The technique of amplification helps Luke to take advantage of his audience's belief and his reference to the kingdom to create a vivid connection between this parable and the parables of the Silent Sower (Luke 13:18–19) and the Industrious Woman (Luke 13:20–21). It also deepens the idea that the internalization of Jesus's message entails the journey toward God's heavenly realm. For us, the kingdom of God, that is, God's heavenly realm, is meant to become a reality now! Used as a rhetorical device, the kingdom theme in the context of the eschatological expectation creates an immediate response.

Internalizing Jesus's Message in the Parables

BUSINESS LANGUAGE (19:12–14)

With the phrase "So he said" (19:12a), Luke captures his audience's attention and begins to tell Jesus's parable. The evangelist puts before our eyes the scene of a "certain nobleman" (19:12b), clarifying the status of the "man" (*anthrōpos*) by distinguishing him as "a nobleman" (*eugenēs*). His creative narrative portrays the nobleman going to "a distant country to get royal power"; this statement explicitly enhances the audience's "imagination" (*phantasia*). To add vividness to the story, Luke provides the reason for the man's distant travel: "to get royal power for himself" or "a kingdom for himself." The motive of the nobleman's long journey vividly pictures his advantageous status; he is a rich man and can quickly gain royal power (or a kingdom) for himself through some kind of business transaction. Without describing the arduous trip and emphasizing the time passing, Luke states that the nobleman returns with royal power, insinuating that he has become wealthier.

Within the context of the first-century business world, Luke features the nobleman summoning ten of his servants to entrust them with business while he is away. The evangelist uses the *ekphrastic* techniques of *clarity* and *style* to achieve "vividness" (*enargeia*). First, he provides the specific number of servants and "pounds" (*mnas*, lit. "minas") as he writes, "[he] gave them ten pounds" (19:13a). In Luke, as Tönsing notes, the nobleman's command is explicit: "do business" or "put the money to work" (*pragmateusasthe*), whereas Matthew in the Parable of Joy left open what exactly was expected. That the nobleman "hands over" or "entrusts" (*paredōken*) his wealth to the servants clearly implies an expectation that they will do what the nobleman would have done with his money: increase it.[61]

According to Johnson, the Greek word *mna* means a coin equaling approximately a hundred drachmas or denarii, that is, an "equivalent of about 100 days' wages for a common laborer."[62] So, Luke's detail of the "ten pounds" and the repetition of the word "ten" provide vividness for the audience's imagination: ten pounds to ten servants. Luke brings before the audience's eyes the scene where each of the ten servants receives a pound (see vv. 16, 18, 20). This description makes clear that one pound is a considerable but not an enormous sum of money.[63] Next, the nobleman speaks, saying directly to his servants, "Do business with these until I come back" (19:13b).[64] Luke rhetorically highlights the type of task or work that the ten servants must engage in, prioritizing the importance of the servants' actions over the nobleman's getting royal power.

Luke's basis of persuasion is much like what is found in the *progymnasmata*. He gives a sense of realism to his narrative of the commercial enterprise entrusted to the ten servants by connecting his parable with Greek virtue ethics and the historical context. Skillfully, Luke produces vividness before the eyes of his readers to incite personal transformation by way of internalizing Jesus's true message. To achieve his goal, the evangelist uses two important rhetorical features of "descriptive speech" (*ekphrasis*): amplification and verisimilitude. By adding the phrase "the citizens of his country" in 19:14a, Luke produces an extension of the hatred that goes beyond the ten servants' own hateful feelings in 19:20–21. In the Greek ethical systems (virtue ethics), "hatred" is often associated with envy, leading toward the harming of another person.[65] Within the historical context, Luke continues to enhance the realism of the scene in 19:14a. With the statement, "the citizens of this country…sent a delegation after him," Luke implies that his audience is familiar with the common practice of sending a delegation to Rome; indeed, it is attested in the writings of two first-century Jewish authors, Philo and Josephus.[66] Luke also knows that such practices were sometimes strongly despised.[67]

The Positive Response (19:15–19)

In vv. 15–19, the parable begins to unfold the heart of Jesus's teaching. To create an *ekphrastic* narrative, Luke repeats key rhetorical elements to connect it with the preceding section. The business language he uses is similar to the business language used in Matthew's Parable of Joy. The phrase "When he returned, having received royal power" (19:15a) is a repetition of 19:12b, "to get royal power for himself and then return," showing the success of the nobleman's journey. This clever detail builds a sense of continuity to enhance the visual images that will later clarify the message of the Lukan Jesus. Once the nobleman returns, he orders his servants to whom he entrusted money (pounds) "to be summoned so that he might find out what they had gained by trading" (19:15bc). This creates clarity, which further strengthens Luke's point: the *positive responses of the servants*. Luke uses the technique of conciseness to focus on the servants' responses and not on the nobleman's behav-

Internalizing Jesus's Message in the Parables

ior. His vivid description in v. 15bc creates a picture of the business deal between the master and his servants.

Luke presents the dialogue between the nobleman and his servants in an orderly fashion.[68] As in the Parable of Joy in Matthew, we encounter two positive ways to respond to Jesus's message. For the first positive example, Luke writes, "The first came forward and said, 'Lord, your pound has made ten more pounds.' He said to him, 'Well done, good slave! Because you have been trustworthy in a very small thing, take charge of ten cities'" (19:16–17). For the second example of a positive response, Luke concisely and vividly states, "Then the second came, saying, 'Lord, your pound has made five pounds.' He said to him, 'And you, rule over five cities'" (19:18–19).

The evangelist increases the vividness of the dialogue through a series of repetitions that link both the positive dialogue (19:15–19) with the two first parts of the parable (19:11 and 19:12–14) and the two positive responses in 19:16–17 and 19:18–19 with each other. The repetition of the words "summoned" (vv. 15c, 13), "servants" (vv. 15b, 13, 17b), "came" (vv.16, 18), "pounds" (vv. 13b, 16b [twice], 18b), "said" (vv. 13c, 14b, 16a, 17a, 18a, 19a), "lord" (vv. 16b, 18b), "made" (vv.16b, 18b), "ten" (vv. 13b, 16b, 17c), "five" (18b, 19b), and "cities" (vv. 17c, 19b) highlights the genuine interaction and the positive relationship between the nobleman and the servants. The repetition also increases the positive impact of the servants' business deals. In the first example, the servant received a pound (19:13, 16b), and he impressively made "ten more pounds" (19:16b). The vividness of Luke's description puts before our eyes the impressive amount of ten pounds—the equivalent of about one thousand days' wages for a common laborer! The servant's response amazes the readers and hearers more than the response in Matthew's Parable of Joy, where the servant doubled the five talents entrusted to him. Similarly, in the second example the servant received one pound and made five pounds. We again clearly visualize an enormous sum! The servant's proper behavior in responding to his master's order produces great amazement; the hyperbole creates images in our minds that enable us to see that one pound has now become five pounds! In both examples, the servants have shown the expected response and the correct behavior in business.

Luke's strong commendations of "well done, good slave" (19:17a) and "because you have been trustworthy" (19:17b) emphasize what truly matters for the Lukan Jesus: the practice of virtues. The positive response reflects the practice of virtues (well done, you are a good servant!) and the absence of vices. The nobleman praises and commends his servants' virtues, such as fidelity, trust, goodness, responsibility, efficiency, and obedience. Thus, because of the servants' positive *responses*, the nobleman entrusts them with the charge of "ten cities" (19:17c) and "five cities" (19:19), each according to his own capacity and abilities.

Before our eyes, the servants' expected responses are described by the nobleman as "a tiny thing," something unexpected to our imagination. We understand and internalize the notion that being reliable in "a very small thing" (a pound) is as great as being reliable in a big thing (ten cities). In both examples, we have seen that reliability in performing the right external actions leads to specific results worthy of praise and reward. Both the *ekphrastic* and *enargetic* techniques (repetition, clarity, narrative, conciseness, verisimilitude, style, and imagination) employed by Luke highlight the nobleman's generosity and the servant's fidelity and obedience. Through these rhetorical techniques we are able to internalize the message of Jesus's parable: positive action requires human effort, and reward is an expression of one's virtues. Luke's use of rhetorical devices leads his audience's imagination and reflection to the true message, which is necessary to achieve human transformation and happiness.

THE NEGATIVE RESPONSE (19:20–25)

Luke provides an opposite example to the two positive responses in 19:16–19. This time, his rhetorical narrative combines techniques that challenge his audience with the effect of the servant's response. Luke uses two rhetorical elements, the *enargetic* device of repetition that connects back to the preceding sections in the parable (19:11–19) and the farming images in the parable of the Silent Sower (see chapter 1). Luke's vivid description also highlights the shocking dialogue between the nobleman and the third servant. Luke uses the unexpectedly aggressive dialogue to create suspense and deception in our minds, redirecting our perspectives toward internalization and persuading us toward personal transformation.

To increase the attention and interest of the audience, Luke changes the repeated and sequential pattern used in 19:16a, "The first came," and in 19:18a, "Then the second came," to, "Then the *other* came, saying" (19:20a). This stylistic change redirects the audience's attention

Internalizing Jesus's Message in the Parables

and focus to "the other" and his words. We visualize in our minds "the other," not as the third servant but as the third *example* of a servant who received "one pound" (19:13). Luke then vividly presents the scene of the servant's response to his master: "Lord, here is your pound. I wrapped it up in a piece of cloth, for I was afraid of you, because you are a harsh man; you take what you did not deposit, and reap what you did not sow" (19:20b–21). Although the parable began with ten servants (19:13), and this is just the third servant heard from, the rhetorical-poetic approach heightens the servant's negative response. First, Luke repeats the word "pound" in 19:13, 16, 18, and he provides a detailed description of the servant's action, "I wrapped it up in a piece of cloth" (19:20c), to amplify evidence and contribute to credibility. His descriptive language dramatically shows the servant's action of hiding the pound in a cloth.[69] These elements of *enargeia* trigger our imagination and arouse our emotions. Luke aims to increase the visual images in our minds and persuade us to take his same view through internalization.

With the servant's explanation in Luke 19:21, "for I was afraid of you, because you are a harsh man; you take what you did not deposit, and reap what you did not sow,'" Luke skillfully delivers what will trigger a response from his readers. The phrase "for I was afraid" provides the reason *why* the servant did not engage in business trade with the pound. As Luke develops the servant's speech, he brings to light the servant's true character using two modes of amplification. First, the servant confronts his master with a direct invective, "because you are a harsh man" (19:21a), accusing him of being a "severe" (*austēros*), cruel master, whose actions in his eyes are rapacious. Luke's vivid description directs us toward the servant's judgmental words. Secondly, Luke's amplification is a repetition. Luke appeals to the image of business or banking (withdrawing/depositing) when he writes, "you take what you did not deposit" (19:21b), and combines it with the agricultural image "and reap what you did not sow" (19:21b). By combining two images (business and farming) with a series of repetitions, for example, "afraid," "you," "harsh man," "you did not," "reap," and "sow," Luke brings before his audience's eyes the importance of taking action. When something is entrusted, one must respond accordingly, like the sower and the woman did in Luke's previous parables.

With the servant's invective language against his master, Luke leads his audience's "mind" (*nous*) and "imagination" (*phantasia*) to see the response of the servant as negative. Luke persuades his audience not to follow the example of *this* servant, even though from the peasant's point of view the servant's actions seem reasonable.[70] The rhetorical-poetic character defies the conventional point of view; *the unexpected becomes the expected.* Luke's elaborate language in 19:20-21 shows a behavior and attitude that should be avoided. The evangelist develops an appropriate emotional, visual presence through words that make the impact of the scene real. As if we were present, we witness the servant's vituperative statement, which is full of vices. In this way, we come to internalize the notion that the Lukan Jesus moves beyond what is familiar or conventional.

Luke dramatically reinforces Jesus's message in the parable through the nobleman's long and vivid reply in 19:22-25:

> [22]He said to him, "I will judge you by your own words, you wicked slave! You knew, did you, that I was a harsh man, taking what I did not deposit and reaping what I did not sow? [23]Why then did you not put my money into the bank? Then when I returned, I could have collected it with interest." [24]He said to the bystanders, "Take the pound from him and give it to the one who has ten pounds." [25](And they said to him, "Lord, he has ten pounds!")[71]

Describing a severe and provocative confrontation, Luke provides an elaborate rhetorical representation of the master's judgment against his servant in which the evangelist shows the master's total disagreement with his servant. His representation reinforces for his readers the negative effect of the practice of vices, as he puts into the nobleman's mouth the words, "I will judge you by your own words, you *wicked* slave!" (19:22a). This judgment by *his owns words* dramatically captures the wicked servant's vituperative statements in the previous verse (19:21). This condemnation of an unacceptable response reveals the servant's true character; his accusations—*you are* a harsh man; *you take* what you did not deposit; *you reap* what you did not sow—are now understood in the context of v. 22a: "you *wicked* slave!" The nobleman explicitly and directly judges his servant. Luke cleverly *repeats* the agricultural metaphor of "reaping" and "sowing" (19:21b, 22c) so that we strengthen the association of this parable with the parable of the Silent Sower. Likewise, to create a sense of reality in the scene, Luke emphasizes business language, specifically the banking action of depositing. The servant's wrong action of "wrapping the pound up and hiding it in a piece of cloth" (19:20) has demonstrated his true character: this servant is full of vices, and there is nothing good in either his action or his words.

To prove to his readers the negative dimension of the servant's action and insulting words, Luke uses the technique of amplification along with repetition. The immediate series of repetitions in 19:22bc, "You knew, did you, that I was a harsh man, taking what I did not deposit and reaping what I did not sow?" reinforce the master's condemnation in 19:22a, "I will judge you by *your own words*." Luke warns his readers that following the wicked servant's example can cause this severe condemnation to happen to them too. Therefore, the repetitions of past aorist forms framed in a rhetorical question are a technique of vividness, fundamental to transporting Luke's readers into the scene and seeing themselves as the "servant," who is being judged by his master. Luke wishes to persuade them (and us) to practice virtues and avoid vices.

The repetition and amplification in the next verses enhance the vicarious visual experience for Luke's readers. Luke uses amplification in the rhetorical question in 19:23–24, "'Why then did you not put my money into the bank? Then when I returned, I could have collected it with interest.' He said to the bystanders, 'Take the pound from him and give it to the one who has ten pounds.' (And they said to him, 'Lord, he has ten pounds!')" The master's statement contains rich *ekphrastic* elements that will help readers to internalize the message of Jesus's parable. Luke wants his audience not only to know and understand Jesus's parables (chapter 1) but also to appreciate the necessity of possessing virtues, which are essential to move to the next level in the journey to happiness, which is a virtue for spiritual transformation.

Expanding the nobleman's response to his servant, He repeats the metaphor of banking (vv. 22c and 23a), a common business practice in the first century CE. The evangelist shows his recurring technique of placing his stories within a historical context while also challenging his audience.[72] By refusing to do business, the servant explicitly disobeys his master. The servant's attitude and behavior make him not only a *disobedient* servant but also a *wicked* person.

When Luke writes, "Then when I returned, I could have collected it with interest" (19:23b), we see the nobleman's explicit intention to gain more wealth. Luke's vivid description stirs the emotions through the crude realism that represents the reality of many peasants and villagers in the ancient business world. In the language of the nobleman, we finally see what is truly honorable and what is not. With the repetition of "return" (vv. 13, 15, 23), Luke offers his audience a sense of focus and a broader picture rather than simply plain sets of actions that put the master on the wrong side (e.g., he is morally evil). Indeed, Luke's vivid description of the master's position in 19:23c allows us to envision the conversation in our minds. Using the *ekphrastic* technique of *clarity*, Luke realistically shows what behavior is expected through the pictorial image of "claiming interest" in the business world. This imagery dramatically presents "interest" as the offspring of money.[73] Thus, symbolically, "interest" indicates a positive response, not a reflection of the master's greedy character.

Luke's rhetorical representation of the servant's negative response highlights vices, like disobedience, wickedness, laziness, unfaithfulness, envy, selfishness, anger, and unhappiness. Nothing good comes out of the servant's response (his action and words). Like Matthew, Luke persuades his audience not to follow this example. With *ekphrasis* and *enargeia*, Luke masterfully depicts, and thus reveals, the servant's shameful *action* (wrapping the pound up in a piece of cloth), his questionable *behavior* (being afraid), and his angry/unhappy *attitude* (his vituperative claims). However, this is not the end for Luke; the rhetorical extension in vv. 24–25 adds further to the stylistic character of his narrative. Luke writes, "He said to the bystanders, 'Take the pound from him and give it to the one who has ten pounds.' (And they said to him, 'Lord, he has ten pounds!')" This lively detail helps his vivid speech to be persuasive. His use of repetition (pound [twice], ten [twice], Lord), surprisingly captures the nobleman's generosity.

The virtue of generosity is the highlight here; Luke's addition (amplification) twice emphasizes the master's good heart: first by repeating twice the "ten pounds" entrusted to the servants, and secondly by commanding the "bystanders" to give the one pound to the servant who has ten pounds (19:24). As we picture the reward of another pound to the servant who already produced ten pounds doing business, we can clearly see in our minds the nobleman's generosity. This generosity plays an important rhetorical role; it prioritizes the nobleman's virtue and his goodness (toward those who respond positively) over the conventional understanding of the master-servant relationship in the business world. Repetition in Luke's descriptive narrative creates vividness, and thus brings before the eyes the hyperbolic description of the money. Because ten pounds (*minas*) are equivalent to about a thousand days' wages for a common laborer, the bystanders' reply to the nobleman, "Lord, he has ten pounds!" (19:25), makes perfect sense.

The Lukan Jesus shows the necessity of practicing virtues and avoiding vices; virtues derive from a positive response, and vices flow from a negative response. The servant's virtues primarily reveal the master's unlimited generosity to those who respond accordingly, and the servant's vices reveal the master's wrath, his rejection of those who respond negatively. The internalization of the message of Jesus's parable occurs when the human mind/heart is sincerely moved to emotion. The individual who reads the story within the rhetorical-poetic tradition experiences an unexpected conclusion, acknowledging and thus internalizing the idea that Jesus's true message often contradicts the cultural message.

THE TEACHING MOMENT (19:26–27)

Luke concludes his parable with a teaching moment, and it comes from the nobleman's mouth: "I tell you, to all those who have, more will be given; but from those who have nothing, even what they have will be taken away. But as for these enemies of mine who did not want me to be king over them—bring them here and slaughter them in my presence" (19:26–27).[74] This forensic statement wraps up the message of the Lukan Jesus in the parable. It is straight and clear.[75] The harshness of the evangelist's rhetoric is not a surprise for us, because by now we have internalized Jesus's message. Taking action is the correct response for those who are ready to give generously as expected by the master. Dramatically, Luke once more presents the nobleman's generosity as a reward for a positive response.

Thus, Jesus's message is that those who have—that is, those who give generously—will be given more. The reference to *having* refers to the possession of virtues, not material possessions. The vividness of the dramatic language allows us to see that we possess *more* virtues when we give a *positive response*. Our individual effort *will be rewarded abundantly* as was the servant's good response. The emphatic phrase "I tell you" (19:26a) assures us that the master will keep his word; God is faithful. However, the nobleman dramatically condemns those who *respond negatively*, "those who have nothing" (19:26b). Because they display vices and not virtues, "even what they *have* will be taken away" (19:26b). This amplification evokes the wicked nature and power of vices, showing the individual's inability to produce goodness when vice empowers human nature.

Luke hopes that his audience internalizes the fact that possessing vices is like possessing nothing. He warns his audience to be aware of the dangers of vice and rejects the notion that producing profit for one's master is a dishonorable act. Such rejection of the servant's wrong choice is depicted in the dramatic images that Luke presents in his final description: "But as for these enemies of mine who did not want me to be king over them—bring them here and slaughter them in my presence" (19:27). We internalize the message through the language, such as "*enemies*," "who *did not want* me," and "*slaughter* in my presence"; these words are equally as shocking as the individuals who possess vices and not virtues. The harsh measures employed by Luke (cf. Josh 10:16–26; 1 Sam 15:32) convince his audience of the need to practice virtues and avoid vices in order to achieve happiness. At this stage in the spiritual journey, we have learned that *expected* behaviors and *expected* attitudes sometimes are not part of Jesus's message in his parables. Thus, internalizing the message of his parables means accepting the challenges presented in the parables and moving beyond the cultural ways of doing things. Jesus subverts *then* and *now* cultural and social patterns and expected human behaviors. The kingdom of God, anticipated immediately by Luke's audience, will also appear now in all those who continue journeying toward God's heavenly realm. God, like the nobleman, desires to give abundantly to those who respond positively by practicing virtues. Therefore, the best name for this story is the Parable of the Generous Nobleman.

Conclusion

In this chapter, I illuminated the Parable of Joy (Matt 25:14–30) and the Parable of the Generous Nobleman (Luke 19:11–27) to highlight the importance of internalizing the message of Jesus's parables. Through the powerful tools of ancient classical rhetorical-poetic composition outlined in the *progymnasmata*, Matthew and Luke highlight their characters' ethical attitudes and responses. The features of vividness, amplification, repetition, clarity, style, imagination, and conciseness revealed the true message of both parables. Within the cultural context of the business world of the first century CE, Matthew and Luke

Internalizing Jesus's Message in the Parables

launched a dramatic performance that allowed their audiences, and us, to mentally imagine three human responses, in which two are vividly described as positive and one as negative. In each example, the rhetorical techniques employed highlighted both the servant's responses and the master's ethical character. As a result of the amplification and repetition features, both the possession and practice of virtues have been presented as central in the process of the internalization of Jesus's message.

Like other ancient Greek writers, Matthew and Luke use "vividness" (*enargeia*) to persuade their audiences by working on their emotions, so that they would feel personally affected. The evangelists' realism "placed before the eyes" how to respond to Jesus's message by practicing virtues and avoiding vices. Indeed, they made their readers feel as if they were participants at the events they described by using the technique of *ekphrasis* where *enargeia* was the aim.[76] The Parable of Joy in Matthew strongly privileged the virtue of joy, viewed as a reflection of the kingdom of heaven, and the Parable of the Generous Nobleman praised the virtues of generosity and faithfulness. Both evangelists in their rhetorical techniques gave close attention to individual behavior, character, and response through a common first-century context, that of a business transaction. In the journey toward God and the heavenly realm/kingdom, the path is virtue. Internalizing the message of Jesus in his parables means realizing that the possession of virtues is essential in the quest for happiness. The desire to practice virtues and avoid vices assures us that we have deepened and assimilated Jesus's true message. By becoming lovers of virtue, we become ready to experience the internal wrestling that comes with the growth in virtue.

3

Wrestling within the Human Heart

Growth in Virtue

The parables of Jesus raise disagreeable feelings, such as discomfort, conflict, and helplessness. We must experience these feelings to move on to transformation. By using the rhetorical techniques of *ekphrasis* and *enargeia,* the evangelists, Mark, Matthew, and Luke, generate these feelings as they tell the parables of Jesus, urging their audiences to strive for what truly matters: a holy and virtuous life, in times of persecution (Mark), in times of internal and external problems (Matthew), and in times of divisions between "the haves" and "the have-nots" (Luke).[1]

To lead us into a spiritual wrestling experience, we will look at three parables of Jesus. Two come from Luke's special material, identified as "L"; these are found in Luke 16:19–31 and 16:1–8. Likewise, another parable is chosen from Matthew's special material, called "M"; it is found in Matt 20:1–16. The reader needs to be aware that we will examine these three parables in this order: Luke 16:19–31, Matt 20:1–16, and Luke 16:1–8. The rationale for this order is that the level of discomfort and internal wrestling is presented as a crescendo from mild to strong.

As in the two preceding chapters, the *ekphrastic* and *enargetic* features reflected in each parable will be highlighted to offer a new interpretation of the parables. As before, the parables will remain unnamed until the end of the discussion.

Luke 16:19–31: Human Perspectives in Question

This parable, unique to Luke, is one of the highlights among the parables of Jesus because of its revealing contrast between the earthly and heavenly worlds.[2] It is placed within the Travel Narrative (9:51–19:27) after a short exposition on the law and the kingdom of God (16:14–18) and before some sayings of Jesus (17:1–10). As Jesus journeys toward Jerusalem, he confronts the Pharisees' attacks by delivering a series of statements in chapter 16, where this parable occurs.[3] Therefore, it is in the context of the theme of rejection that the Lukan Jesus tells this parable.

Table 3.1: Luke 16:19-31
Earthly Realm *Introduction*: [19]There was a certain rich man. He was clothed in purple and fine linen, making good cheer every day in splendor. [20]And at his gate lay a certain poor man named Lazarus, covered with sores, [21]who longed to satisfy his hunger with what fell from the rich man's table; even the dogs would come and lick his sores.
Death: [22]The poor man died and was carried away by the angels to be with Abraham. The rich man also died and was buried.
Heavenly (Hades) Realm *Revelation Unfolds*: [23]In Hades, where he was being tormented, he looked up and saw Abraham far away with Lazarus by his side. [24]He called out, "Father Abraham, have mercy on me, and send Lazarus to dip the tip of his finger in water and cool my tongue; for I am in agony in these flames." [25]But Abraham said, "Child, remember that during your lifetime you received your good things, and Lazarus in like manner evil things; but now he is comforted here, and you are in agony. [26]Besides all this, between you and us a great chasm has been fixed, so that those who might want to pass from here to you cannot do so, and no one can cross from there to us." [27]He said, "Then, father, I beg you to send him to my father's house—[28]for I have five brothers—that he may warn them, so that they will not also come into this place of torment." [29]Abraham replied, "They have Moses and the prophets; they should listen to them." [30]He said, "No, father Abraham; but if someone goes to them from the dead, they will repent."

The Power of Transformation

> *Teaching Moment*: ³¹He said to him, "If they do not listen to Moses and the prophets, neither will they be convinced even if someone rises from the dead."

In this parable, the Lukan Jesus tells a *vividly descriptive story* of two men and their fates in the afterlife, here described as Hades and the angelic world. What is striking in the story is the contrasting and spatial imagery, which are strongly reflected in the lifestyles of the two men. Indeed, in the context of the rhetorical techniques of "descriptive speech" (*ekphrasis*), the evangelist dramatically depicts the two men—an unnamed rich man and Lazarus—and the reversal of their fortunes.[4] Luke's narrative is carefully balanced, and his stylistic narrative features are depicted (1) in the *orderly* introductory scenes in the worldly realm, and (2) in the *conversations* occurring *progressively* in the "other world."

In the story we visually capture two states of life in the earthly world and two reversed fates in the afterlife. Luke's hope is that Jesus's story would trigger a change of disposition that would enable the audience to become people of good character; to become a virtuous individual, one must exhibit good behavior with a disposition to action. To achieve his aim, the evangelist divides the story into three parts: an introduction, which contains two scenes occurring in the earthly world (16:19–22); a conversation, which is a long scene occurring in the heavenly world (16:23–30); and a brief teaching moment (16:31). This structure highlights the rhetorical-poetic elements of each section, facilitates our imagination, and stirs our emotions.

INTRODUCTION (16:19–22)

Luke begins his parable with a vivid description of two characters, "a certain rich man" and "a certain poor man Lazarus" (16:19–22). Both Luke's narrative and rhetorical style show a well-thought-out presentation of the physical, material state of two men living in the earthly realm. These two scenes are purposely balanced to capture the readers' and hearers' attention. Luke's rhetorical approach, first, focuses on a certain "rich man" (*anthrōpos plousios*, 16:19a). Immediately, Luke enhances the man's material status and life with a series of vivid representations to heighten our imagination of the scene. Using the *enargetic* device of amplification, Luke nurtures the imagination when he writes: "He [the rich man] was clothed in purple and fine linen, making good cheer every day in splendor" (16:19bc). Luke produces a vivid and detailed picture in the mind of his audience of the rich man's place within his social context;[5] his clothing is "purple and fine linen" (16:19b). In the Jewish tradition, this small yet important detail represents his royal status, or at least his royal favors and wealth (e.g., Judg 8:26; Sir 45:10; Esth 1:6; 8:15).[6]

Luke's audience, by mentally visualizing the purple garment worn over the rich man's linen undergarments, experiences a sense of amazement at the man's luxurious living. The audience knows that "purple was rare and expensive because of the difficult process of obtaining the best dye from marine snails."[7] In the first-century-CE world, linen was usually imported from Egypt and was extremely expensive.[8] Moreover, with the phrase "making good cheer every day in splendor" (16:19c), Luke expands the amplification to detail the luxurious lifestyle of *that* particular rich man. Luke's application of this rhetorical device allows the readers and hearers to capture in their mind's eye the brilliance and splendor of how a certain rich man dresses and banquets sumptuously. According to Johnson, that this man feasts *every day* shows the kind of opulence and overdone sumptuousness of his lifestyle (cf. Amos 6:4–7).[9]

Next, in 16:20a, Luke introduces "a certain poor man named Lazarus." The evangelist follows the same stylistic form to rhetorically create a sharp contrast between "a certain *rich* man" and "a certain *poor* man" in the audience's "imagination" (*phantasia*). Luke adds to his vivid description by providing two important elements of amplification. The first is the *name* of the poor man—"Lazarus." This name, as Johnson points out, is the Greek form of Eliezer (or Eleazar) and means "My God helps."[10] Interestingly, this is the same name as Abraham's servant in Gen 15:2. The second is the *location* of the poor man, Lazarus; Luke describes that he *lay* (lit. *was laid*) at the rich man's *gate* (16:20a). His use of amplification permits Luke to create a picture and clearly communicate the boundary that exists between the two men in the earthly world. His description exposes the reality of degraded individuals, like Lazarus, who constituted about 5 percent of the population, most of whom lived just outside the city walls.[11] The gate at which Lazarus lay (or was laid) reflects the actual living situation of the rich man, surrounded by a wall, probably designed to keep the "have-nots" physically separated from "the haves." Likewise, the use of the passive form "was laid" (*ebeblēto*) allows us to imagine Lazarus's helplessness and his confinement to the rich man's gate; Lazarus's sickbed is literally the rich man's gate. The word "gate" (*pulōn*) also increases the vividness of the image of the rich man's mansion, walled in as many elite houses were.

Luke's second amplification dramatically represents Lazarus's dire physical condition. Luke states that Lazarus is "covered with sores" (16:20b) and "longed to satisfy his hunger with what fell from the rich man's table" (16:21a).[12] The food that falls from the table is not food that falls accidentally but pieces of bread used to wipe hands that are then thrown under the table.[13] The author uses his rhetorical weapons to visually present powerful images of Lazarus's miserable and wretched condition. His depiction would certainly heighten the *enargetic* character to arouse his audience's feelings, emotions, and imagination. On one side of the gate, we observe an *unnamed* rich man, who lives luxuriously, but paradoxically is devoid of love of humanity (*philanthrōpia*), a key virtue in connection to justice. He is senseless toward Lazarus's basic physical needs. On the other side of the gate, we see a *named* man, Lazarus, whose painful human condition is that of a person dumped at a rich man's gate sick, covered with sores, and famishing.[14] The clarity in Luke's rhetorical representation captures our imagination and leads us to a higher dimension of reflection. Luke, strategically and masterfully, sets Lazarus's human condition in direct opposition to the rich man's fortunate position in this earthly realm.

Further amplifying Lazarus's unfortunate life, Luke focuses on the sores of Lazarus. His statement, "even the dogs would come and lick his sores" (16:21b), increases his rhetorical-poetic representation of Lazarus as a completely miserable human being. Graphically, Luke depicts Lazarus's outcast condition in society (e.g., Exod 22:31; 1 Kgs 21:19, 24).[15] The picture *imagined* by the audience—that of the dogs licking the running sores of Lazarus—is probably that of roaming street dogs that detect and taste the fresh meat that the sores on Lazarus would represent to them. The first-century audience knew that Lazarus's sores and the dogs licking his sores would have rendered him ritually impure. In that milieu, the dogs were considered unclean animals; they were not household pets helping him but scavengers seeking nourishment.[16] In this extreme, inhuman depiction, the dogs are waiting for Lazarus's death to consume his dead flesh.[17] Luke uses grotesque images of first-century *realism* as a way of persuasion. For example, the constant and unfulfilled longing for food that is expressed as the desire to be fed with the scraps that fall from the table is a clear representation of people in extreme poverty; the suffering from sores represents the affliction and cries of the poor; and the association of Lazarus with dogs, as these unclean animals lick his wounds, clearly represents human degradation.

Notice that the rich man is not portrayed as a bad or wicked individual; he is merely introduced as a wealthy and royal person who sumptuously enjoys his earthly life. Similarly, the poor man Lazarus is not particularly good and virtuous; he is simply poor and ignored by the rich man. But the graphic pictures in both scenes form in our minds the observation that the rich man fails to see the reality that (extreme) poverty exists around him and so does nothing to alleviate it.[18] Interestingly, in these initial scenes neither of the two men speak; they are simply two characters living two completely different ways of life. These two lifestyles are, according to Luke, what deserve emphasis and reflection, for they will ultimately cause a *struggle* within the human heart.

To emphasize the importance of one's way of life in the earthly world, Luke briefly describes the fate of both men after their deaths. First, we learn that Lazarus "died and was carried away by the angels to be with Abraham." Then, "The rich man also died and was buried" (16:22). The fact that Luke speaks of the death of "the poor man" and not of "the rich man" first indicates that Lazarus's fate is what truly matters in the story. This interpretation is attested by Luke's use of the phrase "poor man" rather than the name "Lazarus," and is further heightened by the longer description of the poor man's death and what happened immediately afterward. In the case of the rich man's death, Luke shows that the rich man's death is unimportant, just saying he is "buried" (16:22b).

Like the theme of reversal in the beatitudes (Luke 6:20–26 // Matt 5:2–12; cf. Luke 1:46–55), Luke shows us the reversal of conditions at the deaths of the two men. While the rich man dies and is just "buried," the poor man is taken literally "to Abraham's bosom."[19] Indeed, the transition from the earthly to the heavenly realm (v. 22) is when Luke begins to unfold and reveal the core of the parable. So, the events happening in this intelligible realm or *kosmos noētos* (16:23–30) will be key to stirring the feelings that will create a struggle within our hearts and bring before our eyes the virtues necessary for spiritual growth.

Revelation Unfolds in Conversation (16:23–30)

In the spiritual dimension of the heavenly realm (Hades), Luke displays his sophisticated writing skills by presenting a dialogue between the rich man and Abraham, who was introduced at the point of transition between the earthly and the heavenly worlds (16:22). As Luke masterfully unfolds this conversation, he reveals what could create discomfort in our hearts: Lazarus did absolutely *nothing* and was carried away by angels to Abraham's bosom in the heavenly realm; the rich man likewise did *nothing* and went to Hades.[20] This tragic fate should be the beginning of an internal wrestling experience in our hearts and minds. Luke's descriptive dialogue of the interaction between the rich man and Abraham uses the form of classical composition highly praised among students of the *progymnasmata*.

Both Luke and the audience enter the unseen world. The "rich man" is "buried," meaning he is in Hades (*hadēs*),[21] the invisible abode of the departed spirits or the realm of the dead in the Jewish tradition. Using amplification, Luke explains that the rich man is "being tormented" in Hades (16:23a), disclosing that the furnace of hell is the opposite of the paradise of delight (Abraham's bosom).[22] Luke sets this scene before his audience's eyes to stimulate mental imagination and to point to two realities on the earthly level: the rich man's way of life on earth had bad consequences, and Lazarus's state of life had good consequences. Thus, Luke describes that from the tormenting place (Hades) in the invisible realm, the rich man "looked up and saw Abraham far away with Lazarus by his side" (16:23b). The rhetorical language of the "bosom of Abraham" is an image of honor and intimacy between Abraham and Lazarus (cf. John 1:18). Within the context of the eschatological banquet (13:28–30), Luke wants his readers to imagine that Lazarus has a place of honor at the table next to Abraham.[23]

Rhetorically speaking, the Lukan Jesus's parable establishes certain truths and initiates reflection and action.[24] To do that, Luke turns in the scene of 16:24–30 to what most readers may find shocking, although it reveals a deeper message: the *passivity* of Lazarus and the *lack* of virtues of the rich man. Therefore, the rhetorical character of vv. 24–30 highlights the significant hidden meaning of the story. Luke's rhetorical-poetic technique emphasizes important rhetorical elements: explicit names (Lazarus [four times], Father [three times], Abraham [five times], Moses [two times], and the Prophets [two times]); repetitions like "tormented"/"torment," "agony," "far away"/"great chasm," "send," "them," "they," "pass"/"cross," and "you"; and the language device of speaking—Abraham and the rich man converse; both speakers

(Abraham and the man) name Lazarus; the man intercedes; and Lazarus remains silent.

Luke invites his audience into a vivid, imaginative experience of the "rich man" in the unseen world by bringing before their eyes his despair in Hades. Using the aorist passive participle *phōnēsas* of the verb "to call out" or "to cry out" (*phōneō*), the evangelist appeals to the sense of hearing to stimulate the emotions and feelings of his audience, as he writes, "He [the rich man] called out" (16:24a). Immediately, the wretched man expresses his anguish and pain "where he was being *tormented*" (16:23a) and pleads, saying, "Father Abraham, have mercy on me," and requests that Abraham send Lazarus for water, "for I am in agony in these flames" (16:24bc). The graphic representation of the "man" in despair in the unseen world (Hades) creates a scene of reversal in the reader's mind; the rich man now endures an experience similar to the experience of "the poor man" in the earthly world. The man's cry "have *mercy* on me" in the heavenly realm points to his lack of the virtues of mercy and compassion toward the poor man, Lazarus, in the earthly world (16:20–21). Interestingly, at this point Luke no longer refers to the unnamed man as a "rich man."

In Hades, the unnamed man loses his earthly status; he is now referred to as "he" (*autos*). Also, in his revealing speech, "he" *speaks* the name of "Lazarus," who is until this point silent! His request to "Father Abraham," the first patriarch of Israel,[25] to "*send* Lazarus to dip the tip of his finger in water and cool my tongue" is vividly described. In the mind of the reader, every word spoken—"dip," "tip," "finger," "water," "cool," "tongue"—is meant to stimulate the "imagination" (*phantasia*) to see the sharp contrast between the hunger (or starvation) of the "poor man" in the earthly realm (16:21) and the thirst of the "man" in the unseen world (16:24b).[26] The reader also understands that the man's request to provide him relief from his horrible condition directly opposes what he failed to do for Lazarus when they both were on earth (16:19–21). His dramatic statement "for I am in agony in these flames" (16:24c) amplifies Luke's powerful representation of the man's experience of "being tormented" (16:23a). With the language of "flames," Luke connects the man's suffering in the flames and his "torment." Ironically, the man's desperate request to Father Abraham asks that Lazarus may practice toward him the virtues that he on earth did not practice toward the poor man. Luke's rhetorical-poetic devices allow the reader to identify virtues related to the virtue of "love of humanity" (*philanthrōpia*): mercy, compassion, kindness, generosity, solidarity, justice, and service.[27]

In 19:25–26, "Abraham" speaks directly to the man with a shocking revelation for the reader. Luke develops Abraham's words in such a way that the evangelist juxtaposes the earthly realm and the heavenly realm based on the examples of the "rich man" and the "poor man." By using this rhetorical structure, Luke heightens not only the different conditions of their lives in the earthly realm but also creates a sharp line between them in the afterlife (heavenly realm/Hades). Abraham does not grant the man's wish. Even though Abraham acknowledges the kinship relation when he addresses him as "child," he shockingly denies the man's request for mercy! The patriarch justifies his negative response with the situation of reversal between the two realms as shown below.

Table 3.2. The Earthly Realm and the Heavenly Realm	
Earthly Realm: During Lifetime on Earth	
You (rich man)	Lazarus (poor man)
Good things	Bad things
Inclusivity; not "gate"	
Heavenly Realm: Afterlife (Hades; Abraham's bosom)	
Agony	Comfort
"You"	"Us" (Abraham/Lazarus/Angels)
Division; "great abyss"	

The contrast between a *lifetime* in the earthly realm and *now* in the heavenly realm helps us to learn about the afterlife. We come to understand that the man had already received his share of "good things," and we also understand that it is right or just that Lazarus *now* receives goodness and remains in bliss and does not cross over to where the man is being tormented. We likewise learn that the "chasm" or abyss between the man in *Hades* and Lazarus with Abraham (and the angels) is too great to cross over; the man is too "far away" (16:23b). Moreover, it is impossible for Lazarus to make the journey. God has "fixed" the separation between the two dimensions (heaven/Hades) in the unseen world.

The rhetorical-poetic techniques employed by Luke lead us deeper into the real meaning of this parable of Jesus. Through the lens of *ekphrasis* features, the vividness of Abraham's discourse contrasts the "good things" during a *lifetime* on earth (16:19) with the suffering, agony, and misery *now* (19:22–23). Likewise, the vividness of Abraham's speech puts before our eyes the "bad things" experienced by Lazarus on earth (16:20–21) in contrast to his present consolation in the heavenly realm (16:22a).[28] With these contrasts, we become aware that both the "rich man" and the "poor man" have literally done nothing to receive either a punishment (rich man) or a reward (Lazarus).[29] Luke captures our imagination by creating in our minds a sense of nothingness that would give us a transcendent emotional experience of both men's fate in the afterlife.

Such feelings produce a sense of confusion that should lead us to ask, why is Lazarus rewarded and the rich man punished? How are we the readers called to understand this parable? That Lazarus is mentioned for the last time in 16:25b highlights his passivity in the story. At first glance, Lazarus's passivity appears to be the result of his lack of virtues; but it is the rich man who lacks virtues—love of humanity, mercy, compassion, generosity, kindness, and the like. However, we still internally wrestle with the question, what has Lazarus done to deserve such an honorable place in the heavenly world? We view the question as a matter of *doing* and not of *being*. Thus, we wrestle with the notion that Lazarus's passivity on earth is viewed as virtuous and thus rewarded in heaven. In the rhetorical situation, our own imaginative experience causes us to struggle to become convinced that it is okay to receive "bad/evil things" in the earthly realm. The Lukan Jesus speaks of the divine reversal in the beatitudes; bad things in the earthly realm lead to comfort, peace, joy, and happiness in the heavenly realm, and good things in the earthly realm lead to torment, thirst, hunger, and flames in the unseen world (represented as Hades).

How do we as modern readers understand this shocking revelation? The vivid language in vv. 25–26 emphasizes two pivotal points that can lead us to spiritual growth in virtue. First, in the process of wrestling, we come to perceive the need for inclusivity in the earthly realm, where the (invisible) boundary or "gate" that separates "the haves" from "the have-nots" is eliminated (see table 3.2). Having a "gate" avoids the need to practice virtues; for example, the rich man on earth lacked virtues such as mercy and compassion because he built an invisible "gate" between him/his family/friends ("the haves") and Lazarus ("the have-nots"). The Lukan Jesus exhorts his audience and us to move from our comfort zones and break through the invisible gates around us to create an inclusive society where "the haves" and "the have-nots" become one family of brothers and sisters. Secondly, the wrestling experience can transport us imaginatively into the heavenly realm to see the "great chasm" (16:26) between the man and Abraham, Lazarus, and the angels. The strong image of a "chasm" or "abyss" (*chasma*) shows us two realities in the heavenly world: there is a sharp division in the afterlife, and the division between Hades and the heavenly place of Abraham, Lazarus, and the angels is already "fixed" by God's divine providence (see figure 1). The Lukan Jesus reveals that the afterlife is not about inclusivity but about *exclusivity*; either one is *comforted* in peace or *tormented* in agony.

In 16:27–28, Luke's visual description continues to highlight the parable's true meaning. Now, "he" (the man) speaks to Father Abraham to intercede for his "five brothers." Using the vivid technique of repetition of "send" (v. 27; see v. 24) and "torment" (v. 28; see v. 23), the evangelist depicts the man's petition from the unseen world (Hades). Invoking the kinship relation "father" (16:27a), the man asks Abraham to send Lazarus to warn his five brothers. They must repent, or they will end up like him in Hades, the place of torment in flames (16:27–28). Luke connects the man's request ("I beg you") on behalf of his own brothers (16:27) with the language of "send Lazarus" (16:24) in his request that Abraham send Lazarus to his own self. We see then that a person who lacks virtues on earth will likewise lack them in the afterlife. In vv. 27–28, Luke's vivid description highlights the man's vice of selfishness; even in the unseen world of Hades, the man still thinks of himself (*my* brothers, *my* father's house). In fact, his attitude is that of one who is unrepentant to the end, for his concern is his own elite family ("five brothers") only rather than those poor people who, like Lazarus, may remain starving and sick at his gate, in his city.[30]

In an orderly rhetorical fashion, Luke narrates Abraham's second response to the man in Hades. The patriarch *speaks*, "They have Moses and the prophets; they should *listen to them*" (16:29). Here Luke uses the *ekphrastic* element of conciseness to highlight both "Moses and the prophets," important Jewish figures in Hebrew Scriptures. This technique allows the evangelist to appeal to the authority of the Jewish Torah to evoke the teachings concerning the care for the poor (e.g., Exod 22:21–22; 23:9; Lev 19:9–10, 33; 23:22).[31] Luke calls upon the fundamental obligation of "covenantal fidelity" in light of the prophetic force.[32] According to God's laws, the obligation to help the poor and miserable applies to all Jews without exception.[33] From within the Jewish tradition, Abraham powerfully states, "they should *listen to them*." His clear statement strategically associates the importance of listening to the teachings of Moses and the Prophets

(16:29) with the phrase "that he may *warn* them" (16:28). His purpose is to show that—in contrast to the rich man—the readers and hearers are exhorted to a greater humane response to God's material blessings. With the rhetorical connection between the phrases "warn them" in 16:28b and "listen to them" in 16:29b, the Lukan Jesus delivers a severe warning to us: we will be in grave danger if we follow the rich man's example on earth. Indeed, his warning is strengthened with a dramatic subjunctive, "they *should listen to them*" (16:29b). Appealing to the sense of hearing again, the Lukan Jesus exhorts his audience to the necessity of hearing the teachings of Torah and its intrinsic connection with obedience.[34]

For the third time the man intercedes for his own family: "No, father Abraham; but if someone goes to them from the dead, they will repent" (16:30).[35] This is the third time that the man calls the patriarch's name (vv. 24, 25, and 30). Luke uses this repetition to emphasize the authority of Abraham's statements in light of the Torah's teachings. The man's insistence on appealing for his five brothers is argumentative; he objects to what Abraham has just said in v. 29 in addition to what he (Abraham) said in vv. 25–26.[36] The man's statement, "*No*, father Abraham; but if someone goes to them from the dead, they will repent" (v. 30), assumes that repentance is only accessible in the earthly realm. Now, in the heavenly realm, according to the Lukan Jesus, not "even the proverbial visitor from the dead would convince the elite to recognize the needs of the poor."[37] The evangelist highlights two crucial points: first, *mercy* (v. 24) and *repentance* (v. 30) are important virtues that belong to the earthly realm only; second, Luke develops a threefold relationship: Torah (Moses and also the Prophets)–virtues–repentance. The word "repent" (*metanoein*) describes the proper response to the listening (hearing) of God's Word through a prophet (e.g., Luke 10:13; 11:32; 13:3–5; 15:7–10). We come to understand that the rich man's fate (punishment) is the result of his *lack of virtues*, his *lack of practice* of the teachings of Torah, and his *lack of repentance* during his lifetime on earth.[38]

Teaching Moment (16:31)

Luke's story ends with a short but effective teaching moment, where the words of Abraham manifest the inability to change a way of life if there is no disposition to listen. Abraham says, "If they do not *listen* to Moses and the prophets, neither will they be convinced even if someone rises from the dead" (16:31). The repetitions of "they," "listen," "Moses and the prophets," and "from the dead" reaffirm that even a messenger (Lazarus) from the heavenly realm would not be able to bring the five brothers to repentance. The language "from the dead" (16:31c) creates a vivid depiction in our minds. We see that both Lazarus, who is silent and passive, and the rich man are used as rhetorical devices to unfold a hidden truth. In the words of Abraham, we visualize the appropriate attitude to have on earth. We also see the strong emphasis on the sense of hearing (listening), explicitly expressed by Abraham and the man, in close connection with the teachings of the Torah concerning the poor (do not neglect the needs of the poor!). In the journey of spiritual growth, listening and obedience to Jesus's teachings about the poor and the opportunity for repentance are three important qualities belonging to the earthly realm. They encourage the practice of virtues, especially love of humanity, and its companion virtue of justice toward the poor (the "have-nots").

Therefore, the parable is not about what the poor man, Lazarus, does or does not do. He is a rhetorical device to teach us about inclusiveness between the wealthy and the poor and the acceptance of bad things in the earthly life. Similarly, the parable is not about the man's rich status on earth but is used to reveal the deeper meaning of Jesus's message. The strong feelings of discomfort with a provoking revelation are a point of reflection, a valuable moment of grace to find new meaning in virtues. Luke's vivid descriptive parable has helped us to see the importance of possessing and practicing the virtues of love of humanity, mercy, charity, kindness, generosity, selfishness, justice, and obedience. It has also helped us to see that repentance happens on earth and not in the afterlife. Wrestling with these truths helps us to form a virtuous character, to become a lover of virtue. This parable, thus, is properly called the Parable of the Necessity to Love Humanity.

Matt 20:1–16: The "First" and the "Last"

The Parable of the Necessity to Love Humanity has revealed the ethical elements required to practice virtues and aroused strong, uncomfortable feelings and emotions. Matthew's parable is equally discomforting. The parable in 20:1–16 is unique to Matthew and originally belonged to his special material (M).[39] Within the context of Matthew's Gospel, this parable is the last parable in Matthew and is located in the section that concludes Jesus's ministry in Judea and Perea (chapters

19—20). Matthew places it before the prediction of Jesus's death (20:17-19) and after the story of a rich young man (19:16–30), which ends with Jesus's statement, "many who are *first* will be *last*, and the *last* will be *first*" (19:30). This statement captures the attention of Jesus's audience for his parable in 20:1–16. The placement of this parable gives an important clue about its true meaning.

Table 3.3. Matt 20:1–16 The Kingdom of Heaven Is Like
Introduction: ¹For the kingdom of heaven is like
Process of Events: a landowner who went out early in the morning to hire laborers for his vineyard. ²After agreeing with the laborers for the usual daily wage, he sent them into his vineyard. ³When he went out about nine o'clock, he saw others standing idle in the marketplace; ⁴and he said to them, "You also go into the vineyard, and I will pay you whatever is right." So they went. ⁵When he went out again about noon and about three o'clock, he did the same. ⁶And about five o'clock he went out and found others standing around; and he said to them, "Why are you standing here idle all day?" ⁷They said to him, "Because no one has hired us." He said to them, "You also go into the vineyard."
Given Directions: ⁸When evening came, the owner of the vineyard said to his manager, "Call the laborers and give them their pay, beginning with the last and then going to the first."
Distribution of Wages: ⁹When those hired about five o'clock came, each of them received the usual daily wage. ¹⁰Now when the first came, they thought they would receive more; but each of them also received the usual daily wage.
The Focus Revealed: ¹¹And when they received it, they grumbled against the landowner, ¹²saying, "These last worked only one hour, and you have made them equal to us who have borne the burden of the day and the scorching heat." ¹³But he replied to one of them, "Friend, I am doing you no wrong; did you not agree with me for the usual daily wage? ¹⁴Take what belongs to you and go; I choose to give to this last the same as I give to you. ¹⁵Am I not allowed to do what I choose with what belongs to me? Or are you envious because I am generous?"
Teaching Moment: ¹⁶So the last will be first, and the first will be last.

This parable follows the theme of discipleship and can easily relate to the parables about the kingdom and judgment. Some scholars have cataloged this parable as "a marvelous parable about the grace of God" and as an example of "God's extraordinary forgiveness and grace."[40] Jülicher and Fuchs argue that this parable presents the gospel in "a nutshell," indeed, "the climax" of Matthew's Gospel, and Montefiore claims that it is "one of the greatest parables of all."[41] Snodgrass, however, believes that "all of these are hyperbole" and considers the parable as "one of the three most difficult parables" (along with the parables in Luke 16:1–13 [see discussion in chapter 4] and Matthew's account of the banquet feast in 22:1–14). In the study of this puzzling parable, different approaches have offered new insights. Here we will highlight the rhetorical-poetic techniques, which we will examine in six sections: (1) introduction, v. 1a; (2) the process of events, vv. 1b–7; (3) the description of directions, v. 8; (4) the distribution of wages, vv. 9–10; (5) the revelation of the focus point, vv. 11–15; and (6) the teaching moment, v. 16.

Introduction (20:1a)

Matthew begins his parable with a phrase unique to Matthew, "For the kingdom of heaven is like a landowner" (20:1a). The formulaic introduction "the kingdom of heaven is like" is frequently used in Matthew (see 13:31, 33, 44, 45, 47),[42] and also highlights two important rhetorical features. First, Matthew repeats the emphasis on God's heavenly realm, already introduced in the parables in chapter 1 (Matt 13:31–32; Matt 13:33), to maintain a consistent narrative and style. Matthew expresses the heavenly realm as the "kingdom of *heaven*" and not the "kingdom of God" as in Mark and Luke. Matthew returns to the image of God's heavenly realm as a similitude; the kingdom "is like" (*homoia*) a "landowner" (*oikodespotē*, lit. "master of a house," the one who runs the whole estate and pays out of his own pocket). This formula triggers in our imagination a strong connection between the mustard seed and leaven similitudes and the landowner similitude here. His rhetorical strategy not only helps produce *enargeia* but also creates a sense of familiarity and readiness on the part of the reader.

Once again, the Matthean Jesus puts before the eyes of his audience a scene common to the experience of Mediterranean peasants and villagers. The first-century audience knew their level on the domestic economic ladder; day laborers were near the bottom and were among the poorest persons in society. They were usually landless peasants, who were either noninheriting sons or persons who had lost their ancestral lands through debt and drifted into cities and villages looking for work. Since loss of land often meant loss of family and the supporting network that implied, such individuals were usually desperate. Indeed, survival was a bitter struggle.[43]

Process of Events (20:1b–7)

In the parable—the heavenly realm of God is like a landowner—Matthew presents a detailed description of the sequence of hirings (20:1b–7) in order to focus the audience's attention on the landowner's activity—his *going out* and *sending into*—and the response of the "laborers" (*ergatas*)—their *going to* and *into*—both in relation to the landowner's "vineyard" (*ampelōna*). The evangelist employs key rhetorical-poetic techniques of *ekphrasis* and *enargeia*. His narrative creates a balance between both the landowner's *going out/sending into* and the laborers' *going to/into* and the time *of hiring* and the vineyard. This skillful arrangement gradually increases the time sequence and the laborers' state of being, which in return will also increase the images presented to our mind.[44]

Matthew wants to achieve an emotive effect in his audience through vividness when writing about the two main characters, the landowner and the laborers. The evangelist uses repetition of key language—"landowner," "laborers," "time," "hiring," "go to," "go out," "usual wage," "sending into," "go into," "vineyard"—to intensify the *ekphrastic* elements of clarity and style. These features enhance "imagination" (*phantasia*) and thus increase *enargeia*. Structurally, the process of events shows that the landowner "went out" five times "to hire laborers for his vineyard" (20:1b). Using the amplification device, thus evoking clarity and imagination, Matthew specifies the time at which the landowner goes out, for example, "early in the morning" (v. 1b) or "about nine o'clock" (v. 3).

The description of time helps readers grasp the hiring scene more realistically. Jesus's Jewish audience would have imagined that "early in the morning" would have been early enough to enlist laborers who would begin their work at sunrise (cf. Ps 104:22–23), typically about 6 a.m.[45] The audience knew that the hours were counted from sunrise; the usual working day for a laborer was from sunrise to sunset (twelve hours).[46] Hence, for example, the third hour would have been at 9 a.m., the sixth and the ninth hours (v. 5) at noon and 3 p.m., and the eleventh hour at (v. 6) 5 p.m.[47] The landowner's repeated action of going out (20:1b, 3a, 5a, 6a) is rhetorically placed in parallel with his sending to (20:2b, 4a, 5b, 7b) the vineyard (20:1b, 2b, 4a, 7b), as well as with the

The Power of Transformation

laborers going to/into (v. 4b) the vineyard to work. The combination of the hours and the action of "he went out," "he sent to/into," and "they went to/into" puts before our eyes the visual images of the interaction between the landowner and the laborers throughout the day.

To evoke greater realism and imagination, Matthew uses amplification. The first element highlighted in his vivid representation is the "usual daily wage," which is repeated throughout the parable (vv. 2a, 9b, 10b, 13b). Matthew imaginatively transports us into the context of the agrarian society of the first century CE. The amplification, a denarius a day, not only creates realism and gives clarity to the scene depicted but also reinforces the amplifications of the statements, "after *agreeing* with the laborers" (20:2a) and "whatever is *right*" (20:4b). These two extra details emphasize the landowner's right character and establish a connection between the just payment (landowner) and the usual daily wage (laborers). Thus, Matthew sets up the "contract" between the landowner and the laborers in the five encounters. At this point in the parable, we have clearly developed a mental image of the hiring process, which has been repeated five times. In fact, this gloss is enhanced with the rhetorical phrases, "he did the *same*" (20:5b) and "you *also* go into the vineyard" (20:4a, 7b). Therefore, with the rhetorical techniques of amplification and repetition, Matthew does not need to specify the wage (a denarius a day) after the first group of laborers is hired. We know that the other four groups had the same wage agreement.

Matthew also uses the technique of *amplification* to capture the laborers' state of being and their interaction with the landowner. The first image that the evangelist vividly describes is that of the laborers' spatial position. Three times we hear that the laborers are "*standing idle* in the marketplace" (20:3b), "*standing* around" (20:6a), and "why are you *standing* here *idle* all day?" (20:6b). Matthew portrays the laborers physically for his audience's eyes; they are standing "idle" (*argos*, lit. "without work" or "unemployed"). The vivid text creates visual images of laborers who have no permanent employment.[48] Within this context, the repeated hirings (five times), which entail the going back and forth of the landowner, are necessary glosses of *ekphrasis* and *enargeia*. Rhetorically, they are the basis for Matthew's clarity and the point of the parable.

In the last hiring, Matthew highlights the vivid socioeconomic situation of the laborers with a rhetorical question, "why are you standing idle here all day?" (v. 6b). For the first time, the laborers speak, "because no one has hired us" (20:7a). The difficult situation of the fifth group of laborers is vividly portrayed in the language Matthew uses. Now the evangelist creates a direct and reciprocal connection between the laborers and the landowner: "*they* said to *him*" (20:7a), and "*he* said to *them*" (20:7b). The sequence of hiring ends with the words of the landowner, "you also *go into* the vineyard" (20:7b), as the parable had started with the landowner's "going out" to hire workers (20:1b). Matthew emphasizes the landowner and his words, and the audience is able to see the scene in relation to the whole process of *going out* and *sending to/into* (landowner) and *going to/into* (laborers) the vineyard. The vivid verbal picture of hiring laborers, so familiar to people in the first century, is now brought before our eyes to stimulate emotions followed by an internal wrestling experience in our hearts and minds.[49]

GIVEN DIRECTIONS (20:8)

Matthew now has his audience ready to be internally moved by the unexpected in Jesus's parable. However, before the evangelist proceeds to the heart of the parable, the moment of challenge that will stir an internal struggle, he uses the rhetorical device of amplification to set up the scene. In 20:8, Matthew writes, "When evening came, the owner of the vineyard said to his manager, 'call the laborers and give them their pay, beginning with the *last* and then going to the *first*.'" We mentally imagine this short scene happening on the landowner's property, unlike the previous scene (20:1b–7), which occurred in the marketplace. Two features are worthy of being mentioned: the series of repetitions and the time sequence. The repetitions of "owner" ("landowner"), "vineyard," and "pay" ("usual daily wage") are placed in the middle of the verse (20:8b). These key words will help us to become spectators in the coming scene in vv. 9–10.

More significant is the time sequence that Matthew presents to his audience before (20:8a) and after (20:8c) the series of repetitions (20:8b), in which the "owner" (*kyrios,* lit. "master" or "lord") of the "vineyard" tells his "manager" to call the "laborers" to "pay" them their daily wage. The sequence begins with the phrase "When evening came" (20:8a), which is meant to put the audience at ease in a familiar context, since it was customary to pay a day laborer the very evening of his work (see Lev 19:13). In the middle of the verse (20:8b) Matthew shows his powerful rhetorical-poetic skills when he adds the shocking yet revealing phrase, "beginning with the *last* and then going to the *first*"

(20:8c). The key words of *last* and *first* in combination with "beginning" and "then"—*beginning-last* and *then-first*—create a sense of confusion, alerting us to the coming message of Jesus. Thus, the directions given to the manager trigger our emotions and feelings as we envision the sharp contrast between the *last* and the *first* and the priority of the last over the first. We also experience the surprise when those hired *last* receive the usual daily wage, and *then* the laborers hired *first* receive the *same* wages. It is in this temporal dimension of contrast and surprise where we find ourselves wrestling.

Distribution of Wages (20:9–10)

In the distribution of wages, we experience the climax of the story. We have been prepared for this moment, and the Matthean Jesus expects a proper response and understanding. Concisely in two verses (20:9–10), the Matthean Jesus describes the payment procedure: "When those hired *about five o'clock came*, each of them received the usual daily wage. Now when the *first came*, they thought they would receive more; but each of them also received the usual daily wage." Unexpectedly, the distribution of wages is made beginning with the *last* hired and ending with the *first*. One would expect that those hired "early in the morning" (v. 1) would come *first*, and those hired "about five o'clock" (v. 6) would be *last*. Matthew is precise in repeating the time, "about five o'clock," because it emphasizes the reversal that is occurring. With the use of amplification, "each of them also received the usual daily wage" (v. 10c), Matthew puts vividly before our eyes the moment when those hired last each receive one denarius, which is, as he says, the usual daily wage. In the process of internal wrestling, we know that one denarius is earned in a twelve-hour workday—from sunrise to sunset (Ps 104:22–23)—and that a denarius was subsistence pay at best.[50] This is exactly what Matthew wants to emphasize by making the other laborers and us into spectators through the process of payment. The other laborers would naturally believe that they will receive more—even though they originally agreed to a denarius, the usual daily wage (20:2).

But with this common, logical notion, the Matthean Jesus wants to challenge his audience (then and now), for in the following verse (20:10) comes the unexpected and surprising twist in the parable that will stir internal and emotional wrestling. With the conjunction "now" (*kai*, lit. "and"), Matthew changes his rhetorical tone and puts before our eyes the image of the first laborers who came to the vineyard to work. Those who first came "thought they would *receive more*" than one denarius. To increase imagination and give vividness to the shocking, unconventional experience, Matthew repeats the conjunction "but" and "also" (*kai*) to heighten the fact that "each of them also received the usual daily wage," that is a denarius. With a series of repetitions, Matthew develops a parallel between the first laborers hired "early in the morning" and the others hired later. This is clearly observed in his vivid statements: "each of them received the usual daily wage" in 20:9, and "but each of them *also* received the usual daily wage" in 20:10. The key rhetorical word is *kai* (here translated as "also"); it points back to the agreement clearly established with the first group of laborers hired in 20:2 as well as echoing the expression "*whatever* is *right*" in 20:4.

In this way, we learn, as we individually wrestle with and internalize the true message of Jesus's parable, that Jesus expects from each of us the dramatic action of the landowner—abundant *generosity*.

THE FOCUS REVEALED (20:11–15)

The equal payment of one denarius to the last group of laborers creates suspense in the reader's mind, since those laborers who were hired before five o'clock (20:2–5) have maintained silence up to this point in the story. The feelings of suspense change as the laborers grumble against the landowner when their human expectations are disappointed (20:11a).[51] As Matthew describes the feelings of the laborers in their dialogue with the landowner, the true natures of both the landowner and the first laborers are revealed. Matthew uses the technique of *enargeia* to highlight the laborers' argument over their wages (20:11–12), and he employs rhetorical questions to unfold the landowner's virtuous character.

Three rhetorical points are worth mentioning. First, the language changes drastically as Matthew relates the laborers' disappointment and objection. The vivid description that they "grumbled against the landowner" (lit. "master of the house") expresses the negative feelings of the laborers and exposes their unvirtuous character. Second, their objection indirectly accuses the landowner of injustice. They confront the landowner, complaining, "These last worked only one hour, and *you* have made them *equal* to us who have borne the burden of the day and the scorching heat" (20:12). These unvirtuous laborers forget the agreement made with the landowner when they were hired (20:2, 4). Third, the laborers, and those who do not have the capacity to internalize Jesus's parables, consider this equal or reciprocal treatment as unfair.[52]

The harsh language, which we are meant to visualize, represents the vivid reality of the experiences of laborers working in the field under the hot sun. Hence, at first glance, the laborers' objections sound reasonable; after all, these first laborers had worked twelve hours in the scorching heat, not one.[53] However, the rhetorical techniques Matthew uses help us, who are wrestling with the scenario, to visualize the laborers' wrongness and unvirtuous characters. This is particularly represented in their outraged statement, "you have made them equal to us" (20:12). These individuals possess the vices of arrogance, selfishness, injustice, and envy. Their understanding of justice and equal treatment lacks a sense of equity, reciprocity, community, and love of humanity. In this parable, the Matthean Jesus teaches a kind of higher justice that goes beyond the standards of the justice practiced and commonly expected in the Mediterranean agrarian society. For the Matthean Jesus, all the laborers sent at different times into the vineyard are equal in the eyes of the landowner in terms of human dignity, as human beings are before God today. Matthew's vivid description and *enargetic* techniques heighten the focus of this parable.

But if the audience has not yet understood the point, Matthew presents the truth of the parable and the landowner's righteous character in a series of rhetorical questions. The description of the landowner's response to the first laborers is represented in a twofold statement. Initially, the landowner responds to "*one* of them" to bring his response to a more personal level to effect reflection. He assures them (and us too) that he did them no wrong; there is no injustice. Interestingly, he calls the laborer "friend" (*hetaire*), a vocative masculine singular in Greek, to denote that the first laborers are the ones who are wrong, that is, unjust.[54] Therefore, Matthew succinctly exposes the real identity of these laborers; they are insolent and deceitful individuals who are being confronted.[55] The landowner acted rightly and did not cheat them, since *they* agreed with *him* for the usual daily wage (20:13). Rather, he was generous with the last laborers who worked only one hour. He is also fair as he tells the first laborers, "Take what belongs to you and go" (20:14a). The repetitions—"last," "them," "you," "agree," "usual daily wage," and "go"—are meant to enhance our participation as spectators of this scene by seeing ourselves as "*one* of them" (20:13a) to whom the landowner speaks. The repetitions also prepare us to see the climactic moment of the parable.

Second, unlike the first laborers' negative character, the landowner's virtues are exposed. He is the focus of this climax. His ability (and power) to choose to give to the last hired laborers (who worked only one hour) the same as he gave to the first hired laborers (who worked twelve hours) reveals his generosity (20:14b) and determination to distribute his wealth according to each laborer's needs. With the landowner's question—"Am I not allowed to do what I choose with what belongs to me?" (20:15a)—Matthew brings the audience to the most challenging part of the parable where he reveals the identity and nature of the landowner. The landowner is a vivid metaphor for God, who is generous and just and *chooses what to do with what belongs to God*, which is all. Nonetheless, the measure of God's choosing and giving is ruled by the virtues of generosity, reciprocity, love of humanity, equity, justice, and compassion, and not by human standards. The next rhetorical question, "Are you envious because I am generous?" (20:15b), vividly represents an image of the first laborers' vices, which are selfishness, envy, jealousy, and lack of generosity. They do not (cannot) see beyond these detrimental vices. The literal translation of the Greek would be, "Is your eye *evil* because I am *good*?" Matthew creates a vivid contrast between the landowner's *virtues* (goodness) and the first laborers' *vices* (evil). The audience imaginatively sees the relation of the vice of envy with the evil eye (cf. Sir 14:9–10), and the relation of the virtue of generosity with goodness.[56] In the process of internal wrestling, we come to embrace virtues and view them as the "means" to achieve right attitude and behavior. Even if events seem unfair or unjust by human standards, the possession and practice of virtues maintain one's character on the right path toward "likeness to God," that is true happiness.

Teaching Moment (20:16)

Now, in the last part of the parable, the Matthean Jesus utters the message of his parable: "So the last will be *first*, and the first will be *last*" (20:16).[57] This statement is Matthew's last rhetorical weapon to move his audience and thus provoke internal transformation and the desire to practice virtues and avoid vices. The depiction of the landowner's generosity and compassion for the unemployed is, as Herzog notes, a striking picture of the divine generosity that gives without regard to the measures of strict justice.[58] In the end, the landowner is more than just; he is extremely generous, an indication that he has excelled in the practice of virtue; indeed, he is a lover of virtue. Jesus's wise saying repeats two important words of the parable, that is, "last" and "first" (see also 19:30). Matthew frames his parable around these two adjectives; it is in 20:16 that we finally learn that this parable is about a contrast between two choices (virtues and vices), and how to distinguish the correct choice.

Furthermore, the lesson of the parable is about "place." Matthew's rhetorical-poetic language throughout the parable evokes a sense of contrast between the "last" and "first" *place* in terms of virtues and vices. Under the *last* place Matthew puts the virtues of generosity, justice, reciprocity, compassion, love of humanity, and the like; and under the *first* place, the evangelist puts the vices of envy, injustice, selfishness, lack of compassion, and lack of love of humanity. Moreover, Matthew develops a set of contrasts between the pronouns "I" and "you," in which the "I" represents a vivid metaphor for God in the heavenly realm and the "you" represents the laborers in the earthly realm. For the Matthean Jesus, the kingdom of heaven involves the virtue of generosity, the actions of the "I" (present in the metaphor of the landowner), and the quality or capacity of a just/right choice according to God's (heavenly) standards. According to Sri, "being generous with those in need, therefore, is not only an act of mercy; it is also an act of justice."[59] At this point, we arrive at a deeper level of wrestling and come to assimilate God's divine measures of justice and equality. In the process of this deeper wrestling within the human heart, the human soul can gain a genuine disposition of acceptance of God's divine choices; that sincere acceptance requires the possession of virtues, especially generosity and love of humanity. In this parable, the Matthean Jesus teaches us Who God is and how God acts. Therefore, an appropriate name for this parable is the Parable of the Landowner's Choice of Generosity.

Luke 16:1–8: A Puzzling Parable

This story is often regarded as the most puzzling and difficult of the parables in the Synoptic Gospels. This parable appears only in the Gospel of Luke and derives from the special material "L." Luke places his parable within the Travel Narrative (9:51–19:27), in which Jesus is on his way to Jerusalem. The parable is directed to Jesus's disciples

(16:1a), and probably to the Pharisees and scribes, too, since they were there hearing everything (15:1–2); indeed, in 16:14 Jesus calls them "lovers of money."[60] The rhetorical-poetic analysis of the parable, using tools employed in the *progymnasmata*, will offer a new window through which one can better appreciate Jesus's message.

As Jesus gets closer to Jerusalem, in Luke 16:1–8 he tells his audience a parable, once again about a master and his servant, who is a manager.

Table 3.4. Luke 16:1–8
Setting the Story: ¹Then Jesus said to the disciples, "There was a rich man who had a manager, and charges were brought to him that this man was squandering his property. ²So he summoned him and said to him, 'What is this that I hear about you? Give me an accounting of your management, because you cannot be my manager any longer.'
Monologue: ³Then the manager said to himself, 'What will I do, now that my master is taking the position away from me? I am not strong enough to dig, and I am ashamed to beg. ⁴I have decided what to do so that, when I am dismissed as manager, people may welcome me into their homes.'
Astute Action: ⁵So, summoning his master's debtors one by one, he asked the first, 'How much do you owe my master?' ⁶He answered, 'A hundred jugs of olive oil.' He said to him, 'Take your bill, sit down quickly, and make it fifty.' ⁷Then he asked another, 'And how much do you owe?' He replied, 'A hundred containers of wheat.' He said to him, 'Take your bill and make it eighty.'
Teaching Moment: ⁸And his master commended the dishonest manager because he had acted shrewdly; for the children of this age are more shrewd in dealing with their own generation than are the children of light."

The lesson of this parable is difficult to understand. We may find ourselves in a state of discomfort, challenged to a greater disposition of the heart. The big question is: what is the point of Jesus's teaching? We are totally stunned by the actions of both the master and the manager, and we wrestle in our hearts trying to find an answer. The analysis of Luke's use of rhetorical-poetic techniques learned in the *progymnasmata* helps us not only to have a better grasp of the parable itself and its message but also to arrive at the right place in order to experience human transformation. In the context of Greek rhetoric, then, the analysis of this parable will highlight Luke's descriptive speech and the technique of vividness to bring to the surface the complexity of the manager's and the master's actions. We will analyze the parable in four parts: (1) the setting of the story, vv. 1–2; (2) the manager's monologue, vv. 3–4; (3) the manager's astute action, vv. 5–7; and (4) the unpredicted conclusion and lesson, v. 8.

THE SETTING OF THE STORY (16:1–2)

Luke begins his story by introducing the two main characters, a certain man who was rich (*plousios*) and the manager of his household (*oikonomos*, also "steward") in v. 1b. For Luke's first-century audience, the association of a rich man with a manager would be common in their agrarian society. Wealthy landowners usually employed estate managers who had the authority to engage in different transactions, such as renting property, making loans, and forgiving and liquidating debts in the name of the master.[61] In first-century Roman Palestine, Marulli points out that "a large population of peasants (90 to 95 percent) were obliged to work for the elite class of owners (1 to 2 percent), to whom they were mostly linked through the often unpopular work of retainers or stewards."[62] The Lukan Jesus takes advantage of this well-known economic practice to bring before his disciples' eyes images of both the manager's and the rich man's activities (vv. 1c–2). The manager is accused of dishonesty, and Luke vividly describes his situation saying, "*This man* was squandering his property" (16:1c).

From the beginning of the story, we perceive the negative action of the manager: he *is* squandering property. Indeed, Luke writes it in the present participle tense, "*is* squandering" (*diaskorpizōn*). As manager, who has been given control over the business of the rich man's estate, the man is to make sales and loans with honesty and honestly collect, forgive, and pay off debts for his master. He earns his own living by commissions or fees resulting from the various transactions entrusted to him by his master.[63] Therefore, if the manager "is squandering" the property of his master (16:1c), he is acting dishonestly toward his master. So far, the manager's character reflects only vices such as dishonesty, recklessness, deceitfulness, foolishness, insincerity, and mismanagement.

Luke next presents the rich man's response (16:2). The landowner summons the manager, and Luke uses the technique of amplification in a rhetorical question, "What is this that I hear about you?" to increase *enargeia* and the mental images of the master's action—"give me an accounting of your management"—and his decision—"you cannot be my manager any longer." Similarly, the repetition of the words, "management" and "manager" (Greek *oiokonomon, oikonomias, oikonomein*) heightens the representation of the rich man's position, evoking two immediate actions: (1) the records of the manager's work are demanded, and (2) the manager is dismissed, which probably also implies that the manager will have to leave his residence on the estate.[64] Luke has structured his narrative stylistically; the manager is introduced together with his fraudulent, dishonest action, and then the rich man is introduced together with his action and his decision.

THE MANAGER'S MONOLOGUE (16:3–4)

After the introduction of the two main characters of the parable in 16:1–2, Luke focuses on the manager only, where he skillfully develops a monologue to rhetorically present the manager's internal thoughts in 16:3–4. The monologue device is a Lukan characteristic that appears in a number of his parables, for example, in 12:17, 45; 15:17–19; 18:4–5; and 20:13.[65] In this parable, the manager asks himself, "What will I do, now that my master is taking the position away from me? I am not strong enough to dig, and I am ashamed to beg. I have decided what to do so that, when I am dismissed as manager, people may welcome me into their homes" (16:3–4). The vivid presentation of his internal monologue highlights important rhetorical features: repetition and amplification (two *enargetic* elements), the rhetorical question "what to do," and the theme of hospitality. As the manager talks to himself, he repeats twice the fact that his master has taken away his position as manager; indeed, the word "manager" is repeated in 16:3 and 16:4. His thinking, "my master is taking the position away from me" (16:3b) and "I am dismissed as manager" (16:4a) strongly echoes what Luke puts in the rich man's mouth in 16:2c, "you cannot be my manager any longer." In the internal monologue, the evangelist emphasizes the master's decision to immediately fire his manager so that we can vividly see in our imagination the gravity of the manager's wrongdoing.

Another important *enargetic* feature reflected in the manager's monologue is amplification, when Luke vividly presents the manager's physical strength and socioeconomic status: "I am not strong enough to dig, and I am ashamed to beg" (16:3c).[66] Interestingly, as the manager talks to himself about his personal condition, he reveals two important social realities; he can dig, or he can beg. He could be sent away to do

The Power of Transformation

hard labor, such as digging in a stone quarry or construction. Here Luke brings before his audience's eyes images of the most difficult work in ancient Palestine. The manager knows that he does not have the physical strength to do such unwanted, grueling labor. Likewise, with the statement, "I am ashamed to beg," Luke shows another unwanted reality of many ancient people. Begging was considered the most humiliating practice in antiquity; "it is better to die than to beg" (Sir 40:29).[67] Therefore, the fear of digging and begging influences the manager to hastily think of what he would do.

The manager talks internally to himself, asking "what to do" (16:3a), and then he "decides *what to do*" (16:4a). Luke emphasizes this phrase by repeating it twice in his narrative, providing us with the clue that will lead us to focus on the parable. What the manager does will ultimately be central to Jesus's lesson. Luke's narrative style creates suspense for the audience when the manager says to himself, "I have decided what to do" (16:4a) but does not reveal what that is. What the audience knows, however, is that whatever he does will make him so liked by the people that he will be "welcom[ed] into their homes" (16:4b). Luke provides an element of surprise to stir our emotions, keeping us in suspense until the last part of the parable in 16:8. Luke gives a special rhetorical emphasis on what the manager will do, bringing before our eyes the scene of a difficult but common human experience. We can see ourselves wondering "what to do," enticing us to take action. In this context, the manager's internal question (v. 3b) and determination (v. 4a) show an appropriate reaction to a personal crisis that can be applied to our own difficult experiences.

Luke connects what the manager will do with the theme of hospitality, a virtue highly esteemed in the early Christian communities. Luke describes that the manager's yet unknown action will stir people's hearts to "welcome him" into their homes. For the audience, the manager's statement, "welcome me into their homes," denotes hospitality; it implies being taken in as a guest with table fellowship and all of the attendant assumptions that accompany it (cf. Luke 15:2).[68] Luke asserts that the dishonest manager's action will spur certain people to practice toward him the virtue of hospitality. His doing will supersede his fraudulent action against his master (16:1–2), and the people's hospitality will become a reciprocal response. In the Lukan parable, this reciprocal response is significant, something to engrave on our minds when we wrestle internally.

The Manager's Astute Action (16:5–7)

Luke now switches to the interaction of the manager with new characters, the "master's debtors." Three characters are involved in the scene: the master (v. 5ac), the debtors (vv. 5ab, 7a), and the manager (vv. 5ab, 6b, 7ac). The manager brings in several debtors of his master, "one by one" and asks each one how much he owes to the master. In 16:5–7 Luke describes the dialogue between the manager and the debtors as a series of rhetorical questions in which stylistically and concisely he creates a perfect balance between the questions (twice) and the responses (twice). Luke explicitly reveals the astute action of the manager, depicting the calculated manner in which the manager puts into action his clever plan. In this scene, the quick wit of the manager comes to the fore, his first virtuous trait. According to Aristotle, wit is a virtue, an excellent trait of character that is conducive to living well and flourishing.

The manager summons the first debtor and asks, "How much do you owe *my* master?" (16:5b); then, he repeats the same question to another debtor of his master, "And how much do you owe?" (16:7a). While both questions are almost identical, the debtors' answers are not. The first debtor responds to the manager saying, "A hundred jugs of olive oil" (16:6a) and the other debtor replies, "A hundred containers of wheat" (16:7b). The two answers are strategically structured to highlight what the manager is actually doing. Luke juxtaposes both responses in order to heighten the large amount of "a hundred." The repetition vividly highlights the amount owed by both debtors because Luke wants to show that the exact amount owed (one hundred) is very large; this is what we will picture in our mind's eye. The extraordinary amount is clearly a hyperbolic rhetorical description that recalls the stories of the mustard seed and pounds (see chapters 1 and 2). The choice of "oil" and "wheat," which are basic staple foods in the Mediterranean first-century world, creates not only clarity but also vividness as we see the debtors' basic needs. According to the cultural information, one hundred *baths* of oil (a bath is a unit of measurement) was the equivalent of about eight hundred or nine hundred gallons. The audience, familiar with the agricultural milieu, imagines the yield of possibly 150 olive trees and the equivalent of about three years' wages for the average worker! Similarly, the audience *sees* the one hundred "containers" (*koroi*) of wheat, which would be almost 1,100 bushels, probably enough to feed 150 people for a year, the produce of one hundred acres of land and equivalent to seven

The Power of Transformation

and a half years of labor for the average laborer![69] These amounts reflect evidence of the heavy indebtedness in first-century Palestine.[70] Luke's familiar scenario places before his audience's eyes the hard reality of many peasants who fell into debt as they tried to feed their families with a marginal livelihood.[71] Luke's realism increases vividness.

Luke presents to his audience the huge debts of the two men and makes the manager's business dealings with them unforgettable. Luke uses *ekphrastic* and *enargetic* features to emphasize the manager's astute actions and to prepare us to correctly understand what he is doing with each debtor. The technique of repetition of the phrase "he said to him" (16:6b and 16:7b), tells the audience that the manager's statements to the debtors are crucial for knowing the deepest meaning of Jesus's parable. The manager orders the first debtor, "Take your bill, sit down quickly, and make it fifty" (16:6b). We are not disconcerted at this point but quite astonished to see the way the manager is dealing with the difficult situation in which he put himself.[72] The phrases, "take your bill," "sit down quickly," and "make it *fifty*" are details that give clarity to our mental image. The amount owed (100 jugs) is approximately a thousand gallons of oil, an immense amount, and the manager "quickly" reduces the bill or debt by half.[73]

The adverb "quickly" is used rhetorically to show the manager's determination and steady mind that what he is doing is right. The debtor will now have to pay only 50 percent of his debt! We can imagine the joy on the debtor's face! What a generous master and manager! Note that during the imperial period, wealthy owners, not managers, commonly reduced debts such as rents and arrears in order to enable and encourage their repayment as well as secure the longevity of their tenants and their own long-term profitability.[74] As we wrestle to fathom the parable, with the help of the rhetorical techniques used by Luke, we can observe the manager's virtuous character and the master's indirect action. In the eyes of the debtor and the audience, both the manager and master (indirectly) have shown their virtues of generosity, compassion, humaneness, and love of humanity. To increase vividness, Luke uses the same business language (16:6b) when the manager speaks to the second debtor: "Take your bill and make it *eighty*" (16:7c). For us, the emotional impact of the parable is intensified as we visualize the tremendous generosity of the master, who through the kindness of the manager's action, has reduced the debtors' charges. The amount of debt forgiven, though different in percentages, is in both cases approximately five hundred denarii.[75]

To create a sense of realism, thus authority in his story, Luke offers his audience a historical context for the expression "take your bill" by employing a common practice in that cultural context. The expression "your bill" (*sou ta grammata*) "must have been the copy of the bill in possession of the lender, most likely a legal one-sided document on papyrus signed by the debtor himself."[76] Therefore, the manager offers a copy of the bill to each debtor. The bills have been in the manager's possession, and he acknowledges their indebtedness. With authority he hands them their notes for them to rewrite the amount that they owe. This situation clearly envisions the master, and the manager acting on his behalf, handing over money or goods to each debtor. The modern reader understands two points: (1) the manager shows his initiative in the real world and is actively engaged in the business transactions that bring forgiveness, joy, and peace of heart to the debtors; and (2) the manager, and through him the master, shows the virtues of generosity, benevolence, compassion, humaneness, and love of humanity. In return, the debtors will show reciprocity and hospitality—"[they will] welcome [the manager] into their homes" (16:4). Thus, what is emphasized here is not the debtors' position—whether they know that the manager has been fired[77]—but the manager's action and the virtues that flow from it.

THE TEACHING MOMENT (16:8)

Sometimes we wrestle internally trying to accept the ways God mysteriously acts in the human realm. The lessons that come through Jesus's parables reveal the importance of human action toward our neighbor. Indeed, in the Lukan parable, we encounter an unpredicted lesson, where the manager receives unexpected praise. Luke writes, "And his master commended the dishonest manager because he had acted shrewdly; for the children of this age are more shrewd in dealing with their own generation than are the children of light" (16:8). This verse involves a conclusion (v. 8a) and a teaching lesson (v. 8b). In the conclusion, Luke mentions the two main characters, the master, or *kyrios* (rich man), and the manager, who is now identified as "dishonest" (*adikias*, lit. "unjust").[78] Luke connects back to the introduction of the parable, where both individuals are introduced: "There was a *rich man* who had a *manager*" (16:1–2). This rhetorical tactic allows Luke to place both the master and the manager before our eyes again, but this time their virtuous actions are highlighted (16:5–7). With the descriptive adjective "dishonest" referring to the manager (16:8a), Luke would throw to the audience our last test. It is a direct measure of whether we have become conscious of the importance of the practice of virtues and the avoidance of vices.

Is the manager truly *dishonest*? The answer is no. While squandering his master's property *was* certainly viewed as dishonest (16:1), he immediately reflected on how he could redeem himself, and at the same time, do good on behalf of his master's debtors and enhance his master's reputation (16:5–7). Steffen has argued that the manager protected his master "not to continue to be disobedient to the law" (Exod 22:25; Lev 25:36–37; Deut 23:19–20), and that the master commends the manager because the manager's action helped him to be obedient to the Jewish law.[79] The unexpected commendation from his master is certainly opportune. Even though at the beginning of the story the manager was not a virtuous person, in the end, his imperfection compelled him to do good, not exactly selfishly. His action positively reached out to his neighbors in need and favored his own master. We can see the greater extension and dimension of his action.

Using the technique of *encomia* (an expression of praise), Luke says in 16:8a that the manager is "commended" because he acted "shrewdly" (*phronimōs*). What a vivid image of such an unpredicted action! The Greek word *phronimōs* is an adverb that means "wisely" and "prudently." It is a cognate of the noun *phronēsis*, the main virtue in the list of the Greek ethical systems and one of the four cardinal virtues. We have discussed that "prudence" (*phronēsis*) is "the virtue" *par excellence*, and Socrates argued that if one possesses this virtue, one has all the other virtues. With the commendation of the master, Luke clearly intends to show his audience that the manager possesses prudence and has excelled in the practice of virtues; in his business dealings he has shown qualities that derive from the virtue of prudence. He truly deserves to be commended and praised for his virtue. From his prudence stems his generosity, benevolence, compassion, cleverness, unselfishness, humaneness, and love of humanity.[80] The manager has placed his *master* in an honorable position; as a result, the master is also able to show these positive virtues, too. The master will certainly be commended far and wide![81] And the manager's prudent action has also led the debtors to express virtues of reciprocity, thankfulness, joy, and hospitality. The author of Proverbs depicts prudent people as ones who consider their steps (14:15). In other words, prudence or practical wisdom allows one to perceive, amid the complexities of life, what way of acting will most lead to goodness, and act accordingly.[82]

In 16:8b the Lukan Jesus announces the parable's lesson: "for the children of this age are more shrewd in dealing with their own generation than are the children of light" (16:8b). Here Luke uses repetition twice—"the children of" and "prudence"—as he contrasts two groups and their dimensions of life, the children of "this age" and the children of "light." This is an intricate, puzzling saying, but if we comprehend the Lukan Jesus's lesson, it must be taken as a sign that the human soul, which has been challenged and has wrestled intensely, has arrived at the gate to further experience and human/spiritual transformation. The human soul is now ready to encounter true happiness. While scholars offer different interpretations of this difficult saying,[83] the rhetorical features employed by Luke highlight two crucial points. The term "children of this age" is meant to be understood as life in the world, here in the earthly realm where Jesus's audience lived, and where we now live. We can see ourselves as the children of this age who realize that now is the time to act prudently, like the manager, and do virtuous actions that will benefit not only ourselves but also those in need. However, "the children of light" are in the heavenly realm; their time to do good and noble actions has passed. As in the Parable of the Necessity to Love Humanity in Luke 16:19–31, people have their chance to practice virtues, to be prudent and wise, in the earthly realm, not in the heavenly realm. Out of his sinful action at the beginning of the story, the manager gives us a lesson to practice virtues in this earthly world, virtues that will form our character and make us better human beings. Since this parable emphasizes the virtues, especially the virtue of prudence, it is apropos to name it the Parable of the Prudent Manager.

Conclusion

In this chapter we have interpreted rhetorically three of the most difficult parables of Jesus: the Parable of the Necessity to Love Humanity (Luke 16:19–31), the Parable of the Landowner's Choice of Generosity (Matt 20:1–16), and the Parable of the Prudent Manager (Luke 16:1–8). In each of these parables, the rhetorical techniques of descriptive speech and vividness have transported us into the scenes of Jesus's stories. Hopefully, the experience of internal wrestling stirred by the evangelists' use of vividness has developed an aspiration to practice virtues and avoid vices. At the same time, these rhetorical tools have evoked in us emotions that have prepared us for a transformation of the heart centered on the virtues of love of humanity, generosity, and prudence.

The lesson in the Parable of the Necessity to Love Humanity (Luke 16:19–31) focused on being rather than doing, and the Lukan Jesus has taught us about the importance of a disposition to repentance here in the earthly world. It is here on earth that human beings must repent and practice virtues. Similarly, the Parable of the Landowner's Choice of Generosity (Matt 20:1–16) showed the need to practice a higher level of generosity toward our neighbors and other human beings. The Matthean Jesus challenged us to go beyond the ethical (social) norms, and he has invited us to a greater understanding of justice and a greater love of humanity.

We have come to acknowledge the need to listen, to be generous, and to seek the virtues akin to love of humanity, justice, generosity, and prudence or practical wisdom. The virtue of prudence is particularly highlighted by Luke in the Parable of the Prudent Manager (Luke 16:1–8). Interestingly, the Lukan Jesus chose not only a cardinal virtue from the list of Greek ethical virtues but the chief virtue among them to teach the right action that human beings must practice toward God and neighbors. As in the Parable of the Necessity to Love Humanity, the lesson in the Parable of the Prudent Manager focuses on *doing* and on the pursuit of virtues here on earth. The *doing* must reflect the *being*.

4

Transformation and Happiness in Virtue

In Jesus's parables, we have encountered both virtues and vices. The virtues are both moral *excellences*, in philosophical terms, and the middle way (or *mean*) between excess and deficiency to lead us toward God. (Aristotle calls them "means"; Plato and the Stoics refer to them as cardinal or generic virtues.) The emphasis on the rhetorical character of the parables has served as the instrument to dig deeper into the spiritual treasures that each of Jesus's parables reveals. Happiness (*eudaimonia*) is a central virtue for human transformation. If we desire holiness, we must learn to possess the virtue of happiness. To show in detail the process of spiritual transformation and the path to happiness through the parables of Jesus, we will look at three parables: Luke 15:11–32; Luke 18:1–8; and Matt 18:23–35. Through rhetorical analysis, we will gain the necessary tools and *know the virtues* that will help us to achieve the final goal, transformation, which is also expressed in terms of happiness and salvation. Thus, the rhetorical techniques of *ekphrasis* (descriptive speech) and *enargeia* (vividness) will be analyzed in close connection to the understanding of virtues in the ethics of Greek philosophers.[1]

In ancient Greek ethics, virtue ethics involved the practice of virtues and the avoidance of vices. Especially in Plato, Aristotle, the Stoics, and the Middle Platonists, the practice of virtue was believed to be paramount in the formation of a noble character and the acquisition of human perfection. The goal of human life was the achievement of a life of "happiness" (*eudaimonia*). In fact, ancient Greek philosophers were called *eudaimonists*.[2] In chapter 3, we learned that on the journey toward the divine realm (heaven), we must practice virtues in the earthly world, among them the virtues of trust, love of humanity, justice, compassion, generosity, and prudence or practical wisdom. Now, as we look at the process of *transformation*, we will familiarize ourselves with other virtues necessary to acquire and achieve the goal of human life. The rhetorical-poetic approach applied to these three parables will bring to the fore key virtues. For example, in the parable of Luke 15:11–32, we are introduced to the experience of true joy, a virtue akin to happiness, and the middle path that leads human beings to bliss and divine experience.

The virtues vividly represented in Luke 15:11–32, Luke 18:1–8, and Matt 18:23–35 are meant to guide us toward the middle path to find true joy and happiness. As virtues are now the focus, the rhetorical approach in this chapter will highlight three important points: the vivid descriptive elements, the individual's character, and the virtues and vices evoked in each of the parables under discussion. While in the previous chapter we encountered the virtue of prudence or practical wisdom as the *key cardinal virtue*, in this chapter we learn that *happiness* is the most important virtue of all. The Lukan Jesus speaks of this virtue in terms of the virtue of *joy*, in Luke 15:11–32, and the way to acquire this virtue is through the practice of other virtues, vividly described in Luke 18:1–8 and Matt 18:23–35. In these last two parables, we learn *how* to pray and *how* to forgive. Only then will we be ready to *become virtue-loving souls*, for we will learn that the possession and practice of virtues are the middle way to God. Thus, being spiritually *transformed* means becoming truly holy. The virtue-loving soul will attain the heavenly, divine realm of God. Again, the three parables will be named at the end of each analysis.

Luke 15:11–32: The Necessity of Genuine Relationships

Most people are familiar with the Lukan story in 15:11–32.[3] This parable appears only in Luke's Gospel and is attributed to his special source "L." It is the last of the so-called "parables of the lost" (15:1–7; 15:8–10; 15:11–32), placed within the Travel Narrative (chapters 9:51—19:27), and responds to those Pharisees and scribes who reject Jesus as prophet and savior, along with his teachings (cf. 15:1–2).[4] After the Lukan Jesus assures his mixed audience (Jewish Christians and Gentile

Transformation and Happiness in Virtue

Christians) that there is great joy among God's angels when a sinner repents, he tells them another parable to make his point.

Table 4.1. Luke 15:11–32
Unexpected Departure: [11]Then Jesus said, "There was a man who had two sons. [12]The younger of them said to his father, 'Father, give me the share of the property that will belong to me.' So he divided his property between them. [13]A few days later the younger son gathered all he had and traveled to a distant country, and there he squandered his property in dissolute living. [14]When he had spent everything, a severe famine took place throughout that country, and he began to be in need. [15]So he went and hired himself out to one of the citizens of that country, who sent him to his fields to feed the pigs. [16]He would gladly have filled himself with the pods that the pigs were eating; and no one gave him anything. [17]But when he came to himself he said, 'How many of my father's hired hands have bread enough and to spare, but here I am dying of hunger! [18]I will get up and go to my father, and I will say to him, "Father, I have sinned against heaven and before you; [19]I am no longer worthy to be called your son; treat me like one of your hired hands."'
Awaited Return: [20]So he set off and went to his father. But while he was still far off, his father saw him and was filled with compassion; he ran and put his arms around him and kissed him. [21]Then the son said to him, 'Father, I have sinned against heaven and before you; I am no longer worthy to be called your son.' [22]But the father said to his slaves, 'Quickly, bring out a robe—the best one—and put it on him; put a ring on his finger and sandals on his feet. [23]And get the fatted calf and kill it, and let us eat and celebrate; [24]for this son of mine was dead and is alive again; he was lost and is found!' And they began to celebrate.
Unexpected Attitude: [25]"Now his elder son was in the field; and when he came and approached the house, he heard music and dancing. [26]He called one of the slaves and asked what was going on. [27]He replied, 'Your brother has come, and your father has killed the fatted calf, because he has got him back safe and sound.' [28]Then he became angry and refused to go in. His father came out and began to plead with him. [29]But he answered his father, 'Listen! For all these years I have been working like a slave for you, and I have never disobeyed your command; yet you have never given me even a young goat so that I might celebrate with my friends. [30]But when this son of yours came back, who has devoured your property with prostitutes, you killed the fatted calf for him!' [31]Then the father said to him, 'Son, you are always with me, and all that is mine is yours. [32]But we had to celebrate and rejoice, because this brother of yours was dead and has come to life; he was lost and has been found.'"

Hultgren points out that this parable is the longest in the Gospels and consists of three main parts: (1) the departure of the younger son from his father to a faraway country, where he is wasteful and eventually in want (15:11–19); (2) the homecoming of the son and his welcome by his father (15:20–24); and (3) the episode between the father and the elder brother (15:25–32).[5] This parable is an example story contrasting two types of responses to a situation, as Getty-Sullivan argues,[6] and an example of an expected attitude and the clear reflection of virtues that a father and a son possess.

AN UNEXPECTED DEPARTURE (15:11–19)

Luke begins his parable with the *unexpected departure* of a younger son, after he requests his inheritance from his father (15:11–19). According to Roman customs, a person's inheritance is transferred to heirs only at death, and in Jewish law, the inheritance or property (*ousia*) goes to heirs at the death of the one who passes it on (e.g., Num 27:8–11; 36:7–9; Deut 21:15–17).[7] When the younger son requests his inheritance, he is acting contrary to the basic ethos of the house.[8] Forbes rightly asserts that it is unthinkable that a Middle Eastern son would ever ask for an inheritance, let alone be given it. He adds, "Normally the father would explode with rage, for this is the ultimate insult. It is even more remarkable that the son was able to sell his share." According to the Jewish law, the younger son also rejects his duty to honor his father and mother (Exod 20:12; Deut 5:16) because by leaving his father, he casts aside his obligation to care for him in old age (cf. Mark 7:11–13). Therefore, to request one's inheritance while the parent still lived was atypical; likewise, it was inconceivable in the first century that a parent would respond to such a request.[9] According to the laws of inheritance in the Torah (Deut 21:17) and the Mishnah,[10] a double portion of the father's property would go to the elder brother; thus, the younger brother would receive one-third of the property only. In the parable, however, the father divides his "living" (*bios*) and the younger son receives his "sharing" (*meros*). The father's living probably consisted of the father's real estate (farm and its furnishings) and personal property.[11]

Traveling to a distant country (15:13–16) implies that the younger son distances himself from his father, his brother, and his community, not only geographically but also psychologically and emotionally. The expression "distant country" (*chōran makran*) in 15:13a would probably refer to a place *outside* Palestine (cf. 19:12), a country populated mostly by Gentiles (non-Jews).[12] Forbes notes that the phrase "distant country," which was probably authentic, is designed to "stress the alienation" of the younger son from his family.[13] In that distant place the younger son experiences a "wild and disorderly life" (*asōtōs*) that ends in the loss of all his property and consequently goes downhill. As severe famine strikes (16:14a),[14] the younger son has no control of the events affecting his life and finds himself in a dire situation. He hires himself out to work for a "citizen" (*politēs*) of that country, a Gentile who raises pigs and sends him into the fields to feed them.[15] Even though his status is probably like that of an indentured servant[16]—a status above that of a slave—to feed pigs is a degradation of the worst sort. In Jewish law and tradition, pigs are considered unclean animals (Lev 11:7; Deut 14:8),[17] and according to the Mishnah, no one is allowed to rear swine. In the Babylonian Talmud, the person who does so is accursed.[18] Hultgren points out that the "very idea of wishing to be fed from the 'pods' eaten by pigs—and therefore being envious of the pigs!—but being refused, is even more degrading than the act of feeding the pigs itself."[19]

In the worst situation of his life, when the younger son is in absolute misery, he "came to himself" or "to his senses" (15:17a) and sought how he could best get himself out of this horrible situation (15:17–19).[20] The younger son remembers that the "hired servants" (*misthioi*) at his father's house have plenty of food. Luke shows the son's descriptive scene of his actual life and adds color to the story (emphasizing his horrible plight and his imaginary dream), so important to the main purpose of this chapter.[21] The son's statement "I am dying of hunger!" (15:17c) vividly describes the younger son's impending death, which anticipates his father's dramatic statements about his son who died (15:24, 32). Strikingly, the younger son's willingness to go back to his father (15:18–19) and become one of his father's servants shows his disposition to have a status lower than sonship and equal to the slaves and servants of his father's household and farm (15:19). After composing his homecoming speech of *repentance* in the form of a soliloquy, the younger son returns to his father determined to ask for forgiveness. The younger son's remorseful statement, "I have sinned," in 15:18b alludes to the LXX, particularly Exod 10:16 and Ps 51:6. The *confessional* phrase "against heaven" is a reference to "against God," for the term "heaven" is often used as a pious way to refer to God (Luke 15:7).[22] It is important to note that Luke does not say *what* the younger son's sin is, thus keeping us in suspense;[23] however, his previous actions would likely be considered an act of great *insolence* (cf. 15:30).[24]

An Awaited Return (15:20–24)

In the *awaited return* scene (15:20–24), Luke vividly presents the younger son overcoming his weaknesses and returning to his father's home. Here the evangelist presents the father *seeing* his son coming home, and while the son is still at a distance, the father "*was filled with compassion toward his son*" (15:20).[25] The expression of compassion exemplifies the divine compassion that is revealed through Jesus's story. For the first-century audience, the expected response would have been that the father simply lets his son arrive home, fall on his knees, and implore forgiveness. In response, the father would respond with words of forgiveness and a review of expectations. Then, the younger son would be on probation around the home for a time; perhaps he could remain there until he could earn enough to leave as an independent person once again. But, for us, the unexpected happens; immediately upon seeing his younger son, the father *runs* to meet him—an outlandish behavior—pulling up his robe and exposing his legs. His action would have been considered shameful in an honor-shame Semitic society. Even in the Greco-Roman context, a proud, decent person would have usually made "slow steps."[26] Prior to the son saying anything, the father "puts his arms around" him and *kisses* him (15:20c; cf. Gen 33:4), making it impossible for the son to greet his father properly, fall at his feet, and make his speech of repentance.[27] The two verbs "filled with compassion" (v. 20b) and "kissed him" (v. 20c) highlight the virtuous character of the father, reflecting his compassionate heart, a compassion that precedes his son's *prayer* (or confession),[28] and his forgiveness. The three vivid descriptions of the father's behavior—running, embracing his son, and kissing him prior to the son's speech—powerfully evoke in the audience's mind reconciliation and grace on the part of the father, who has no clue of the son's motives. The father expressively shows his delight and joy to have his son home again.[29]

The son's speech of repentance in 15:21, depicted on his feet and in his father's arms, is word for word what he had practiced in his monologue, except that it is interrupted. The son does not have the chance to say the last line, "treat me like one of your hired hands" (15:19b). The statement "I am no longer worthy to be called your son" (15:21c) is enough for his father; indeed, his response is to treat him as *more than* a son (15:22), a special guest! Through amplification, Luke achieves *enargeia* by describing three symbolic gestures that show this distinctive treatment: the father bestows on his son the "best robe" (15:22a), expressing the son's status of *honor* (see Gen 27:15; 41:42; 1 Macc 6:15); he gives a "ring" (15:22b), showing he is receiving *authority* (see Gen 41:42; 1 Macc 6:15; Esth 3:10; 8:2); he puts "sandals on his feet" (15:22b), reflecting the bestowal of his *freedom*. These three symbolic gestures restore the son fully to the family and community. The father's declaration, "for this son of mine was dead and is alive again; he was lost and is found!" (15:24), is the climax of the scene. The vivid language of lost and found links the parable to the exclamations of the shepherd (15:6) and the woman (15:9) in the preceding parables (15:1–7 and 15:8–10).[30]

An Unexpected Attitude (15:25–32)

The scene in 15:25–32 shows the *unexpected attitude* of the elder son when Luke describes the dialogue between the father and the elder son. Luke captures the father's firm attitude and character when he risks humiliation and shame by leaving his guests inside the house and going outdoors to plead with his elder son to come in and join the celebration. Surprisingly, the elder son, who supposedly is obedient and a hard worker, becomes angry and unexpectedly disobeys his father's request; he "refused to go in" (15:28a). His refusal demonstrates that his family relationships are less than adequate, as Forbes has claimed,[31] and also reveals his true feelings toward both the father and his work (15:29–30). He angrily protests the father's virtuous attitude and loving behavior toward the younger son. Luke vividly describes the elder son's outburst toward the father as he wrongfully claims he is the "obedient one" (15:29c), saying, "I have never disobeyed your command" (cf. Deut 26:13). He disrespects the father for not being grateful for his obedience (15:29d), "yet you have never given me even a young goat so that I might celebrate with my friends"; and he humiliates the father for what he sees as foolishness (15:30), "But when this son of yours came back, who has devoured your property with prostitutes, you killed the fatted calf for him!"[32] The elder son shows *no virtues at all*! Such derogatory expressions as "this son of yours," "devoured," "your property," and "with prostitutes," portray what the elder son has felt during all those years he has worked, according to his perception, "like a slave" for the father. Instead of viewing his service to the father as an opportunity to practice virtues, he has nurtured vices of defiance, scorn, hatred, anger, and unhappiness. The audience comes to perceive the elder son in this critical scene as a "son" who does not see the father as *his father*; he derogatively speaks of "this son *of yours*" and never calls him "father" or "my father," as the younger son did. It is the father who affectionately addresses the elder son as "son" and sees him not as a slave but as *his* son and co-owner of the land; the father says, "you are always with *me*, and *all that is mine is yours*" (15:31).

The parable ends with the father's joyful words of excitement inviting *his* elder son to participate in a happy experience saying, come in, we have to celebrate and rejoice, because "this brother *of yours*," who has been dead and lost, "has come to life and has been found" (15:32). We never hear whether the elder son joins the celebration or if the two brothers reconcile. A good name for this story is the Parable of the Son's True Repentance and the Father's Forgiveness.

The Path to Transformation in Virtue

Two virtues are needed to achieve *transformation*—a *prayerful attitude* and *forgiveness*. In the beautiful parable of the Son's True Repentance and the Father's Forgiveness, Luke rhetorically presents two attitudes and two relationships to spell out these virtues. Three features are used to achieve Luke's goal: the descriptive and vivid elements, the behavior and character of the two sons, and the virtues and vices reflected in each son. With the help of the *ekphrastic* and *enargetic* techniques, we will realize that the way each son *sees himself* in relation to the other as his "brother" and in relation to God (father) affects whether he practices virtues and avoids vices. Another Lukan parable (Luke 18:1–8) will help us to learn about the virtue of a prayerful attitude, that is, *how* to pray, and a Matthean parable (Matt 18:23–35) will teach us about the virtue of forgiveness. These two virtues—a prayerful attitude and forgiveness—are crucial in these three stories and will reveal the correct understanding of human transformation and the importance of virtues in our relationship with God and neighbors.

What we shall examine here will help to enlighten our minds as we view Jesus's parables as stories that speak to us about what attitude the characters in the stories reflect. We will now focus our attention not on the unexpected or challenging experiences in the parables but rather on the *expected attitude*. Virtues are the middle path to happiness—a privileged virtue that has the power to lead us toward a genuine transformation. Happiness is a sign that we have spiritually entered the heavenly realm, the intelligible world where God dwells and where we become *perfect*. In a Christian expression, transformation, happiness, and the intelligible world are ways to talk about holiness, salvation, afterlife, and heaven.

THE YOUNGER SON AND THE FATHER'S JOY

As mentioned above, ancient Greek philosophers were known for being *eudaimonists*, for they believed that *happiness* was the goal of human life. Now, in Luke's Parable of the Son's True Repentance and the Father's Forgiveness (15:11–32), the rhetorical-poetic emphasis highlights Jesus as a philosopher, a *eudaimonist*, who speaks of the virtue of joy and exhorts his followers to experience the delights of this virtue. The way the evangelist leads his audience toward the final steps to happiness, thus, transformation, is through a series of "real" imaginary experiences with each of the three major characters: the father, the younger son, and the elder son. The Lukan descriptive elements, such as the *enargetic* features of repetition, amplification, clarity, mimesis, and imagination, arouse our "imagination" (*phantasia*) to create mental images that "bring the scene before our eyes." Throughout the parable, Luke develops specific scenes into a familiar rhetorical description in order to achieve *enargeia*, textualizing images as if they were real, to increase his representational powers. The complex interactions of the father with each of his sons illustrate two different attitudes and two views of themselves in relation to the father to ultimately show the emergence of the younger son's dramatic transformation.

Through *ekphrastic* techniques and *enargeia*, we observe the relationships of the father with his two sons (15:11) and put the relationships into the context of virtue ethics to mentally see what each son does in the circumstances presented. Luke uses clarity to enhance each son's conversation with the father and their attitudes toward each other. The depiction of the scenes in which the younger son directly interacts with the father is found in 15:12 and 20–21. The single scene in which the elder son and the father have a conversation is found at the end of the parable in 15:28b–32. Luke's clear and vivid *ekphrasis* allows us to imagine each scene. As we imagine what is vividly described, we are transported into the scenes, where we can visualize complex situational experiences such as the *initiative of the younger son* in 15:12; 15:15; 15:17–19, 20, and 21, and *his virtuous heroism* in 15:18 and 21.

The Power of Transformation

We also visualize the younger son's *lowest point of despair* in 15:17 and his *humble prayer to his father* in 15:21. These experiences are points of reflection in which we capture through imagination *who* is the main character in the story and to whom we must pay heed. It is in and through the younger son that the Lukan Jesus speaks about happiness or joy; in fact, the language of "celebration," "joy," and "rejoice" comes forth from the father's mouth always in reference to the younger son.[33] Thus, careful attention must be given to the younger son rather than the elder son. The rhetorical elements employed in the scenes with the younger son must be followed closely.

The Lukan Jesus uses the younger son's experiences, both negative and positive, and the response to his father's loving expression to present the climactic event of transformation. The three symbolic gifts given by the father to his youngest son—the best robe, the ring, and the sandals (15:22)—represent the father's extravagant gesture of acceptance toward his younger son,[34] but also the human transformation that derives from the practice of virtues (forgiveness, love, compassion, joy, hospitality [father], humility, and courage [younger son]).

The younger son is a reflection in which we can see ourselves as in a mirror and come to understand true human nature. What we as humans truly are—imperfect beings in constant need of reconciliation with our Father God—is depicted in the younger son's life. A poor choice in 15:12b ("give me the share of the property that will belong to me") did not prevent the son from getting up and returning to the right path (15:18a), which is virtue. His determination to return is only possible with virtues, especially humility, acceptance, and courage.

The younger son's decision to ask for the share of his father's property (15:12b) was socially unacceptable; indeed, it was a shameful and greedy act.[35] Luke's concise technique employed in 15:11–12 is, however, overpowered by the detailed and vivid features of amplification and repetition in 15:13–22. In this way, the rhetorical elements enhance the virtues that the younger son shows outwardly, rather than the vices. For us who are invited to join in the process of transformation, the parable centers solely on the actions (15:11–12), the attitudes, and the virtues of the younger son, exposed in his going away, his rising up, and his returning to his father. These key actions required not only determination but also virtuous attitudes. In return, these become ethical reflections that gradually disclose the father's true nature and relationship with his children. Luke develops his vivid description in such a way

Transformation and Happiness in Virtue

that for us, who are now spectators in the story of the younger son, the awaited event is a celebration! We eagerly await the moment when the younger son experiences transformation through his father's loving and sumptuous actions.

Luke does not use the language of "happiness" (*eudaimonia*), the virtue intrinsically connected to the goal of human life in Greek philosophical ethical systems. However, the evangelist is working within the context of the virtue ethics of ancient philosophers. The notion of acquiring happiness in order to attain the divine realm, or in Luke's familiar language the kingdom of God (Luke 12:22–34), is present in Luke's mind.[36] In the parable Luke centers the scenes of celebration (15:23–24, 32) on the virtue of joy:

> [23]"And get the fatted calf and kill it, and let us eat and *celebrate*; [24]for this son of mine was dead and is alive again; he was lost and is found!" And they began to *celebrate*....
>
> [32]"But we had to *celebrate* and *rejoice*, because this brother of yours was dead and has come to life; he was lost and has been found."

These important, joyous scenes are the climactic moments in the parable, and Luke enhances them with repetition and amplification to "bring before the eyes" the moments of great joy in the celebration. The repetitions of "fatted calf" (vv. 23, 27, 30), "celebrate" (vv. 25, 24, 29, 32), and "found" (vv. 24, 32) transport us into a higher dimension of ethics. Even in the dreary scene of the elder son in 15:25–31, the joy of the celebration is conveyed in the words of "music and dancing" (v. 25), "safe and sound" (v. 27), and "rejoice" (v. 32).

Luke captures vividly the images of the spiritual impact that the joyous celebration will produce in the virtue-loving souls' emotions.[37] Luke goes even further when he glosses his rhetorical techniques with vivid images illustrated in phrases like "let us *eat* and *celebrate*" (v. 23), "was dead and has come to *life*" (v. 32), and "he was lost and has been *found*" (v. 32).[38] The evangelist creates a threefold relationship in the words "celebrate-life-found," so important on the way to transformation. The language of "lost" and "found" echoes not only the finding of Jesus in the Jerusalem Temple (2:46) but also the previous parables in Luke 15:1–7 (when a person loses and finds a sheep) and in 15:8–10 (when a woman loses and finds a silver coin). In this parable, a son who dies (symbolically) and is found *again* cannot but have a deep resonance for us who are visualizing ourselves in the younger son. By creating a contrast between *dead* and *alive/life* and *lost* and *found,* the evangelist develops the younger son's process of transformation—from a negative, unexpected behavior (15:11–19) to a positive, virtuous, and intimate relationship with his father. This progression on the path to virtue brings joy and celebration.

Two Sons and Two Attitudes: Virtue and Vice

In the parable, Luke's rhetorical-poetic approach puts in parallel the attitudes of the two sons and their relationship with the father. The vivid emphasis on each son's encounter with the father highlights *what the father does* to his younger son rather than *what the younger son did* at the beginning of the story (15:11–12). We imagine in our minds (*phantasia*), as if they were real, the two distinct sons. As Luke develops his narrative focused on the two sons' attitudes, he reveals two different relationships, the younger son with *his* father, and the elder son with *the* father. What is quite remarkable is that we are able to distinctly see a specific, crucial moment that will ultimately enlighten the emphasis on virtues around the younger son-father relationship, something that will motivate "imitation" (*mimesis*). Here, the element of *mimesis* makes it possible to see or imitate the father and younger son in a new way and to go beyond the human comparative perspectives of the two sons.[39]

At the beginning of the parable, the younger son's actions portray him negatively. A superficial reading may certainly lead to that view. However, Luke's rhetorical techniques bring forward the younger son's actions as a rhetorical device that prepares us to find the middle way, that is, the path of virtue. We see ourselves in the younger son, as in a mirror, feeling emotions of sympathy. Significantly, the truth and reality of human nature are revealed in the younger son: all human beings sin. At certain points in life, all humans are like the younger son. Thus, instead of looking at the younger son's greediness (materialism), we observe the younger son with understanding, a virtue akin to prudence or practical wisdom. In this parable, Luke has skillfully engraved the reflection of the younger son on our eyes and hearts. It is he (not the elder son) who, with his exemplary determination to repent, will lead us to experience happiness, a virtue akin to joy.

Transformation and Happiness in Virtue

As Luke vividly presents the long scene of the younger son in 15:14–21, the virtuous attitude and character of the younger son shine in three ways: his humiliation (vv. 14–16), his internal reflection in soliloquy (vv. 17–19), and his exaltation (vv. 20–21). Luke aims to show that the son's virtue derives from his experience of humiliation (his sin) and culminates in his experience of exaltation (his coming back to his father), represented in the language of "celebration and rejoice" (vv. 22–24, 25, 32). When Luke brings before our eyes the scene of the tragic situation of the younger son (15:14–16), he vividly heightens the worst scenario of the younger son's life. The descriptive language of "severe famine," "throughout that country," "be in need," "hired himself," "to feed the pigs," "filled himself with the pods that the pigs were eating," and "no one gave him anything" amplifies the son's lowest point of his humiliation (necessary to his exaltation). As a consequence of his own choice, the younger son experiences dishonor before his father, family, and community; we see him experiencing degradation, spiritually a sinful condition before God. However, in the younger son's personal reflection (15:17–19), his humiliation produces virtuous fruits. Indeed, we see no vices in the younger son's experience of humiliation as well as in his internal reflection and exaltation.

In the younger son's internal reflection, visualized as a link or threshold between humiliation and exaltation, Luke powerfully captures the younger son's initiative as he "came to himself" (v. 17a) in an internal soliloquy.[40] At the point of death, dramatically articulated in the expression, "I am dying of hunger!" (v. 17c), the younger son shows his great determination (and courage): "I will get up and go to *my father*" (v. 18a). This is a moment of grace rooted in the trustful and unbroken relationship with his father, as he repeatedly calls him "my father" or "father" throughout the narrative (vv. 17, 18 [twice], 19 ["your son"], 21 [also "your son"]). Luke masterfully depicts the fact that the younger son has never lost his relationship with his father. Even in the most painful moments of alienation, despair, and humiliation, he never sees himself as one who broke ties (physically or spiritually) with his father. Only one who possesses virtues can be empowered to show such a noble, courageous, and graceful character in a dire situation. This is also the moment when the younger son begins to show his repentance, a virtue that helps him acknowledge his sinful human nature (what a lesson for us!) and pray for forgiveness.[41] In 15:17, Luke explains two important points that lead to the younger son's repentance and supplication for his father's forgiveness; first, the son knows his father's abundant generosity, as he says to himself, "How many of *my father's* hired hands have bread enough and to spare," and second, "food"—"I am dying of hunger!"—triggers his return to his father.[42]

Through this process of internal reflection, the younger son offers a precious moment of true prayer (15:18–19):

> [18]I will get up and go to *my father*, and I will say to him, "Father, I have sinned against heaven and before you; [19]I am no longer worthy to be called your son; treat me like one of your hired hands."

Only his deep and sincere love, his possession of virtues, and his spiritual experience allow the younger son to utter such a powerful and profound prayer. To get to this moment of grace, the younger son is at the level of genuine transformation that will reach its culmination in his father's actions of putting his arms around him and kissing him. The presence of the father-son relationship dominates the "prayer moment" vividly described in three progressive parts.

First, the younger son expresses his guilt: "*Father*, I have sinned against heaven and before you" (15:18c, 21b). The younger son vividly acknowledges his sinfulness against "heaven," a word that refers to God (see 15:7; 12:33; 6:23), and his own father. The evangelist stylistically illustrates the son's humble acceptance of his wrongdoing by connecting the relationship with God in the heavenly realm to his relationship with human beings in the earthly world.[43] That the Lukan Jesus does not specify the nature of the son's sin in his prayer of repentance is important, because he attempts to let us connect our own sinfulness with our Father God in an act of repentance. Second, the younger son accepts having damaged the father-son relationship: "*I* am no longer worthy to be called *your son*" (15:19a, 21c). With humility he shows his true repentance and recognizes that he has disrupted his relationship with his father. We recognize in the son's prayer his virtues and noble character—humility, repentance, prayerful attitude, and the recognition of sin and human nature. Third, the son's personal resolution illuminated in the statement "treat me like one of your hired hands" (15:19b) shows his disposition to accept punishment that may come together with his father's forgiveness.[44] He genuinely accepts the consequences of his sinful action.

Transformation and Happiness in Virtue

As the younger son meets and experiences firsthand his compassionate and loving father, Luke repeats verbatim the first two parts of the younger son's prayer in 15:18–19—"Father, I have sinned against heaven and before you; I am no longer worthy to be called your son." However, Luke omits the third part of the prayer, "treat me like one of your hired hands," because he wants to depict the father's unlimited forgiveness to evoke a sense of divine love and our emotional response. This is the climactic moment that we have been waiting for. The Lukan Jesus reveals to his audience God's true nature and humanity's need for God's forgiveness. We visualize a Father God who teaches us how to forgive, and whose forgiveness is graphically carried out in the following verses (15:22–24). Luke's rhetorical description highlights two important aspects of the son's return: (1) the younger son's powerful prayer initiated by his repentance, and (2) the father's forgiveness coming out of his great compassion, which makes possible the younger son's exaltation and experience of joy. In our journey to happiness, as we strive for salvation, we need to learn these two important lessons—how to pray and how to forgive.

In contrast to the younger son's transformation, the scenes with the elder son in conversation with the servants and the father (15:25–32) reveal the elder son's unvirtuous attitude and his vicious character toward both the younger son and the father. In his encounter with the servants (vv. 25–27), the elder son learns that his "brother has come" (v. 27); this knowledge—the younger son's return to his father, family, and community—brings to the surface the elder son's true identity. Luke's vivid description highlights nothing good about the elder brother; what we see is that the elder is full of hatred. Luke exposes the elder son's real feelings toward his brother and father in words and phrases such as being "angry," and his "refusal to go in." The son's imperative addressed to the father—"Listen!"—shows his disrespect for his father. His manner of viewing his work "as a slave"; his arrogant attitude, "I have never disobeyed your command"; his hidden resentment toward his father, "you have never given me..."; his lack of relationship with both his father and brother, "this son *of yours*"; his attempt to hurt his father intentionally, "who has devoured your property with prostitutes"; and his envious attitude toward his father's actions for his younger son, "you killed the fatted calf *for him*!" all reveal the elder son's lack of virtues and love.[45] Forbes explains it this way: "He [the elder son] sees himself as the model son, serving his father obediently," but he never understood "what a

The Power of Transformation

father-son relationship was also meant to be."[46] I would add: the elder son never understood what a brother-brother relationship was meant to be either.

Luke presents the vicious character of the elder son and puts "before the eyes" his vices and wickedness. Nothing, absolutely nothing, connects the elder son and his father (he never says "my father") or the elder son and the younger son (he never says "my brother"). Sadly, the elder son never sees himself in close relationship to either of them; he does not see himself as a son of *his father* (something that the younger son always does even in his humiliation). His unhappiness leads him to reject the celebration; for we who imagine the scene, unhappiness (vice) and celebration cannot be reconciled. In essence, the elder son rejects the virtue of joy, essential to the attainment of transformation. Both his stubbornness and selfishness impede any desire to attend the blissful celebration. His resentment and greed lead him to see himself not as a son but as a slave, alien to his father, brother, family, and community. Furthermore, the elder son shows no initiative, an important attitude in the process of transformation and a skill that the younger son possesses.

We may wonder, why did the elder son not *ask* his father to have a celebration with his friends? The elder son resentfully reproaches his father, saying, "Listen! For all these years I have been working like a slave for you, and I have never disobeyed your command; *yet you have never given me even a young goat so that I might celebrate with my friends*" (15:29). The elder son insults his father, not only by refusing to join the feast but also by addressing him without a title. In that cultural milieu, this insult is even worse than the one given by the younger son, because this is public.[47] We also learn at this point that the elder son has never learned how to pray truthfully and has not experienced genuine repentance; his arrogance and envy have never allowed him to ask for forgiveness. Unexpectedly, he lacks virtues and noble character. The elder son, despite having been with his father, never got to *know* his father, and never developed a relationship with him. Indeed, he treats his father as a stranger. Nor does he claim any relationship with the younger son; "this son *of yours*," he says (15:30).

The father listens to the sons and grants the younger son forgiveness. The father sees both brothers as his sons (15:27, 32), but he relates with the younger son, who also knows his father and sees himself as his father's son. Interestingly, even the servants see the elder son as the father's son (15:27), while he himself never does. The special relationship between the father and the younger son is represented by the virtues they both possess and practice. The father shows the virtues of compassion, mercy, love, care, forgiveness, hospitality, and joy; the younger son exhibits the virtues of repentance, humility, trust, courage, fellowship, acceptance, determination, love, and joy. Sadly, the elder son lacks all these virtues; instead, he possesses only vices, such as anger, disobedience, disrespect, stubbornness, greed, selfishness, and unhappiness. Forbes highlights the vice of jealousy in the elder brother, recalling the brothers in the Joseph story (Gen 37—50) and the thematic elements of famine and reconciliation in connection with the younger son.[48] Significantly, it is the father who offers the virtue of joy to both sons, but only the younger son welcomes his father's offer. Through and in the father's foregiveness, the younger son experiences transformation and thus experiences the virtue of joy expressed in the celebration, the music, the dance, the food, and the feasting with great rejoicing.

Luke's stylistic narrative with its *ekphrastic* techniques presents Jesus as a *eudaimonian* philosopher like the Greek thinkers.[49] Indeed, as we experience spiritual moments, we also embrace joy, a virtue akin to happiness and the middle path, leading us to the final goal of human life (salvation/heaven). We associate the virtue of joy with the experience of transformation, and we understand repentance, prayerfulness, and forgiveness as virtues important for attaining the heavenly realm, or in Luke's language, the kingdom of God.

The Parable of the Son's True Repentance and the Father's Forgiveness is about what the father *expects* from his children and how the father, younger son, and elder son *see* or understand relationships. The father sees the two sons as *his children*, and the younger son sees the father as *his father*; however, the elder son sees the father and younger son as *this father of yours* and *this son of yours*. Between the father and the younger son, we see an intimate relationship and an honest attitude toward each other (*my* son, *my* father). This sense of *belonging* captures our minds through the vivid words of the narrator, the younger son, and the father.

In this parable, Jesus teaches correct attitude and virtuous character toward God and our brothers and sisters. Luke exhorts us to identify ourselves with the younger son and to practice the virtues exemplified by him in the parable. It is not then about an appearance of "virtue" (as exposed in the elder son) but about failure (humiliation) and return (exaltation). The virtue of humility in this parable urges us to recognize that human beings are sinners, like the younger son. But thanks to that sinful condition, human beings need God so that they (1) can repent and ask forgiveness through prayer, and (2) come to know (knowledge) the virtue of humility and the tremendous love that God has for each of us. The next two parables will show us how to maintain a relationship with God, a good attitude, and a true character through prayer and forgiveness.

Luke 18:1–8: A Prayerful Attitude

The parable in Luke 18:1–8 appears only in Luke's Gospel and derives from his special "L" material.[50] It is located almost at the end of the Travel Narrative (9:51–19:27). Luke places two parables concerning *prayer* together (18:1–8 and 18:10–14). The second parable addresses a wide audience and focuses on those who trust in themselves for righteousness and despise others.[51] The first parable in Luke 18:1–8 is brilliantly placed immediately after Jesus's eschatological discourse in 17:22–37 and directed to his disciples, urging them not to "lose heart" (18:1) in light of the coming crisis.[52] Jesus states that the kingdom he proclaims is not yet the end-time, that there must be a period in which the disciples will "long to see one of the days of the Son of Man and will not see it" (17:22).

The Lukan Jesus sees the need to teach his disciples how to pray and exhorts them to "pray always" (18:1) by using an example of a widow in a short parable:

> ¹Then Jesus told them a parable about their need to pray always and not to lose heart. ²He said, "In a certain city there was a judge who neither feared God nor had respect for people. ³In that city there was a widow who kept coming to him and saying, 'Grant me justice against my opponent.' ⁴For a while he refused; but later he said to himself, 'Though I have no fear of God and no respect for anyone, ⁵yet because this widow keeps bothering me, I will grant her justice, so that she may not wear me out by continually coming.'" ⁶And the Lord said, "Listen to what the unjust judge says. ⁷And will not God grant justice to his chosen ones who cry to him day and night? Will he delay long in helping them? ⁸I tell you, he

will quickly grant justice to them. And yet, when the Son of Man comes, will he find faith on earth?"

The emphasis on persistent prayer is distinctive in this parable,[53] in which the Lukan Jesus tells his disciples to pray at all times and never give up (see 21:36).[54]

Through Luke's description, we visualize a judge, who does not act according to the prevailing codes of honor and shame.[55] Indeed, the story underscores that this judge eschews honor in regard to the divine (18:2) and the human (18:2, 4).[56] Luke depicts him as "ruthless by any human estimation"[57] when he writes, "[he] neither feared God nor had respect for people" (18:2). In his Jewish milieu, the judge is obligated to fear the Lord. This obligation applies to every Jew (Lev 19:14, 32; Deut 4:10; 6:13; 14:23; 17:13; 19:20).[58] In Judaism, fearing God and obeying the commandments are intrinsically connected (Deut 5:29; 8:6; 10:12; 13:4; 31:12), and by keeping the commandments one learns how to fear God (Deut 6:2; 17:19). Furthermore, the judge does not have "respect for people" (18:2; see also 18:4). For Luke's first-century audience, not having respect for anyone meant, as Hultgren asserts, that the judge had "outright contempt for those who came before him."[59] The ideal judge shows a righteous character (Sir 35:12–15), exhibits no partiality, listens to the one who is wronged, and does not ignore the "supplication of the fatherless, nor the widow when she pours out her story" (Sir 35:14, speaking of God as judge). In this parable, Luke presents us with an unrighteous judge.

Luke's rhetorical techniques help us to also visualize the widow, who comes before the judge to have her case settled against an adversary (18:3). We are able to see ourselves as the widow, who together with orphans and sojourners are considered the most vulnerable people in the first century CE. Within the honor-shame society, a widow is subject to oppression and delayed justice. Nonetheless, the woman "boldly faces the impervious judge, voicing her demands until she achieves justice on her own behalf. She marches into the arena of adjudication—clearly the domain of men by mores of her culture."[60] We are not told what the issue is between them; scholars argue that she may have had a lawsuit against one of the heirs of her husband's property, or perhaps she is being evicted from her home as widows sometimes were (cf. 20:47). We are told that the widow bravely seeks justice, not revenge; however, the judge has no sense of justice, nor does he abide by the commandments and exhortations to take up the widow's case (18:2–4a).[61]

According to Jewish law, Jews must take special care of widows (Deut 10:18; 14:29).[62] In Deuteronomy there is a clear command: "You shall not prevent the justice due the sojourner or the fatherless, or take a widow's grant in pledge" (Deut 24:17). There is also a curse: "Cursed be he who prevents the justice due to the sojourner, the fatherless, and the widow" (Deut 27:19). In the Jewish Scripture, doing justice for "widows" is a major theme. For example, in the prophetic books, justice for widows expresses covenantal loyalty (e.g., Mal 3:5; Isa 1:17, 23; 10:2; Jer 5:28 [LXX]; 7:6; 22:3; Ezek 22:7), and in the Writings, God comes to the aid of widows (LXX Ps 67:5; 145:9).[63]

In this parable, the judge responds only because of the widow's persistence; he helps the widow "only because he cannot take any more of her constant pleading and begging. He had simply had enough."[64] Luke vividly describes the judge's unpleasant feelings when he states, "This widow keeps bothering me" (18:5a), shouting, "Grant me justice against my opponent" (18:3).

The judge ultimately decides to "grant her justice," "so that she may *not wear me out* by continually coming" (18:5b). The Greek verb *hupōpiazō* (translated here as "wear out") is related to the noun *hupōpion*, which has the meanings of "part of the face under the eyes," generally "the face," "a blow in the face," and "a black eye."[65] The word also has a figurative sense, meaning "to slander," or "to besmirch on one's character."[66] The verb itself, however, means to strike someone on the face (under the eyes) in a way that would result in a "black eye" and disfigurement. Luke's dramatic description helps us to mentally observe the unexpected scene: the judge fears that the widow will literally strike him in the face. We can imagine ourselves as an enraged woman hitting the negligent judge over the head and literally "giving him a black eye" (18:5b).[67] Metaphorically, she not only will make him look bad in public but will also defame him for not responding to her continual pleas for vindication.[68] As a result of the widow's persistence, the unrighteous judge grants "her justice" (18:5). A good name for this short story is the Parable of a Widow's Perseverance and Justice.

How to Pray: Faith and Justice

In the Parable of the Son's True Repentance and the Father's Forgiveness, the younger son experiences repentance and joy because he

Transformation and Happiness in Virtue

knows *how to pray* (15:18-19, 21). In the Parable of a Widow's Perseverance and Justice, Jesus teaches a lesson about *how to pray*. Luke's rhetorical elements bring before our eyes Jesus's lesson about prayer. We know that to experience the younger son's virtues (15:20-24)—a prayerful attitude, repentance, humility, forgiveness, reconciliation, and joy—we must, as the Lukan Jesus declares, "pray always and not...lose heart" (18:1). In other words, to follow the widow's example in the Parable of a Widow's Perseverance and Justice (Luke 18:1-8), we must practice the virtues of perseverance, courage, faith, and justice. Luke uses the *enargetic* feature of repetition to vividly present the virtue of justice (18:5, 6 [its opposite, injustice], 7, 8), which is one of the cardinal virtues in Greek philosophical ethical systems. For the Lukan Jesus, too, justice is an important virtue that we must possess and practice.

Luke's dramatic representation of the judge's unrighteous/unjust character also emphasizes the centrality of the virtue of justice. His lack of fear of the Lord (18:2, 4) and his lack of respect for people (18:2, 4), which both are repeated, evoke a contrast between the virtue of justice and the vice of injustice. By calling the judge unjust (18:6), Luke intentionally heightens the contrast between virtue and vice so that the virtue of justice predominates in Jesus's lesson on how to pray. In the context of Aristotle's doctrine of the mean,[69] justice is not only identified as a "mean" virtue but is also linked with God; as the Lukan Jesus affirms, God "*grants justice* to his chosen ones who cry to him day and night" (18:7). At this point, we learn that perseverance in prayer brings justice, and that God is the author and source of justice. Luke follows the tradition of virtue ethics in Greek philosophies and again presents Jesus as a true philosopher who values the generic/cardinal virtue of justice. It is a mean virtue that will confidently lead us toward transformation and ultimately to God.

The evangelist is stylistic and concise in his narrative and highlights the widow's virtuous character; not only is she brave and courageous (18:5-6) but she also has faith, a spiritual virtue. Her determination to come continually (day and night) to the judge with the hope of receiving justice shows her virtues of perseverance, courage, and faith. Justice is another cardinal virtue in the Platonic and Stoic traditions, and a mean virtue in the Aristotelian tradition. Her strong character allows her to confront the judge (she is ready to punch him in the face and leave a black eye) and gives a dramatic picture of her womanhood, a great lesson for us today! Her empowerment is attributed to her virtues, especially that of faith and patience (cf. 18:7). Through the widow's behavior and noble character, the Lukan Jesus offers an unexpected model—a lowly yet courageous widow—to teach us how we must pray. Hence, in the Parable of a Widow's Perseverance and Justice (18:1–8), the Lukan Jesus presents two generic/mean virtues for learning how to pray: the virtue of faith, exemplified by the widow, and the virtue of justice, exemplified by God. Now we see the urgency to acquire and practice the virtue of faith and to avoid injustice, stubbornness, lack of fear of the Lord, and lack of respect. Unlike the judge, we see the need to possess justice, because this virtue will make us like God (18:7–8). These two virtues—faith and justice—relate to prayer. In Luke's notion of virtue ethics (if he might have had one), faith and justice are the two "headings" under which are listed the other virtues: perseverance, patience, courage, bravery, and trust. These virtues are highlighted to teach us how to pray properly and experience genuine joy, the virtue that is essential to acquire spiritual transformation, indispensable for salvation.

Matt 18:23–35: The Spiritual Benefits of Forgiveness

In the Matthean parable of 18:23–35, Jesus teaches about forgiveness.[70] This parable appears only in Matthew, the special material "M," and the evangelist places it at the close of 18:1–35, classified as one of the discourse sections (chapters 5—7, 10, 13, 24—25). As Hultgren notes, chapter 18 consists of teachings of Jesus concerning the relationship of his disciples to one another. Just before this parable, Peter asks Jesus how often he should forgive his brother or sister, and the Matthean Jesus replies that one should forgive "seventy-seven times" (18:22). As part of his response to Peter, the Matthean Jesus tells his disciples this parable:

Table 4.2. Matthew 18:23–35
Petition of Forgiveness: 23"For this reason the kingdom of heaven may be compared to a king who wished to settle accounts with his slaves. 24When he began the reckoning, one who owed him ten thousand talents was brought to him; 25and, as he could not pay, his lord ordered him to be sold, together with his wife and children and all his possessions, and payment to be made. 26So the slave fell on his knees before him, saying, 'Have patience with me, and I will pay you everything.' 27And out of pity for him, the lord of that slave released him and forgave him the debt.

Transformation and Happiness in Virtue

> *Refusal to Forgive*: ²⁸"But that same slave, as he went out, came upon one of his fellow slaves who owed him a hundred denarii; and seizing him by the throat, he said, 'Pay what you owe.' ²⁹Then his fellow slave fell down and pleaded with him, 'Have patience with me, and I will pay you.' ³⁰But he refused; then he went and threw him into prison until he would pay the debt. ³¹When his fellow slaves saw what had happened, they were greatly distressed, and they went and reported to their lord all that had taken place.
>
> *Expected Attitude*: ³²"Then his lord summoned him and said to him, 'You wicked slave! I forgave you all that debt because you pleaded with me. ³³Should you not have had mercy on your fellow slave, as I had mercy on you?' ³⁴And in anger his lord handed him over to be tortured until he would pay his entire debt.
>
> *Teaching Moment*: ³⁵So my heavenly Father will also do to every one of you, if you do not forgive your brother or sister from your heart."

R. T. France argues that this parable is about a king and his slaves to explain how the kingship of God operates (v. 23) and how God's full sovereignty is over those who belong to God's kingship.⁷¹ It speaks of the totally unmerited grace of God, which forgives God's people more than they could ever imagine.⁷² As seen above, I divide this Matthean parable into four parts: (1) the petition of forgiveness, that is, the king's dealing with his slave (18:23–27); (2) the refusal to forgive, which consists of the slave's dealing with his fellow slave (18:28–31); (3) the expected attitude, that is, the lord's dealing with his slave once more in response to what has happened (18:32–34); and (4) the teaching moment (18:35).⁷³

A Petition of Forgiveness (18:23–27)

The Matthean Jesus introduces his parable with a reference to "the kingdom of heaven" (18:23a). This is the last chance for his audience to hear a parable about the heavenly kingdom, and this time it is compared to a "king" (*basileus*) who is about to settle accounts with his slaves (18:23b).

Matthew uses vividness in his story to bring before the eyes of his audience Jesus's teaching about the virtue of forgiveness. Our imagination captures key scenes where a king grants his slave forgiveness, and in return the "lord" or "master" (*kyrios*) expects imitation, which the slave fails to do (18:29–31). The vividness of the scene showing the lord's unlimited forgiveness (18:23–27) is amplified by specific phrases, like "who owed him ten thousand talents" (18:24b), "the slave fell on his knees before him" (18:26a), and "Have patience with me, and I will pay you everything" (18:26b). In the dramatic scene of the slave's plea for forgiveness, we see as "real" a prayerful expression of true devotion. His "falling down on his knees before" his lord powerfully represents both his recognition of his lord's important position and his own humility in his petition for forgiveness.

The slave owes his lord "ten thousand talents," which is an astronomical figure in the first-century world. To be precise, the amount that the slave owes would be equivalent to nearly two hundred thousand years' wages for one individual, or a year's wages for two hundred thousand persons![74] Here, the evangelist uses hyperbole to increase our imagination of the king's unlimited forgiveness. The slave petitions the lord for an impossible forgiveness, humanly speaking, in an act of prayer and with humility; he knows that his debt is ridiculously high, but he still trusts that his prayerful request and humble posture (kneeling before the king) will help him to receive forgiveness. Indeed, "out of pity for him," as Matthew vividly describes, "the lord of that slave released him and forgave him the debt" (18:27). The Matthean Jesus uses the lord's virtuous attitude toward his slave to teach two great lessons to his audience: the virtues of compassion and patience, and how to forgive others (18:26-27). We wonder in awe that the lord forgives the slave the entire debt! However, Matthew's rhetorical device accentuates not the "amount" owed but the genuine, merciful disposition to forgive "from the heart" (18:35b). We come to the realization that this is exactly the attitude that the father had toward his younger son in the Parable of the Son's True Repentance and the Father's Forgiveness (Luke 15:11-32).

THE REFUSAL TO FORGIVE (18:28-31)

Stylistically, Matthew repeats the same words in the amplification employed in 18:23-27 when the slave's fellow slave, who owes him a hundred denarii, begs for forgiveness. Matthew writes, "Then his fellow slave *fell down* and pleaded with him, '*Have patience with me,* and I will pay you'" (18:26ab; 18:29). The evangelist employs the *enargetic* features of repetition (notice the repetition four times of the phrase "fellow slave" in vv. 28, 29, 31, and 33) and amplification once again (vv. 28-29) to reinforce the vividness of the scene. But he also increases the amplification device with the phrase "and *pleaded* with him" (v. 29a) to create a greater impact of the supplication and the meaning of forgiveness. By representing the dramatic gesture of the petition in vv. 28-29, Matthew strengthens the importance of praying and the way to forgive. The prayerful petition of the slave not only is identical to that of 18:26 but also expects the same virtues—compassion, patience, and forgiveness—from the slave who was previously forgiven by the lord.

Surprisingly, the forgiven slave harshly refuses to forgive his fellow slave (18:28–30)! Crossan argues that Matthew emphasizes the slave's lack of mercy and "his sheer stupidity in displaying his lack in such a way at such a time."[75] The evangelist amplifies the slave's negative response with dramatic behavior: "seizing him by the throat" (v. 28c), "Pay what you owe" (v. 28d), "But he refused" (v. 30a), and "he went and threw him into prison until he would pay the debt" (v. 30b).[76] At this point, the forgiven slave shows his true heart and identity; he "practiced" repentance before the lord and requested forgiveness for his own benefit, but now he fails to show the same virtue (forgiveness) toward his fellow slave. In other words, he does not imitate the lord's virtuous character. He receives forgiveness because the lord is infinitely compassionate and does not discriminate among people. The vividness employed creates images in our mind of the forgiven slave's negative attitude toward his fellow slave, his neighbor, who owes him less money than he owed to the lord.

The forgiven slave's vicious reaction toward his fellow slave, who is in a similar situation as he was, reveals that this slave has not learned to forgive. By being forgiven by his lord (God), he has been taught how to forgive. Indeed, Matthew's rhetoric is very explicit when the lord says to him, "*I forgave you*" (18:32b); this slave is supposed to do the same: practice the virtue of forgiveness toward others. The slave excels in virtues and prayer when it is for his own benefit (18:26–27), but he lacks them when he needs to practice them toward his neighbor (18:28–31). His supplication (prayer) before the lord shows his practice of the virtue of piety, but he lacks the virtue of justice toward other human beings who need help like him. In this parable, the Matthean Jesus strongly urges us to have both virtues, piety toward God and justice toward one's neighbors. We perceive that spiritual transformation requires the possession and practice of these two virtues; as Plato's Socrates claims, if one is just, he or she is also pious.[77]

The Expected Attitude (18:32–34)

The slave who was forgiven fails to follow, or imitate, his lord's example of forgiveness (18:32–34). When the other slaves "saw what had happened, they were greatly distressed," and consequently "reported to their lord all that had taken place" (18:31; cf. 17:23; 26:22). Matthew appeals to the presence of a crowd (other slaves) to enhance the believability of the slave's disapproved action. In response, the lord summons the slave to confront his vicious action (18:32a) and his lack of virtues toward his fellow slave. Matthew vividly presents the slave's vices in the phrases "You *wicked* slave!" (18:32b), "I forgave you all that debt because you pleaded with me" (18:32c), and "Should you not have had mercy on your fellow slave, as I had *mercy* on you?" (18:33). The lord demands imitation, but the slave's lack of virtues (e.g., mercy, forgiveness, compassion) does not allow him to be like his lord; thus, in anger his lord punishes his lack of virtues by handing him over "to be tortured until he would pay his entire debt" (18:34). The forgiven slave is expected to be virtuous and just and to extend his virtues of mercy, compassion, and forgiveness toward the slave who owed him a hundred denarii. He showed his piety before his lord in vv. 23–27 for his own benefit only, but that piety was not sufficient to go beyond his own needs, to move beyond his selfishness to unselfishness.

To highlight the role of the lord/king in the parable, Matthew uses the technique of repetition: "king" in v. 23 and "lord" in vv. 25, 27, 31, 32, and 34. This special rhetorical gloss in the narrative allows us to take "lord/king" as a metaphor for God. Therefore, the depiction of the lord's being "angry" in 18:34 is a rhetorical reflection of God's wrath in response to human vices or wicked actions that are against God's ethical commandments. The expression "God's wrath" in Jewish tradition refers to God's feelings against sin, a divine reaction to human provocation, not an arbitrary passion or animosity, for God is slow to anger. Furthermore, God dislikes wickedness, that is, the practice of vices, for God's nature is virtuous. In order to emphasize the practice of virtues and the avoidance of vices, Matthew sharply contrasts the rhetorical phrases "and in *anger*" (vice) in 18:34 with the "out of *pity*" (virtue) in 18:27.

THE TEACHING MOMENT (18:35)

The lord (God) expects imitation from his slave as God does from us, particularly toward our neighbors. In the Parable of the Son's True Repentance and the Father's Forgiveness (Luke 15:11–32), we understand that the elder son needs to learn and cultivate the virtue of forgiveness toward his younger brother; in this parable, the Matthean Jesus shows that the slave whom the lord forgave also needs to learn forgiveness, another central virtue to achieving transformation. This is clear in the parable's teaching lesson when Jesus asserts: "So my heavenly Father will also do to every one of you, if you do not *forgive* your brother or sister *from your heart*" (18:35). In this parable the Matthean Jesus shows that "piety" (*eusebeia*) and "justice" (*dikaiosunē*) must go hand in hand.

How to be like the father (God) and have the genuine capacity to forgive others is a necessary practice learned in the Parable of the Son's True Repentance and the Father's Forgiveness. As Carlston argues, Luke believes that the forgiveness of sins comes from God's gracious act (4:18; 24:47).[78] Looking at the rhetorical features that Matthew employs in 18:23–35, the way to transformation requires learning how to forgive in order to be like God. Thus, forgiveness stems from the practice of two generic/mean virtues: piety and justice, which are necessary to truly imitate God in our relationship with one another (justice) as well as in our relationship with God (piety). Under these two generic virtues are grouped the other virtues, primarily forgiveness, then patience, mercy, and compassion. Importantly, forgiveness must be from the heart. Their opposites, the vices, are treated as "wickedness" of the heart, a refusal to accept the generic virtues of piety and justice. The refusal to forgive means the rejection of compassion and mercy. Having this unvirtuous human character would hinder us from spiritual transformation. It is thus appropriate to call this Matthean story the Parable of Piety and Justice.

VIRTUE AND THE POWER OF TRANSFORMATION

The three parables in this chapter have served to move us toward the highest definition or concept of a virtue ethic found in the parables of Jesus. These parables in Luke and Matthew have revealed two essential factors necessary to be acquired through practice—prayer and forgiveness. In the Parable of the Son's True Repentance and the Father's Forgiveness (Luke 15:11–32), the Lukan Jesus speaks of the younger son's open attitude and his noble character. Throughout the scenes, his virtues, his initiative of repentance, and his strong determination—as represented in his virtue of prayerfulness—empowered him to ask forgiveness of his father and find a harmonious and virtuous balance between his experiences of humiliation and exaltation. We learn how to pray in the Parable of a Widow's Perseverance and Justice (Luke 18:1–8).

Through the widow's example of the virtues of perseverance, courage, faith, and justice, the Lukan Jesus teaches us how to pray properly. We learn how to forgive in the Parable of Piety and Justice (Matt 18:23–35), in which the Matthean Jesus gives us an example of the virtues of mercy, compassion, piety, and justice.

The rhetorical techniques of *ekphrasis* and *enargeia* allow us to freshly highlight in each of these parables the characters' personal attitudes and ethical characters as reflected in the practice of virtues and the avoidance of vices. Three central virtues have been presented: faith, piety, and justice. The virtue of piety is expressed in prayer and petition (toward the father/judge/lord) in all three parables. The virtues of faith and justice are shown in the widow's petition (for herself) to the judge, a metaphor for God, in the Parable of the Widow's Perseverance and Justice (Luke 18:1–8). As Herzog notes, Luke reads the judge as a "God figure" in order to argue "from the lesser to the greater: if the judge responds to the widow, how much more will God respond to the cries and petitions of the saints."[79] The virtues of piety and justice are expected in the forgiven slave toward his fellow slave in the Parable of Piety and Justice (Matt 18:23–35). These three generic/mean virtues must be practiced and possessed as we seek transformation.

The other virtues, which I call "particular virtues,"[80] highlighted in each parable, flow out from the three generic/mean virtues. As we have studied each parable, we have learned a list of excellent virtues and can now identify the main virtues (or headings), as we can see in the table of virtues in chapter 5. The structure of these virtues (both generic/mean and particulars) is very much like the Greek ethical systems of Plato, Aristotle, and the Stoics. Having identified the virtues, we now move into a different ethical dimension of how to live virtuously the teachings of Jesus's parables. We become a lover of virtue in imitation of God, who is Virtue and a Lover of Virtue.

As lovers of virtue, we find ourselves at the entrance of the heavenly realm and see the power of virtues for transformation. We experience an intimate relationship with the Father God, the Lover of Virtue, and we feel compelled to practice piety toward God and justice toward our brothers and sisters. This intimate relationship with the Father evolves around the virtue of piety and is strengthened by faithful and constant prayer (as seen in the widow). The development of the relationship with one another evolves around the virtue of justice and becomes intrinsically grounded in the human heart as we open our hearts to genuine forgiveness and compassion.

In the Parable of the Son's True Repentance and the Father's Forgiveness (Luke 15:11–32), the rhetorical techniques have helped us to distinguish the virtue above all the other virtues. This is joy, a virtue akin to happiness in the Greek ethical systems. Joy is the source, the perfect fountain from which both the generic virtues and the particular virtues bubble forth. Unlike the generic virtues, joy is *the* virtue that belongs in the heavenly realm, for God is the one who offers the virtue to humans, as the father offered joy to his two sons. In the genuine experience of the virtue of joy we can truly celebrate and rejoice because we have finally attained knowledge of God and how to be perfect as the Father is perfect. Spiritual transformation is experienced in virtue, in joy. Hence, it is in this heavenly/divine virtue that we shall attain salvation in heaven.

Conclusion

In this chapter we analyzed the rhetorical elements of three important parables: the Parable of the Son's True Repentance and the Father's Forgiveness (Luke 15:11–32), the Parable of a Widow's Perseverance and Justice (Luke 18:1–8), and the Parable of Piety and Justice (Matt 18:23–35). By digging into the stories, we have experienced the practice of virtues in close connection to each of the characters in the three parables. The vividness in the presentation of each parable has aimed at one goal: to bring before our eyes the centrality of *virtues* in Jesus's parables. As we have learned how to attain true happiness, we have also acknowledged that to be holy and achieve perfection we must become a virtue-loving soul.

Against the background of Greek virtue ethics, the parables of Jesus have brought virtue and its ethical fruits before our eyes and minds. In the Parable of the Son's True Repentance and the Father's Forgiveness, we appreciated the younger son's humble attitude to repent for his wrongdoing, his virtues of courage, humility, and initiative to return to his father. The younger son's awaited action to go back to his father and request forgiveness allowed him to accept his father's joy and celebrate a special moment of union with his father. We see in the father a God who listens, gives in abundance, and expects goodness. In the Parable of a Widow's Perseverance and Justice (Luke 18:1–8), we learned how we must pray with piety in order to receive justice. In the Parable of Piety and Justice (Matt 19:23–35), we learned how we must forgive others.

The key elements to attain spiritual transformation are the virtues of faith, genuine prayer, repentance, and forgiveness. In these qualities the generic/mean virtues surface—piety, justice, and the queen of virtues, joy. All human beings are invited to become virtue-loving souls so that human attitudes and relationships with God and neighbors will be perfected in virtues. The possession of the perfect and divine virtue of joy is a secure path to transformation and, ultimately, the final goal of human life, salvation. Joy leads us to salvation and heaven. In this way, joy is a virtue that truly belongs to the *heavenly realm*; it is this virtue that God possesses. So, when we say that God is a lover of virtue, it means that God is a lover of joy; and when we say God is virtue, it means God is joy!

5

CONCLUSION

At the beginning of this book, we were introduced to an understanding of the *heavenly realm*, or in the evangelists' words, the kingdom of God/heaven. With the heavenly realm, or intelligible world, as our starting point, we used the rhetorical techniques of *ekphrasis* and *enargeia* to help us interpret selected parables of Jesus to reveal the important virtues that would lead us to this realm. We began with the simple experience of knowing and understanding the parables, then looked at how their messages could be internalized. Then, we began to see how the parables called forth a deeper wrestling within the human heart. The true messages of the parables invited us into spiritual growth through the virtues. We learned that in order to pursue the goal of happiness, and thus salvation, we must become virtue-loving souls. We became familiar with the generic/mean virtues, a number of particular virtues, and the queen virtue, joy. We learned two important lessons: (1) that God is Virtue (Joy) and a lover of virtues, and (2) that the virtue-loving soul is called to a higher ethic rooted in joy, the generic virtues, and the particular virtues we see in the table below.

This book also ends in the heavenly world because *joy* is a virtue that belongs to heaven. God is *Virtue* and, according to Jesus, that virtue is *joy*. For the virtue-loving soul, Jesus's parables are a "bubbling fountain" of virtues offering us a higher ethical dimension that secures eternal salvation; that is, virtues prepare us for eternal life in heaven.[1] God is the source of virtues from whom the generic virtues flow—trust, joy, generosity, love of humanity, justice, prudence, faith, and piety. It is quite striking as well as significant to see joy as a generic virtue. You may ask, why? Because *God is Joy*, a virtue akin to happiness. God flows out to human beings to freely share God's divinity with us, a joyful sharing of God's great love. To have "part of" God through the virtue of joy is required to move up to the heavenly realm (heaven). This constant self-gift becomes a source of joy for all who strive for it. Thus, the virtue of joy possesses God and God's power; this divine virtue is God's grace in us. If we have joy, we have God in our hearts.

Table 5.1. Parables and Their Virtues		
Joy The Source or Queen Virtue (Heavenly Realm)		
Faith/Justice and Piety/Justice (Earthly Realm)		
Parables	Generic/Mean Virtues	Particular Virtues
The Trustful Man (Mark 4:26-29)	Trust	Simplicity, patience, confidence, faithfulness, endurance, faith, humility
The Silent Sower (Matt 13:31-32 // Mark 4:30-32 // Luke 13:18-19)	Trust	Simplicity, patience, confidence, reliance, faith, knowledge, understanding, resilience, availability
The Industrious Woman (Matt 13:33 // Luke 13:20-21)	Trust	Simplicity, confidence, industriousness, knowledge, understanding, service
Joy (Matt 25:14-30)	Joy Kingdom of God	Faithfulness, trust, responsibility, goodness, trustworthiness
The Generous Nobleman (Luke 19:11-27)	Generosity	Fidelity, trust, goodness, responsibility, efficiency, obedience, reliability, faithfulness
The Necessity to Love Humanity (Luke 16:19-31)	Love of Humanity	Mercy, compassion, kindness, generosity, justice, service, solidarity, goodness, humaneness, obedience, repentance, attentiveness
The Landowner's Choice of Generosity (Matt 20:1-16)	Love of Humanity Justice	Generosity, equity, reciprocity, compassion, goodness

Conclusion

The Prudent Manager (Luke 16:1-8)	Prudence or Practical Wisdom	Generosity, hospitality, wit, compassion, humaneness, love of humanity, kindness, magnanimity, forgiveness, joy, peace, benevolence, thankfulness, reciprocity, gratitude
The Son's True Repentance and the Father's Forgiveness (Luke 15:11-32)	Joy	Generosity, noble character, prayerfulness, compassion, mercy, fellowship, forgiveness, hospitality, love of humanity, courage, acceptance, understanding, repentance, acceptance, resilience
A Widow's Perseverance and Justice (Luke 18:1-8)	Justice Faith	Perseverance, courage, prayerfulness, bravery, trust, resilience
Piety and Justice (Matt 18:23-35)	Piety Justice	Forgiveness, mercy, compassion, trust, humility, patience

True joy or happiness has to do with an experience of transformation and holiness, a guarantee of salvation. Within the understanding of virtue in ancient Greek philosophical ethical systems, from the virtue of joy, the queen virtue, stems three important generic virtues—faith (*pistis*), piety (*eusebeia*), and justice (*dikaiosunē*). These three virtues are paramount on the way to transformation. In the parables we examined, the virtue of justice is paired with two virtues: faith and piety. Faith and piety are related to our duties toward God; the virtue of justice connects to our responsibilities toward human beings. Both faith/piety and justice complement one another as they bring together, or serve as a "link" between, the heavenly realm and the earthly realm. Only the queen virtue of joy belongs purely to the heavenly world; thus, it is a heavenly virtue and a virtue that God's nature possesses. Therefore, joy is the virtue that guides the virtue-loving soul on the spiritual journey through human struggles and experiences in the earthly realm to bring us finally to the heavenly realm. In this context, the parables that revealed the heavenly kingdom/realm in chapter 1 (the Parable of the Trustful Man, the Parable of the Silent Sower, and the Parable of the Industrious Woman) vividly map the notion of transformation;[2] so too

The Power of Transformation

do the parables discussed in chapter 4 (the Parable of the Son's True Repentance and the Father's Forgiveness, the Parable of a Widow's Perseverance and Justice, and the Parable of Piety and Justice). In other words, as the (mustard) seed transforms into a plant/tree and the leaven transforms the measures of flour, so joy and the other virtues transform us. In essence, salvation or eternal life is ultimately about experiencing joy, and the fulfillment of joy is in the God who loves us even with our brokenness and folly.

The rhetorical analysis of the parables of Jesus using the *ekphrastic* and *enargetic* techniques of the *progymnasmata* that our first-century evangelists knew and used allowed us to encounter the stories of Jesus in a new and higher dimension than through their traditional approaches. As Pheme Perkins claims, they help modern readers to respond virtuously to the stories on many levels with their minds and feelings.[3] The rhetorical techniques of *ekphrasis* and *enargeia* also challenged the traditional names and established themes of the parables. By accentuating the understanding of the virtues in the parables, we can truly appreciate Jesus's parables in their highest expressions. Furthermore, the rhetorical features highlighted in each of the parables can change the way we approach the stories of Jesus. These rhetorical techniques reveal Jesus's true message in these meaningful stories, a result that would not have been seen through a simple cognitive analysis. Obvious and superficial readings have been replaced by studies of human attitudes and responses, virtues, and dispositions, vividly presented in each of the characters and their behaviors. The eleven parables analyzed in this book offered not one but two responses to life: one in virtue and another in vice. Which one are *you* going to choose?

My hope is that through reading this book you have become familiar with ancient rhetorical-poetic techniques learned in the *progymnasmata* that the evangelists knew and used in the composition of their Gospels. I also hope that you will apply the same techniques when reading other parables of Jesus to enrich your theological and ethical understanding of the parables and their meanings. Use these parables that we analyzed in rhetorical fashion as examples for how to interpret the other parables of Jesus. Read Jesus's parables in a way that makes the acquisition of virtues and the avoidance of vices the central message. My aim is that you will remember that these rhetorical features of *ekphrasis* and *enargeia* are also found in the other parables. Study of them will reveal the same truth, other virtues, and creative new connections

Conclusion

between parables. I especially hope that the experience of "reading" and/or "seeing" mentally the parables of Jesus will be a genuine search for joy and bring a deeper feeling of happiness. Happiness is the virtue that encapsulates all the other virtues and, in its nature, holds the divine nature of God. This knowledge will make the virtue-loving soul aware that spiritual transformation has occurred and that the human mind has achieved holiness, and ultimately, eternal life.

NOTES

Introduction

1. Plato, *Min.* 88C; *Resp.* 465D, 613B; *Theaet.* 176A–177A.
2. Plato, *Leg.* 631C–D; 688A–B; 963A–965E.
3. Within the Christian tradition the word *cardinal* in Latin means "hinge." The four virtues are called "cardinal" (or "hinge") virtues because all other human virtues can be seen as subcategories of these foundational four, as we shall see below. See Edward Sri, *The Art of Living: The Cardinal Virtues and the Freedom to Love* (San Francisco: Ignatius Press, 2021), 21.
4. I have chosen eleven parables for this study for their individual function for the purpose of the methodology. The same rhetorical interpretation can be applied to the rest of the parables.
5. With the exception of a few, most scholars agree that the Gospel of John does not contain parables. See Ruben Zimmermann, *Puzzling the Parables of Jesus: Methods and Interpretation* (Minneapolis: Fortress, 2015); Barnabas Lindars, "Two Parables in John," *New Testament Studies* 16, no. 4 (1970): 318–29.
6. John R. Donahue, *The Gospel in Parable: Metaphor, Narrative and Theology in the Synoptic Gospels* (Philadelphia: Fortress 1988), 61–62, 123–25, 200, 205–6.
7. Gerhard Lohfink, *The Forty Parables of Jesus,* trans. Linda M. Maloney (Collegeville, MN: Liturgical Press Academic, 2021), xi.
8. Klyne R. Snodgrass, *Stories with Intent: A Comprehensive Guide to the Parables of Jesus* (Grand Rapids, MI: Eerdmans, 2008), 9.
9. The term *parabolē* became a rhetorical concept with Aristotle; his influence was decisive in the sphere of persuasion (*Rhet.* 2.20.1393b4–8). Cf. Bernard Brandon Scott, *Hear Then the Parable: A*

Commentary on the Parables of Jesus (Minneapolis: Fortress, 1989), 19–20.

10. Brad H. Young, *Jesus and His Jewish Parables: Rediscovering the Roots of Jesus' Teaching* (Mahwah, NJ: Paulist Press, 1989), 4–5; Herman Hendrickx, *The Parables of Jesus: Studies in the Synoptic Gospels* (San Francisco: Harper & Row, 1983), 1–2.

11. Zimmermann, *Puzzling the Parables of Jesus*, 89; also *Kompendium der Gleichnisse Jesu* (Gütersloh: Gütersloher Verlagshaus, 2007).

12. Snodgrass, *Stories with Intent*, 2.

13. Arland J. Hultgren, *The Parables of Jesus: A Commentary* (Grand Rapids, MI: Eerdmans, 2000), 3; Donahue, *The Gospel in Parable*, 5.

14. Rabbinic Judaism refers to the normative form of Judaism that developed after the fall of the Temple of Jerusalem (70 CE). Originating in the work of the Pharisaic rabbis, it was based on the legal and commentative literature in the Talmud, and it set up a mode of worship and a life discipline that have been practiced by Jews worldwide down to modern times. "Rabbinic Judaism," *Encyclopedia Britannica*, September 10, 2019, https://www.britannica.com/topic/Rabbinic-Judaism. For a good study on Jesus's parables in connection to rabbinic parables, see David B. Gowler, *What Are They Saying About the Parables?* (Mahwah, NJ: Paulist Press, 2000), 41–56; David Stern, "Jesus' Parables from the Perspective of Rabbinic Literature: The Example of the Wicked Husbandmen," in *Parable and Story in Judaism and Christianity*, ed. Clemens Thoma and Michael Wyschogrod, Studies in Judaism and Christianity (Mahwah, NJ: Paulist Press, 1989), 42–80.

15. Thoma and Wyschogrod, *Parable and Story in Judaism and Christianity*, 29–31; Young, *Jesus and His Jewish Parables*, 10.

16. For a good overview of scholarly positions, see Gowler, *What Are They Saying about the Parables?* 3–40.

17. Adolf Jülicher, *Die Gleichnisreden Jesu*, 2 vols. (Tübingen: J. C. B. Mohr [Paul Siebeck], 1899; repr. Darmstadt: Wissenschftliche Buchgesellschaft, 1963).

18. Hultgren, *The Parables of Jesus*, 13; Hendrickx, *The Parables of Jesus*, 13.

19. Snodgrass, *Stories with Intent*, 5.

20. A. T. Cadoux, *The Parables of Jesus: Their Art and Use* (New York: Macmillan, 1931).

Notes

21. C. H. Dodd, *The Parables of the Kingdom*, rev. ed. (New York: Charles Scribner's Sons, 1961); Zimmermann, *Puzzling the Parables of Jesus*, 24.

22. Warren Carter and John Paul Heil, *Matthew's Parables: Audience-Oriented Perspectives*, CBQMS 30 (Washington, DC: Catholic Biblical Association of America, 1998), 2–4.

23. Joachim Jeremias, *The Parables of Jesus*, 2nd. rev. ed. (Upper Saddle River, NJ: Prentice Hall, 1972).

24. Young, *Jesus and His Jewish Parables*, 33.

25. Jeremias, *The Parables of Jesus*, 112.

26. William R. Herzog II, *The Parables as Subversive Speech: Jesus as Pedagogue of the Oppressed* (Louisville, KY: Westminster John Knox, 1994); Luise Schottroff, *The Parables of Jesus*, trans. L. M. Maloney (Minneapolis: Augsburg Fortress, 2006), 29–37; Luise Schottroff, *Die Gleichnisse Jesu*, 2nd ed. (Gütersloh: Gütersloher verlagshaus, 2007).

27. Zimmermann, *Puzzling the Parables of Jesus*, 26.

28. Herzog, *The Parables as Subversive Speech*, 27–28; cf. Hultgren, *The Parables of Jesus*, 18.

29. See also Charles W. Hedrick, *Many Things in Parables: Jesus and His Modern Critics* (Louisville, KY: Westminster John Knox Press, 2004); Amy-Jill Levine, *Short Stories by Jesus: The Enigmatic Parables of a Controversial Rabbi* (New York: HarperOne, 2004). Their historical approaches, as Zimmermann notes (*Puzzling the Parables of Jesus*, 29), come back full circle to Jülicher and Jeremias.

30. Robert W. Funk, *Parables and Presence: Forms of the New Testament Tradition* (Philadelphia: Fortress, 1982); Dan Via, *The Parables: Their Literary and Existential Dimension* (Philadelphia: Fortress, 1967); John Dominic Crossan, "Aphorism in Discourse and Narrative," *Semeia* 43 (1988): 121–40.

31. Cf. Hendrickx, *The Parables of Jesus*, 14; Norman Perrin, *Jesus and the Language of the Kingdom: Symbol and Metaphor in New Testament Interpretation* (Philadelphia: Fortress, 1976). See also Paul Ricœur, *Die Lebendige Metapher: Mit einem Vorwort zur deutschen Ausgabe*, Übergänge 12, 3rd ed. (Munich: Fink, 2004).

32. Robert W. Funk, *Language, Hermeneutic, and Word of God: The Problem of Language in the New Testament and Contemporary Theology* (New York: Harper & Row, 1966), 155.

33. Carter and Heil, *Matthew's Parables*, 5.

34. Robert W. Funk, "The Parable as Metaphor," in *Language, Hermeneutic, and Word of God: The Problem of Language in the New Testament and Contemporary Theology* (New York: Harper & Row, 1966), 133–62.

35. Via, *Parables*, 26–69.

36. Jack D. Kingsbury, "The Parables of Jesus in Current Research," *Dialog* 11 (1972): 101–7; John Drury, *The Parables in the Gospels: History and Allegory* (New York: Crossroad, 1985).

37. See Hultgren, *The Parables of Jesus*, 16.

38. George A. Kennedy, *Classical Rhetoric: Its Christian and Secular Tradition from Ancient to Modern Times*, 2nd ed. (Chapel Hill: The University of North Carolina Press, 1999), 143; *Progymnasmata: Greek Textbooks of Prose and Rhetoric* (Leiden: Brill, 2003). Meghan Henning, *Educating Early Christians through the Rhetoric of Hell: "Weeping and Gnashing of Teeth" as* Paideaia *in Matthew and the Early Church*, WUNT 2, Reihe 382 (Tübingen: Mohr Siebeck, 2014), 43–82.

39. See Ruth Webb, "The *Progymnasmata* as Practice," in *Education in Greek and Roman Antiquity*, ed. Yun Lee Too (Leiden: Brill, 2001), 289–316; also, *Ekphrasis, Imagination and Persuasion in Ancient Rhetorical Theory and Practice* (Burlington, VT: Ashgate, 2009). Aelius Theon of Alexandria's *Progymnasmata* are the earliest compositional exercises in Greek and were written in the first century CE, the time period when the earliest books of the NT were written. *Ekphrasis* (descriptive speech) was one of the exercises practiced in *progymnasmata*. *Ekphrasis* appeared in all of the four major Greek rhetorical handbooks (Hermogenes, *Prog.* 10; Aphthonius, *Prog.* 12; Theon, *Prog.* 11; Nicolaus, *Prog.* 12). See Kennedy, *Classical Rhetoric*, 26–28.

40. Mikeal C. Parsons and Michael Wade Martin, *Ancient Rhetoric and the New Testament: The Influence of Elementary Greek Composition* (Waco, TX: Baylor University Press, 2018), 278–79.

41. Studies that focus on rhetorical criticism are: Sunny Kuan-Hui Wang, *Sense Perception and Testimony in the Gospel According to John*, WUNT 2, Reihe 435 (Tübingen: Mohr Siebeck, 2017); Gary S. Selby, *Not with Wisdom of Words: Nonrational Persuasion in the New Testament* (Grand Rapids, MI: Eerdmans, 2016); Robyn J. Whitaker, *Ekphrasis, Vision, and Persuasion in the Book of Revelation*, WUNT 2, Reihe 410 (Tübingen: Mohr Siebeck, 2015); Nils Neumann, *Hören und Sehen: Die Rhetorik der Anschaulichkeit in den Gottesthron-Szenen der Johannesoffenbarung* (Leipzig: Evangelische Verlagsanstalt, 2015).

Notes

42. Theon, *Prog.* 118.7; Quintilian, *Inst.* 8.3.64. Cf. Wang, *Sense Perception and Testimony in the Gospel According to John*, 91–92.

43. Claus Clüver, "Quotation, Enargeia, and the Functions of Ekphrasis," in *Pictures into Words,* ed. Valerie Robillard and Els Jongeneel (Amsterdam: VU University Press, 1998), 36–37.

44. Theon, *Prog.* 119.31–32; Hermogenes, *Prog.* 23; Nicolaus, *Prog.* 68.

45. Theon, *Prog.* 79.20.

46. Nicolaus, *Prog.* 70–71; Quintilian, *Inst.* 8.3.61.

47. Whitaker, *Ekphrasis, Vision, and Persuasion in the Book of Revelation*, 57.

48. Wang, *Sense Perception and Testimony in the Gospel According to John*, 97–101.

Chapter 1

1. For example, see Arland J. Hultgren, *The Parables of Jesus: A Commentary* (Grand Rapids, MI: Eerdmans, 2000), 7–8.

2. "Q" derives from the German word *Quelle,* and its English translation is "source." A good number of biblical scholars argue that there was a hypothetical written gospel in Greek to which both Matthew and Luke had access to write their gospels. Q scholars call this gospel, "the Q Sayings Gospel," written in at least three different stages, and they believe that there are about two hundred "sayings" uttered by Jesus, the wisdom Teacher. For an excellent study on the Q hypothesis, see John S. Kloppenborg Verbin, *Excavating Q: The History and Setting of the Sayings Gospel* (Edinburgh: T & T Clark, 2000); for the reconstruction of the Q document by the International Q Project (IQP), see James M. Robinson, Paul Hoffmann, and John S. Kloppenborg Verbin, eds., *The Critical Edition of Q: Synopsis Including the Gospel of Matthew and Luke, Mark, and Thomas with English, German, and French Translations of Q and Thomas* (Minneapolis: Fortress, 2000).

3. Cf. Mary Ann Getty-Sullivan, *Parables of the Kingdom: Jesus and the Use of Parables in the Synoptic Tradition* (Collegeville, MN: Liturgical Press, 2007), 35.

4. John R. Donahue and Daniel J. Harrington, *The Gospel of Mark,* ed. Daniel J. Harrington, Sacra Pagina 2 (Collegeville, MN: Liturgical Press, 2002), 154.

5. Herman Hendrickx, *The Parables of Jesus: Studies in the Synoptic Gospels* (San Francisco: Harper & Row, 1983), 17.

6. James L. Mays, ed., *Harper's Bible Commentary* (San Francisco: Harper & Row, 1988), 990.

7. For a good analysis on the kingdom language as power in Mark, see Kent Brower, "Mark 9:1: Seeing the Kingdom in Power," *Journal for the Study of the New Testament* 6 (1980): 17–41.

8. George A. Kennedy, *Classical Rhetoric: Its Christian and Secular Tradition from Ancient to Modern Times*, 2nd ed. (Chapel Hill: University of North Carolina Press, 1999), 27; see also Ruth Webb, "The *Progymnasmata* as Practice," in *Education in Greek and Roman Antiquity*, ed. Yun Lee Too (Leiden: Brill, 2001), 294.

9. For a discussion about the meaning of the kingdom of God, see Richard Lischer, *Reading the Parables*, Interpretation: Resources for the Use of Scripture in the Church (Louisville, KY: Westminster John Knox Press, 2014), 20–26.

10. For studies on Middle Platonism, see George Boys-Stones, *Platonist Philosophy 80 BC to AD 250: An Introduction and Collection of Sources in Tradition* (Cambridge: Cambridge University Press, 2018); John M. Dillon, *Middle Platonists: 80 B.C. to A.D. 220* (Ithaca, NY: Cornell University Press, 1996). For an excellent book that describes Philo's view on the heavenly world, see Thomas H. Tobin, *The Creation of Man: Philo and the History of Interpretation*, CBQMS 14; Washington, DC: Catholic Biblical Association, 1983), 119–34.

11. The word "kingdom" (*basileia*) appears twenty times in Mark: 1:15; 3:24 (twice); 4:11, 26, 30; 6:23; 9:1, 47; 10:14, 15, 23, 24, 25; 11:10; 12:34; 13:8, 8; 14:25; 15:43. Bruce M. Metzger, *Exhaustive Concordance: Complete and Unabridged* (Nashville: Thomas Nelson, 1991), 710.

12. See C. Clifton Black, "Mark as Historian of God's Kingdom," *Catholic Biblical Quarterly* 71 (2009): 64–83; Peter Spitaler, "Welcoming a Child as a Metaphor for Welcoming God's Kingdom: A Close Reading of Mark 10.13–16," *Journal for the Study of the New Testament* 31, no. 4 (2009): 423–46; Brower, "Mark 9:1: Seeing the Kingdom in Power"; Schuyler Brown, "'The Secret of the Kingdom of God' (Mark 4:11)," *Journal of Biblical Literature* 92 (1973): 60–74.

13. Mark Allan Powell, *Fortress Introduction to the Gospels* (Minneapolis: Fortress, 1998), 52.

14. See 9:47; 10:14, 23, 24; 12:34.

15. Kennedy, *Classical Rhetoric*, 147.

Notes

16. E.g., Demetrius, *Eloc.* 209.
17. Hultgren, *The Parables of Jesus*, 386.
18. See also Matt 18:14, 35; 20:16; Luke 12:21; 15:7, 10.
19. Hultgren, *The Parables of Jesus*, 386.
20. Max Zerwick and Mary Grosvenor, *A Grammatical Analysis of the Greek New Testament: Unabridged, Revised Edition in One Volume* (Rome: Biblical Institute Press, 1981), 113.
21. There are three other possible readings: "as a man whenever," "as if a man," and "just like a man." Hultgren, *The Parables of Jesus*, 385.
22. It is worth noting that Mark's Gospel was originally written to be performed. For a recent well-researched study, see Danila Oder, *The Two Gospels of Mark: Performance and Text* (Rozzano, Milan: Domus, 2019).
23. Donahue and Harrington, *The Gospel of Mark*, 150.
24. Quintilian, *Inst.* 4.2.123
25. Zerwick and Grosvenor, *A Grammatical Analysis of the Greek New Testament*, 113.
26. Gerhard Lohfink, *The Forty Parables of Jesus,* trans. Linda M. Maloney (Collegeville, MN: Liturgical Press Academic, 2021). Originally published as *Die vierzig Gleichnisse Jesu* (Freiburg im Breisgau: Verlag Herder GmbH, 2020), 63.
27. Cf. Kennedy, *Classical Rhetoric*, 91.
28. Cicero, *Part. or.* 6.2; *Verr.* 2.4.52; 3.18.47; 4.50.110; 4.29.67. See Sunny Kuan-Hui Wang, *Sense Perception and Testimony in the Gospel According to John*, WUNT 2, Series 435 (Tübingen: Mohr Siebeck, 2017), 99.
29. Cf. Donahue and Harrington, *The Gospel of Mark*, 15.
30. Hendrickx, *The Parables of Jesus*, 17.
31. Hultgren, *The Parables of Jesus*, 387.
32. Scholars have pointed out that 4:28 recalls 2:20 where "the good seed bears fruit." See Getty-Sullivan, *Parables of the Kingdom*, 36; Donahue and Harrington, *The Gospel of Mark*, 151.
33. The harvest language has overtones of eschatological urgency. It presents the image of a judge who comes to "harvest" the godless (Joel 3[4]:12–16), and both harvest and sickle are used to describe final judgment in Rev 14:14–20. See Hendrickx, *The Parables of Jesus*, 18–19; Klyne R. Snodgrass, *Stories with Intent: A Comprehensive Guide to the Parables of Jesus* (Grand Rapids, MI: Eerdmans, 2008), 186.
34. See also Rev 13:18–19.

35. Snodgrass, *Stories with Intent*, 186.

36. Some scholars have argued the authenticity of this verse for two main reasons: the first is the connection with Joel 3(4):13, and the second is the identification of the one who harvests with the man who does not do anything in v. 27. For a discussion on this topic, see Hendrickx, *The Parables of Jesus*, 18–19.

37. The word "immediately" appears forty-two times in Mark's Gospel.

38. Snodgrass, *Stories with Intent*, 216.

39. The translation is my own.

40. Hultgren, *The Parables of Jesus*, 399; Powell, *Fortress Introduction to the Gospels*, 62.

41. In Luke's Gospel, Jesus teaches on his way to Jerusalem, the city where his *exodus* will be fulfilled, that is, his passion, death, resurrection, and ascension.

42. Although this is an important topic in the literary study of this parable, it is beyond the scope of this book. For a good study on this topic, see David K. Bryan, "Transformation of the Mustard Seed and Leaven in the Gospel of Luke," *Novum Testamentum* 58 (2016): 115–34, especially 121–26.

43. Luke makes thirty-two references to the kingdom of God. See Metzger, *Exhaustive Concordance*, 710.

44. "Kingdom of heaven" is a Matthean expression and appears for the first time in 3:2. It "refers to the fullness of God's power and presence that will be acknowledged by all creation." Daniel J. Harrington, *The Gospel of Matthew*, Sacra Pagina 1 (Collegeville, MN: Liturgical Press, 2007), 51. However, there are five times when Matthew uses "kingdom of God" (6:33; 12:28; 19:24; 21:31, 43). For arguments concerning the parable's originality, see Hendrickx, *The Parables of Jesus*, 32–39.

45. Snodgrass, *Stories with Intent*, 223.

46. Hendrickx, *The Parables of Jesus*, 33.

47. Demetrius, *Eloc.* 211. Wang, *Sense Perception and Testimony in the Gospel According to John*, 97–98.

48. The same introduction is found in Matt 13:24, 33; 21:33.

49. Bible hub at https://biblehub.com/greek/3908.htm.

50. Ruben Zimmermann, *Puzzling the Parables of Jesus: Methods and Interpretation* (Minneapolis: Fortress, 2015), 247. He adds, "the parable in Mark 4:30–32 seems to limit itself to two aspects. One aspect is its size, as a sharp contrast is drawn between the very small seed and the

meter-tall plant. This is found in particular in the case of 'black mustard' (*brassica nigra*). On the other hand, the parable mentions the aspect of its fast growth and impressive form, which remind one of a tree based on the trunk and the branches."

51. See Hultgren, *The Parables of Jesus*, 395. Snodgrass, *Stories with Intent*, 220–21.

52. Snodgrass, *Stories with Intent*, 218.

53. Demetrius, *Eloc.* 217; Wang, *Sense Perception and Testimony in the Gospel According to John*, 98.

54. Cicero, *Part. or.* 6.20; *Verr.* 2.4.52; 2.3.18.47; 4.50.110; 4.29.67.

55. Usually, a mustard seed weighs 1 mg and has a diameter of 0.9 to 1.6 mm. See Gerhard Lohfink, *Las Cuarenta Parábolas de Jesús*, trans. Robert H. Bernet (Estella, Navarra: Verbo Divino, 2022), 72.

56. As Hultgren (*The Parables of Jesus*, 398) notes, the adjectives *mikroteron* (smaller) and *meizon* (greater) are comparatives, but they function as superlatives, "smallest" and "greatest," both here and elsewhere in the NT. Even when they are translated literally as comparatives, the superlative sense comes out by the double sense of the plural genitive "of all" (*pantōn*)—"smaller than all the seeds" and "greater than all the shrubs."

57. Within a context of persecution, Getty-Sullivan (*Parables of the Kingdom*, 36) argues that Jesus appeals to his audience's imagination and uses the superlative "smallest" as a symbol of faith (cf. Matt 17:20; Dan 4:19–21; Ezek 17:22–23). For the evangelist, Jesus teaches that God's kingdom extends hope to all those suffering from discouragement at the apparent insignificance of faith in the face of great opposition. For a discussion of this parable in light of Ezekiel 17:22–23, see Robert W. Funk, "The Looking-Glass Tree Is for the Birds: Ezekiel 17:22–24; Mark 4:30–32," *Interpretation* 27, no. 1 (1973): 3–9.

58. Snodgrass, *Stories with Intent*, 220.

59. John R. Donahue, *The Gospel in Parable: Metaphor, Narrative and Theology in the Synoptic Gospels* (Philadelphia: Fortress 1988), 13–15, 17.

60. Snodgrass, *Stories with Intent*, 219.

61. E.g., Prov 11:30; Ps 104:12; Dan 4:10–12.

62. Hendrickx, *The Parables of Jesus*, 41.

63. Hendrickx (*The Parables of Jesus*, 35) points out that the shrubs in which the birds take shelter represent a classical image often used in the Bible to symbolize the protection by a powerful king to his subjects

(e.g., Lam 4:20; Baruch 1:12; Ps 104[103]:12; Ezek 17:22–23; Dan 4:12, 17, 21).

64. See also Ezek 31:6; Dan 4:12, 21; cf. Ps 104:12, 16–17; Matt 17:20; Luke 17:6.

65. Cf. Snodgrass, *Stories with Intent*, 223.

66. As Hendrickx (*The Parables of Jesus*, 47) notes, it can be discovered that the smallness of the amount of leaven needed to leaven a great quantity of dough was also proverbial (e.g., Gal 5:9; 1 Cor 5:6).

67. The phrase "twin parables" was already designated by Hultgren, *The Parables of Jesus*, 405.

68. Snodgrass, *Stories with Intent*, 231. Elsewhere in the NT, leaven is a negative symbol (e.g., Matt 1:6 // Mark 8:15 // Luke 12:1; Gal 5:9; 1 Cor 5:6–8).

69. According to Hultgren (*The Parables of Jesus*, 406), it is customary to translate the Greek *zumē* as "yeast" in modern translations (e.g., NEB, NIV, NRSV) in place of the older translation "leaven." In this book the latter is used.

70. In Jer 7:18 baking bread is viewed as a family task. See Snodgrass, *Stories with Intent*, 231; see also *m. Ketubot* 5.5., in Shaye J. D. Cohen, Robert Goldenberg, and Hayim Lapin, eds., *The Oxford Annotated Mishnah*, 3 vols. (Oxford: Oxford University Press, 2022).

71. Hultgren, *The Parables of Jesus*, 406–7.

72. Snodgrass, *Stories with Intent*, 231.

73. Quintilian, *Inst.* 6.3.62; 8.3.67–68.

Chapter 2

1. For a current study on these parables, see Gertrud Tönsing, "Scolding the 'Wicked, Lazy' Servant; Is the Master God? A Redaction-Critical Study of Matthew 25:14–30 and Luke 19:11–27," *Neotestamentica* 53, no. 1 (2019): 123–47.

2. See, for example, Plato, *Prot.* 329C–330A; Aristotle, *Eth. nic.* 7.2.1146a7–8; Plutarch, *Virt. mor.* 441A–B; *Fort.* 97E. For a discussion on this topic, see Nélida Naveros Córdova, *Philo of Alexandria's Ethical Discourse: Living in the Power of Piety* (Lanham, MD: Lexington Books/Fortress Academic, 2018), 85–89.

3. In the Platonic catalog of virtues, prudence or practical wisdom (*phronēsis*) is labeled as "the leader of the entire of virtue" (*Leg.*

688B), "the greatest wisdom" (*Leg.* 689D), "the leader of all the virtues" (*Leg.* 688B), and "the first and chiefest wisdom" (*Leg.* 631C), and temperance (*sōphrosunē*) "the virtue following wisdom" (*Leg.* 631C).

4. Plato, *Prot.* 356D–357B. For a good discussion on the Socratic unity of virtues, see Howard J. Curzer, *Aristotle and the Virtues* (Oxford: Oxford University Press, 2012); Raymond J. Devettere, *Introduction to Virtue Ethics: Insights of the Ancient Greeks* (Washington, DC: Georgetown University Press, 2002).

5. Cf. *Decal.* 52.

6. For studies on the role of the Spirit in Paul's ethical teaching, see Nélida Naveros Córdova, *Living in the Spirit: Paul and the Spirit of God* (Lanham, MD: Lexington Books/Fortress Academic, 2018); Volker Rabens, *The Holy Spirit and Ethics in Paul: Transformation and Empowering for Religious-Ethical Life,* 2nd ed., WUNT 2, Reihe 283 (Tübingen: Mohr Siebeck, 2013 [2010]).

7. John R. Donahue, *The Gospel in Parable: Metaphor, Narrative and Theology in the Synoptic Gospels* (Philadelphia: Fortress, 1988), 105. Donahue notes that this is the longest and most difficult of Matthew's parables. It apparently caused problems in the tradition prior to Matthew. The historian Eusebius gives another account of the parable, which is found in the (now) lost Gospel of the Nazorean (Eusebius, *Theophania* on Matt 25:14f., cited from Wilhelm Schneemelcher, *New Testament Apocrypha*, vol. 1: *Gospels and Related Writings*, rev. ed., trans. R. McL. Wilson [Louisville, KY: Westminster John Knox, 1990], 149). This version is unambiguously written from the Mediterranean peasant point of view. See Bruce J. Malina and Richard L. Rohrbaugh, *Social-Science Commentary on the Synoptic Gospels* (Minneapolis: Fortress Press, 2003), 385–86.

8. Klyne R. Snodgrass, *Stories with Intent: A Comprehensive Guide to the Parables of Jesus* (Grand Rapids, MI: Eerdmans, 2008), 519. The *nimshal* here is unnecessary because the story and the context make the lesson clear.

9. Cf. James Gavigan and Brian McCarthy, *The Navarre Bible: Saint Matthew's Gospel* (Dublin: Four Courts Press, 1993), 211.

10. Daniel J. Harrington, *The Gospel of Matthew*, Sacra Pagina 1 (Collegeville, MN: Liturgical Press, 2007), 353.

11. Some scholars divide the parable into three sections: the distribution of money (25:14–15), the action of the servants (25:16–18), and the reckoning (25:19–30). See Snodgrass, *Stories with Intent*, 523.

12. See Snodgrass, *Stories with Intent*, 527.

13. In the rabbinic material, considerable effort was made to distinguish interest from legitimate increase. See Snodgrass, *Stories with Intent*, 528.

14. Malina and Rohrbaugh, *Social-Science Commentary on the Synoptic Gospels*, 385.

15. Jonathan L. Reed, *Archaeology and the Galilean Jesus: A Re-examination of the Evidence* (Harrisburg, PA: Trinity Press International, 2000), 66.

16. Snodgrass, *Stories with Intent*, 527.

17. For a description of population numbers and building projects in Galilee, see Reed, *Archaeology and the Galilean Jesus*, 69–82.

18. Cf. Reed, *Archaeology and the Galilean Jesus*, 89–93.

19. Reed, *Archaeology and the Galilean Jesus*, 86.

20. See Peter Garnsey, *Famine and Food Supply in the Graeco-Roman World* (Cambridge: Cambridge University Press, 1988), 56–63; Reed, *Archaeology and the Galilean Jesus*, 88.

21. *Inst.* 8.3.61–62. Bernhard F. Scholz, "'Sub Oculos Subiectio': Quintilian on *Ekphrasis* and *Enargeia*," in *Pictures into Words*, ed. Valerie Robillard and Els Jongeneel (Amsterdam: VU University Press, 1998), 78.

22. E.g., Quintilian, *Inst.* 8.3.67–68; 6.2.32; Longinus, *Subl.* 15.2.

23. Cf. Malina and Rohrbaugh, *Social-Science Commentary on the Synoptic Gospels*, 124. Tönsing ("Scolding the 'Wicked, Lazy' Servant," 130) notes that these servants were probably slaves who were expected to do the master's bidding or face the consequences. They did all financial transactions in his name, and the profit belonged to him.

24. Hermogenes, *Prog.* 22. Cf. Aphthonius, *Prog.* 46; Nicolaus, *Prog.* 68.

25. Cicero, *Verr.* 2. 1.19.50–51.

26. It is difficult to be precise about the amount constituted by a talent or its modern equivalent. It can be described as "the wage of an ordinary worker for fifteen years." The point is not the precise amount but that it was a large sum. See Harrington, *The Gospel of Matthew*, 352.

27. Snodgrass, *Stories with Intent*, 528; Arland J. Hultgren, *The Parables of Jesus: A Commentary* (Grand Rapids, MI: Eerdmans, 2000), 274–75.

28. Mary Ann Getty-Sullivan, *Parables of the Kingdom: Jesus and the Use of Parables in the Synoptic Tradition* (Collegeville, MN: Liturgi-

cal Press, 2007), 2, rightly argues that in Jesus's parables there is often an element of surprise, a hook, designed to present something new and different to his audience.

29. Bible Hub, https://biblehub.com/text/matthew/25-16.htm.

30. The first servant "immediately" (*eutheōs*) gets to work with the talent (25:16).

31. See, for example, Prov 31:18; Rev 18:17.

32. See Snodgrass, *Stories with Intent*, 528.

33. Hultgren, *The Parables of Jesus*, 275. When the Romans conquered Jerusalem in 70 CE, they discovered hoards of gold, silver, and other treasures hidden underground (Josephus, *A. J.* 7.115).

34. Pliny, *Natural History*, 36.4.20.

35. Longinus, *Subl.* 15.2; Robyn J. Whitaker, *Ekphrasis, Vision, and Persuasion in the Book of Revelation*, WUNT 2, Reihe 410 (Tübingen: Mohr Siebeck, 2015), 47–48.

36. Tönsing, "Scolding the 'Wicked, Lazy' Servant," 131.

37. Cf. Quintilian, *Inst.* 8.3.61.

38. Malina and Rohrbaugh, *Social-Science Commentary on the Synoptic Gospels*, 385.

39. Cicero, *Verr.* 2. 4.50.110. On the sense of sight in classical rhetoric, see Nils Neumann, *Hören und Sehen: Die Rhetorik der Anschaulichkeit in den Gottesthron-Szenen der Johannesoffenbarung* (Leipzig: Evangelische Verlagsanstalt, 2015), 74–173.

40. Sunny Kuan-Hui Wang, *Sense Perception and Testimony in the Gospel According to John*, WUNT 2, Reihe 435 (Tübingen: Mohr Siebeck, 2017), 93.

41. Theon, *Prog.* 71.

42. Malina and Rohrbaugh, *Social-Science Commentary on the Synoptic Gospel*, 124.

43. On the third servant's response, see Rich Carter, "Buried under Excellent Soil: Matthew 25:14–30," *Lutheran Mission Matters* 27, no. 1 (2019): 147–55.

44. For a recent literary analysis of this parable, see Phillip Porter, "The Parable of the Talents (Matt 25:14–30): Preparing Jesus' Disciples to Lead the Worldwide Expansion of the Mission of Jesus," *Novum Testamentum* 63, no. 3 (2021): 159–76.

45. Malina and Rohrbaugh, *Social-Science Commentary on the Synoptic Gospels*, 124.

46. Snodgrass, *Stories with Intent*, 528.

47. The other three Stoic passions are "grief" (*lupē*), "pleasure" (*edonē*), and "desire" (*epithumia*). This last is the deadliest passion, and according to the Stoics, it must be eliminated.

48. Cf. Hultgren, *The Parables of Jesus*, 176.

49. Malina and Rohrbaugh, *Social-Science Commentary on the Synoptic Gospels*, 385. The law of charging interest was often broken (cf. Ps 15:5; Jer 15:10; Ezek 18:8, 13, 17; 22:12); however, interest could be charged to non-Israelites (Deut 23:20). This notion is supported by rabbinic law, which stated that burying a pledge or deposit was the safest way to care for someone else's money.

50. This passage is similar to its parallel at Matt 13:12; Luke 19:26; 8:18; Mark 4:25; and the Gospel of Thomas, Logion 41, which reads, "Jesus said, 'Those who have something in hand will be given more, and those who have nothing will be deprived of even the little they have.'" Translation is from Robert J. Miller, ed., *The Complete Gospels: Annotated Scholars Version* (Santa Rosa, CA: Polebridge Press, 1994), 312.

51. Hultgren, *The Parables of Jesus*, 277.

52. Concerning the kingdom of God or heavenly realm, see discussion in chapter 1.

53. The "weeping and gnashing of teeth" is Matthean; he uses the same expression in Matt 8:12; 13:42, 50; 22:13; 24:51 within the context of the last judgment. Harrington, *The Gospel of Matthew*, 353.

54. See Donahue, *The Gospel in Parable*, 105.

55. See Hultgren, *The Parables of Jesus*, 273.

56. Joseph A. Fitzmyer, *The Gospel According to Luke X—XXIV: A New Translation with Introduction and Commentary*, Anchor Bible 28A (New York: Doubleday, 1983), 1228.

57. For a comparison between the parables in Matthew and Luke, see Adam F. Braun, "Reframing the Parable of the Pounds in Lukan Narrative and Economic Context: Luke 19:11–28," *Currents in Theology and Mission* 39, no. 6 (2012): 442–48; Holger Szesnat, "Bible Study on Economic Justice: Luke 19:11–28," *The Pacific Journal of Theology* 56 (2016): 19–29; Robert Doran, "The Parable of the Talents/Pounds: Apocalyptic Warning or Economic Critique?" *Biblica* 100, no. 4 (2019): 527–42.

58. Luke Timothy Johnson, *The Gospel of Luke*, ed. Daniel J. Harrington, Sacra Pagina 3 (Collegeville, MN: Liturgical Press, 1991), 292. Similarly, Henry Clarence Thiessen in "The Parable of the Nobleman and the Earthly Kingdom," *Bibliotheca Sacra* 91 (1934): 180–90, argues

that this parable shows Jesus's return to the earthly world to set up his kingdom in which his servants will reign with him.

59. For an interpretation of this parable in light of current social justice issues, see Elizabeth Dowling, "Hearing the Voice of Earth in the Lukan Parable of the Pounds," *Colloquium* 48, no. 1 (2016): 35–46.

60. Cf. Snodgrass, *Stories with Intent*, 527.

61. Tönsing, "Scolding the 'Wicked, Lazy' Servant," 131.

62. Snodgrass, *Stories with Intent*, 528.

63. Johnson, *The Gospel of Luke*, 289.

64. Some commentators have observed that the parable in Luke reflects actual historical events at the time of the death of Herod the Great when his son Archelaus went to Rome to try to obtain the title "king," but was opposed by a delegation of Judeans and Samaritans, who succeeded in preventing it. Malina and Rohrbaugh, *Social-Science Commentary on the Synoptic Gospels*, 305; Snodgrass, *Stories with Intent*, 535.

65. Plutarch, *Mor.* 536e–538e; Johnson, *The Gospel of Luke*, 290.

66. See Philo, *Embassy to Gaius*, and Josephus, *A. J.* 17:299–314.

67. Johnson, *The Gospel of Luke*, 290.

68. At the beginning of his Gospel (1:1–4), Luke states that after he has investigated everything carefully from the very beginning, he has written an *orderly account* of the events pertaining to Jesus.

69. Cf. Acts 19:12; John 11:44; 20:7; Johnson, *The Gospel of Luke*, 290.

70. Malina and Rohrbaugh, *Social-Science Commentary on the Synoptic Gospels*, 385.

71. For an analysis on the cultural setting of peasants, artisans, slaves, and hangers-on, see Richard Q. Ford, *The Parables of Jesus: Recovering the Art of Listening* (Minneapolis: Fortress, 1997), 37–46.

72. Luke's image of banking in 19:23 may be proverbial (cf. Plato, *Laws* 913C; Josephus, *Against Apion* 2.216).

73. Johnson, *The Gospel of Luke*, 291. Taking interest on loans (usury) is forbidden by Exod 22:25; Lev 25:36–37; Deut 23:19. The Mishnah distinguishes usury and increase with more liberal regulations governing relations with Gentiles (e.g., m. Bat. M. 5:1–6).

74. The same pronouncement is also found in Matt 13:12; Mark 4:25; Luke 8:18.

75. According to Doran ("The Parable of the Talents/Pounds," 542), Jesus's intended teaching within the eschatological context is meant to offer a criticism of the developing exploitative economy in

Galilee, particularly as a response to the abusive rule of Herod Antipas. On this topic, see M. H. Jensen, *Herod Antipas in Galilee*, WUNT 2, Reihe 215 (Tübingen: Mohr Siebeck, 2006), 256–57.

76. Plutarch, *Art.* 8.1.

Chapter 3

1. A major theme in the Gospel of Luke is that of social justice, and one way that the evangelist shows that is by presenting Jesus as an example of poverty starting from his humble origins until the end of his life.

2. For the parable's theological interpretation and application, see Gerhard Lohfink, *The Forty Parables of Jesus*, trans. Linda M. Maloney (Collegeville, MN: Liturgical Press Academic, 2021), 126–31; Karen M. Hatcher, "In Gold We Trust: The Parable of the Rich Man and Lazarus (Luke 16:19–31)," *Review & Expositor* 109, no. 2 (2012): 277–83; David B. Gowler, "'At His Gate Lay a Poor Man': A Dialogic Reading of Luke 16:19–31," *Perspectives in Religious Studies* 32 (2005): 260–62.

3. Luke Timothy Johnson, *The Gospel of Luke*, ed. Daniel J. Harrington, Sacra Pagina 3 (Collegeville, MN: Liturgical Press, 1991), 254; Joseph A. Fitzmyer, *The Gospel According to Luke X—XXIV: A New Translation with Introduction and Commentary*, Anchor Bible 28A (New York: Doubleday, 1983), 1125.

4. Fitzmyer, *The Gospel According to Luke X—XXIV*, 1128. In her study on early Christian education in rhetoric, Meghan Henning, *Educating Early Christians through the Rhetoric of Hell: "Weeping and Gnashing of Teeth" as* Paideaia *in Matthew and the Early Church*, WUNT 2, Reihe 382 (Tübingen: Mohr Siebeck, 2014), 124–25, argues that in this parable Luke uses *enargeia* three times: first, when Luke describes Lazarus's earthly suffering; second, when the evangelist depicts the suffering that the rich man undergoes after death; and third, when he describes the rich man's request.

5. Quintilian, *Inst.* 8.2; 8.3.61–71.

6. Cf. Sir 40:4; 1 Macc 8:4; 10:20, 62, 64; 11:58; 14:43–44; 2 Macc 4:38; 1 Esdr 3:6; Mark 15:17, 20; John 19:2.

7. Gerard Lohfink, *Las Cuarenta Parábolas de Jesús*, trans. Robert H. Bernet (Estella, Navarra: Verbo Divino, 2022), 143; Klyne R.

Notes

Snodgrass, *Stories with Intent: A Comprehensive Guide to the Parables of Jesus* (Grand Rapids, MI: Eerdmans, 2008), 425.

8. Bruce J. Malina and Richard L. Rohrbaugh, *Social-Science Commentary on the Synoptic Gospels* (Minneapolis: Fortress, 2003), 295.

9. Johnson, *The Gospel of Luke*, 252. See also "The Dinner at Trimalchio's" in Petronius's *Satyricon*; Juvenal, *Satires* 11:120–60 and Lucian of Samosata, *The Dream*, 7–15.

10. Johnson, *The Gospel of Luke*, 252; Snodgrass, *Stories with Intent*, 425.

11. Malina and Rohrbaugh, *Social-Science Commentary on the Synoptic Gospels*, 295.

12. Cf. Greg W. Forbes, *The God of Old: The Role of the Lukan Parables in the Purpose of Luke's Gospel* (Sheffield: Sheffield Academic Press, 2000), 187.

13. Snodgrass, *Stories with Intent*, 425.

14. Johnson, *The Gospel of Luke*, 252. Human dignity is covered with sores and hunger; in this sense, the rich man is unable to see him as a human person.

15. Johnson, *The Gospel of Luke*, 252.

16. Snodgrass, *Stories with Intent*, 425. Mary Ann Getty-Sullivan, in *Parables of the Kingdom: Jesus and the Use of Parables in the Synoptic Tradition* (Collegeville, MN: Liturgical Press, 2007), 166, notes that dogs could be allowed to feed on the scraps that fall from the table, as the story of the Syrophoenician woman insinuates in Mark 7:24–30 and Matt 15:21–28.

17. E.g., 1 Kgs 14:11; 16:4; 21:24; Ps 16:2; Jer 5:3.

18. Arland J. Hultgren, *The Parables of Jesus: A Commentary* (Grand Rapids, MI: Eerdmans, 2000), 112.

19. Cf. Gen 5:24; 2 Kgs 2:11. The expression "bosom of Abraham" is found only in Luke's Gospel and may derive from the ancient biblical idea of "being gathered to one's people" at death (Gen 49:33; Num 27:13; Deut 32:50; Judg 2:10). Johnson, *The Gospel of Luke*, 252.

20. Hades is the Greek place of the dead, the netherworld of shades, equivalent to the Hebrew *sheol* (LXX Gen 37:35; Ps 6:5; 16:10; Acts 2:27). Johnson, *The Gospel of Luke*, 168.

21. The Greek term *hades* appears ten times in the NT: Matt 11:23; 16:18; Luke 10:15; 16:23; Acts 2:27, 31; Rev 1:18; 6:8; 20:13, 14. It generally refers to a place where the dead remain for only a short time (Acts

The Power of Transformation

2:27; Rev 20:13–14) prior to the final judgment (Rev 20:13). See Hultgren, *The Parables of Jesus*, 113.

22. For a good study on the image of Father Abraham, see Martin O'Kane, "'The Bosom of Abraham' (Luke 16:22): Father Abraham in the Visual Imagination," *Biblical Interpretation* 15 (2007): 485–518.

23. Snodgrass, *Stories with Intent*, 425.

24. Cf. Aristotle, *Poet.* 6.1450a16–17.

25. The other two patriarchs are Isaac and Jacob, who becomes Israel in Gen 32:28.

26. That the wicked suffer thirst in the realm of the dead is traditional; indeed, it is one of their punishments (e.g., Esdr 8:59; 15:58); Hultgren, *The Parables of Jesus*, 114.

27. These virtues are often related to social justice themes and the seven Catholic Social Principles. On these important topics, see Marcus Mescher, *The Ethics of Encounter: Christian Neighbor Love as a Practice of Solidarity* (Maryknoll, NY: Orbis, 2020).

28. For an outspoken depiction of the contrast between the very wealthy and the destitute in the Roman Empire, see Juvenal, *Satires* 1:130–44. Johnson, *The Gospel of Luke*, 252.

29. Along this line, Jocelyn McWhirter, in "Between Text and Sermon: Luke 16:19–31," *Interpretation: A Journal of Bible and Theology* 69, no. 4 (2015): 464, notes that Lazarus was not particularly righteous. The rich man suffers because he was rich; in contrast, Lazarus receives comfort because he was poor (Luke 16:25). The Lukan Jesus has preached this message in the Beatitudes: 6:20–21, 24–25.

30. Malina and Rohrbaugh, *Social-Science Commentary on the Synoptic Gospels*, 295.

31. See also Deut 10:17–19; 14:28–29; 15:1–11; 16:9–15; 24:17–18; 26:12–15; Amos 2:6–8; Hos 12:7–9.

32. Johnson, *The Gospel of Luke*, 253.

33. Hultgren, *The Parables of Jesus*, 114.

34. Johnson, *The Gospel of Luke*, 253.

35. McWhirter ("Between Text and Sermon," 465) argues that the story strongly implies that "this someone is Jesus, the one whom God raised from the dead."

36. Hultgren, *The Parables of Jesus*, 114.

37. Malina and Rohrbaugh, *Social-Science Commentary on the Synoptic Gospels*, 295.

38. Cf. Johnson, *The Gospel of Luke*, 253.

Notes

39. Although this Matthean parable has no parallel in the canonical Gospels, there are rabbinic tales of later dates that show some similarities, e.g., Rabbi Zeira (325 CE), *Y. Ber.* 2:3c. See also Hultgren, *The Parables of Jesus*, 2–3.

40. See Snodgrass, *Stories with Intent*, 363.

41. Snodgrass, *Stories with Intent*, 362.

42. See also Luke 13:18–21; 6:47–49; 7:31–32.

43. Malina and Rohrbaugh, *Social-Science Commentary on the Synoptic Gospels*, 100–101.

44. Quintilian, *Inst.* 8.3.88; Philostratus, *Vit. Apoll.* 6.19.

45. Hultgren, *The Parables of Jesus*, 35–36.

46. See Gustaf Dalman, *Arbeit und Sitte in Palästina*, 7 vols. (Gütersloh: Verlag C. Bertlsmann et al., 1928–41), 1:43–44.

47. Daniel J. Harrington, *The Gospel of Matthew*, Sacra Pagina 1 (Collegeville, MN: Liturgical Press, 2007), 282–83.

48. The laborers' lives and livelihoods were less secure than those of servants/slaves since their employment was seasonal. Unemployment was a continual problem, and many servants/slaves had an easier life because their owners had a financial investment that required protection and adequate care. See Hultgren, *The Parables of Jesus*, 36; Snodgrass, *Stories with Intent*, 369.

49. Quintilian, *Inst.* 4.2123.

50. Snodgrass, *Stories with Intent*, 370. It was estimated that an adult in ancient Palestine needed about half a denarius a day to live.

51. Cf. Harrington, *The Gospel of Matthew*, 283.

52. Cf. Hultgren, *The Parables of Jesus*, 38.

53. Cf. Harrington, *The Gospel of Matthew*, 283.

54. Matthew uses the word *hetaire* also at 22:12 (where the king addresses the man without a wedding garment) and at 26:50 (where Jesus addresses Judas in Gethsemane). The term is not a positive one. Hultgren, *The Parables of Jesus*, 39.

55. Hultgren, *The Parables of Jesus*, 39.

56. Karen Lebacqz, in "Justice, Economics, and the Uncomfortable Kingdom: Reflection on Matthew 20:1–16," *The Annual of the Society of Christian Ethics* (1983): 33, notes that the issue in this parable is about generosity and not justice. It shows that God is primarily merciful, not just. On the other hand, Yung Suk Kim, in "Justice Matters, But Which Justice? In the Case of Jesus' Parables," *Currents in Theology and*

Mission 46, no. 3 (2019): 43, interprets the story in terms of economic justice or distributive justice for all.

57. Many scholars suggest that v. 16 does not belong to the parable proper. As Hultgren (*The Parables of Jesus*, 39–40) says, "It is a floating saying that shows up elsewhere as well, including the verse just prior to the parable (19:30), so the parable is framed by the saying (cf. Luke 13:30)."

58. William R. Herzog II, *The Parables as Subversive Speech: Jesus as Pedagogue of the Oppressed* (Louisville: Westminster/John Knox, 1994), 85–86.

59. Edward Sri, *The Art of Living: The Cardinal Virtues and the Freedom to Love* (San Francisco: Ignatius Press, 2021), 236.

60. Hultgren, *The Parables of Jesus*, 146–47.

61. Malina and Rohrbaugh, *Social-Science Commentary on the Synoptic Gospels*, 292; Hultgren, *The Parables of Jesus*, 148.

62. Luca Marulli, "'And How Much Do You Owe…? Take Your Bill, Sit Down Quickly, and Write…' (Luke 16:5–6)," *Tyndale Bulletin* 63, no. 2 (2012): 200. He adds: "Among the peasants we find tenant farmers and their slaves, day labourers and manumitted slaves who, despite their acquired status of freedman, were *de facto* socially doomed to work and be considered as slaves."

63. Hultgren, *The Parables of Jesus*, 148–49.

64. Hultgren, *The Parables of Jesus*, 149.

65. Hultgren, *The Parables of Jesus*, 150. See also, Philip Sellew, "Interior Monologue as a Narrative Device in the Parables of Jesus," *Journal of Biblical Literature* 111 (1992): 239–53.

66. For a study of this parable in the context of the perspective of Greco-Roman status, see Louis W. Ndekha, "'I Am Not Strong to Dig and I Am Afraid to Beg': Social Status and Status Concern in the Parable of the Dishonest Steward (Lk 16:1–9)," *Hervormde Teologiese Studies* 77, no. 4 (2021): 1–9. For a Latin American interpretation of this parable, see Daniel S. Steffen, "La Justicia del Mayordomo Injusto (Lucas 16:1–13)," *Kairós* 58–59 (2016): 135–55; also J. D. M. Derrett, "Fresh Light on St. Luke 16: The Parable of the Unjust Steward," *New Testament Studies* 7 (1960–1961): 198–219; John S. Verbin Kloppenborg, "The Dishonored Master (Luke 16, 1–8a)," *Biblica* 70, no. 4 (1989): 474–95.

67. Hultgren, *The Parables of Jesus*, 150.

68. Malina and Rohrbaugh, *Social-Science Commentary on the Synoptic Gospels*, 293.

Notes

69. Snodgrass, *Stories with Intent*, 406; Malina and Rohrbaugh, *Social-Science Commentary on the Synoptic Gospels*, 293.

70. Cf. Josephus, *War* 2.426–27.

71. As Malina and Rohrbaugh (*Social-Science Commentary on the Synoptic Gospels*, 349) point out, the main reason for indebtedness was the excessive demand placed on peasant resources. Evidence suggests that about 35 to 40 percent of the total agricultural production was often extracted in various taxes.

72. For an interesting study on the historical context of debt reductions, see Steffen, "La Justicia del Mayordomo Injusto," 143–48.

73. Marulli ("And How Much Do You Owe…?" 201) argues that Jesus uses the debt-remission practice as a symbol of socioreligious justice. Cf. C. S. A. Cheong, *A Dialogic Reading of The Steward Parable (Luke 16:1–9)*, Studies in Biblical Literature 28 (New York: Peter Lay, 2001), 148–49.

74. John K. Goodrich, "Voluntary Debt Remission and the Parable of the Unjust Steward (Luke 16:1–13)," *Journal of Biblical Literature* 131, no. 3 (2012): 553. He argues that the master's praise is better understood through the socioeconomic perspective lens. For the historical context of the story, see pages 559–63.

75. Malina and Rohrbaugh, *Social-Science Commentary on the Synoptic Gospels*, 293.

76. Marulli, "'And How Much Do You Owe…?'" 214.

77. Cf. Hultgren, *The Parables of Jesus*, 151.

78. Many scholars have devoted a good deal of ink to the analysis of the genitive *tēs adikias* in v. 8a and have argued whether it should be taken as a subjective or objective genitive. This is an important topic, though outside the scope of this book's purpose. See Joseph A. Fitzmyer, "The Story of the Dishonest Manager (Lk 16:1–13)," *Theological Studies* 25 (1964): 33; and David De Silva, "The Parable of the Prudent Steward and Its Lucan Context," *Criswell Theological Review* 6 (1993): 264–66.

79. Steffen, "La Justicia del Mayordomo Injusto (Lucas 16:1–13)," 138. My translation.

80. John Dominic Crossan, *In Parables: The Challenges of the Historical Jesus* (New York: Harper & Row, 1973), 110. Crossan notes that the cleverness of the steward consists not only in solving his problem but in solving it by means of the very reason (low profits) that has created it in the first place.

81. Cf. Malina and Rohrbaugh, *Social-Science Commentary on the Synoptic Gospels*, 293.

82. Sri, *The Art of Living*, 70.

83. For different interpretations, see Hultgren, *Parables of Jesus*, 152; Johnson, *The Gospel of Luke*, 245; and Richard Gutzwiller, *The Parables of the Lord* (New York: Herder and Herder, 1964), 86. Gutzwiller offers this interpretation: "The children of darkness are refined and cunning in the use of their means to achieve their aims and often enough do achieve their immoral goals through the cleverness of the procedure. So too the children of light must seek to obtain their moral goals with their moral means just as cleverly and just as zealously. It is therefore neither goal, nor way with way, nor means with means that is compared: rather *the point of comparison is the exertion which is made and should be made on both sides*" (italics in the original).

Chapter 4

1. E.g., Socrates, Plato, Aristotle, and Middle Platonists. On the ethics of Greek thinkers, see George Boys-Stones, *Platonist Philosophy 80 BC to AD 250: An Introduction and Collection of Sources in Tradition* (Cambridge: Cambridge University Press, 2018), 457–507; John M. Dillon, *The Middle Platonists, 80 B.C. to A.D. 220* (Ithaca, NY: Cornell University Press, 1996); A. A. Long and D. N. Sedley, *The Hellenistic Philosophers*, vol. 1: *Translations of the Principal Sources, with Philosophical Commentary* (Cambridge: Cambridge University Press, 2012 [1987]).

2. Plato, *Leg.* 770D–771A; Aristotle, *Eth. nic.* 2–10; 6.13.1145a6. See Nélida Naveros Córdova, *Philo of Alexandria's Ethical Discourse: Living in the Power of Piety* (Lanham, MD: Lexington Books/Fortress Academic, 2018), 157–62. On human happiness as the goal of life, see the excellent work of Julia Annas, *The Morality of Happiness* (New York: Oxford University Press, 1993).

3. Much ink has been spilled on this parable. For a recent survey, see John Carroll, "Sons, Hired Hands, and Slaves: Luke 15:11–32," *Perspectives in Religious Studies* 46, no. 2 (2019): 137–39; Ezra Horbury, "Aristotelian Ethics and Luke 15:11–32 in Early Modern England," *Journal of Religious History* 41, no. 2 (2017): 181–96. For a modern application of the parable, see Rohun Park, "Revisiting the Parable of the Prodigal Son for Decolonization: Luke's Reconfiguration of *Oikos* in

Notes

15:11–32," *Biblical Interpretation* 17 (2009): 506–20; Pat Bumgardner, "Luke 15:11–32," *Union Seminary Quarterly Review* 55, no. 3 (2001): 43–49; P. C. Enniss, "The Forgiving Child: Luke 15:11–32," *Journal for Preachers* 25, no. 2 (2003): 37–41; Greg W. Forbes, "Repentance and Conflict in the Parable of the Lost Son (Luke 15:11–32)," *Journal of the Evangelical Theological Society* 42, no. 2 (1999): 211–29; Charles E. Carlston, "Reminiscence and Redaction in Luke 15:11–32," *Journal of Biblical Literature* 94, no. 3 (1975): 368–90.

4. Bernard Brandon Scott, *Hear Then the Parable: A Commentary on the Parables of Jesus* (Minneapolis: Fortress, 1989), 100.

5. Arland J. Hultgren, *The Parables of Jesus: A Commentary* (Grand Rapids, MI: Eerdmans, 2000), 73.

6. Mary Ann Getty-Sullivan, *Parables of the Kingdom: Jesus and the Use of Parables in the Synoptic Tradition* (Collegeville, MN: Liturgical Press, 2007), 154. Biblical scholars argue whether the father, the younger son, or the elder son is the pivotal player in the story. For different views, see Scott, *Hear Then the Parable*, 105; C. H. Talbert, *Reading Luke* (New York: Crossroad, 1982), 275; R. Pesch, "Zur Exegese Gottes durch Jesus von Nazaret: Eine Auslegung des Gleichnisses vom Vater und den beiden Söhnen (Lk 15, 11–32)," in *Jesus: Ort der Erfahrung Gottes*, ed. B. Casper (Freiburg: Herder, 1976), 179–89; John R. Donahue, *The Gospel in Parable: Metaphor, Narrative and Theology in the Synoptic Gospels* (Philadelphia: Fortress, 1988), 152; Luke Timothy Johnson, *The Gospel of Luke*, ed. Daniel J. Harrington, Sacra Pagina 3 (Collegeville, MN: Liturgical Press, 1991), 240; K. E. Bailey, *Finding the Lost: Cultural Keys to Luke 15* (St. Louis: Concordia, 1992), 109–93.

7. The Greek term *ousia* (inheritance/property/wealth) appears only in this parable (Luke 15:11, 13; cf. Tob 14:13; 3 Macc 3:28). Diogenes Laertius (Lives 9.35) tells of three brothers who divide the *ousia* when one wishes to settle in a distant land. See Forbes, "Repentance and Conflict in the Parable of the Lost Son," 214. For further discussion, see Fritz Schultz, *Classical Roman Law* (Oxford: Clarendon Press, 1951), 203–333.

8. Forbes, "Repentance and Conflict in the Parable of the Lost Son," 215.

9. Hultgren, *The Parables of Jesus*, 73.

10. M. B. Bat. 8:4–5; m. Bek. 8:9.

11. This story is somewhat like the story in Diogenes Laertius (*Lives* 9.35–36), in which a younger son takes a smaller portion (money)

of the family's property (*ousia*) to finance his travels. Cf. Hultgren, *The Parables of Jesus*, 74–75.

12. The only New Testament occurrence of the phrase "a distant country" is in Luke 19:12. Cf. Carlston, "Reminiscence and Redaction in Luke 15:11–32," 370.

13. Forbes, "Repentance and Conflict in the Parable of the Lost Son," 216.

14. Luke uses a similar phrase in Luke 4:25 and Acts 11:28 (the We-source).

15. The other New Testament references of the word "citizen" appear in Luke 19:14 // Matt 25:18–19; Acts 21:39; and Heb 8:11 (Jer 38:34 LXX).

16. J. Albert Harrill, "The Indentured Labor of the Prodigal Son (15:15)," *Journal of Biblical Literature* 115 (1996): 714–17.

17. See also Isa 65:4; 66:17; 1 Macc 1:47; 2 Macc 6:18; 7:1.

18. Menachot 64b.

19. Hultgren, *The Parables of Jesus*, 75.

20. The use of the rhetorical monologue is a characteristically Lukan device. We will also see it in 16:1–8 (cf. 12:17). Carlston, "Reminiscence and Redaction in Luke 15:11–32," 371.

21. Hultgren, *The Parables of Jesus*, 75.

22. See also Dan 4:26; 1 Macc 3:18; Matt 21:25.

23. Demetrius, *Eloc.* 216.

24. Hultgren, *The Parables of Jesus*, 77.

25. The term "compassion" appears only in the Gospels (Mark 1:41; 6:34; 8:2; 9:22; Matt 9:36; 14:14; 15:32; 18:27; 20:34; Luke 7:13; 10:33; 15:20.

26. Hultgren, *The Parables of Jesus*, 78.

27. See Luke 15:7, 10, where the theme of repentance is also present with the same emphasis. Carlston ("Reminiscence and Redaction in Luke 15:11–32," 384–85) notes that Luke has a special interest in repentance and conversion, and for the evangelist, repentance is the moral emphasis of the story. See also Francis L. Filas, *The Parables of Jesus: A Popular Explanation* (New York: MacMillan, 1959), 68–72.

28. Forbes, "Repentance and Conflict in the Parable of the Lost Son," 219.

29. Hultgren, *The Parables of Jesus*, 79.

30. Hultgren, *The Parables of Jesus*, 80.

Notes

31. Forbes, "Repentance and Conflict in the Parable of the Lost Son," 215. See also, K. E. Bailey, *Poet and Peasant* (Grand Rapids, MI: Eerdmans, 1983), 161–66.

32. Hultgren, *The Parables of Jesus*, 80.

33. See also Luke 15:3–7, where the language of joy and rejoice are present as the lost sheep is found.

34. Johnson, *The Gospel of Luke*, 237.

35. Bruce J. Malina and Richard L. Rohrbaugh, *Social-Science Commentary on the Synoptic Gospels* (Minneapolis: Fortress, 2003), 290.

36. We know that this is a major theme in Luke's Gospel. On the theme of the kingdom of God in Luke 12:22–34, see Nélida Naveros Córdova, "Q [Luke] 12:27: The Lilies of the Field and the Kingdom of God," *Catholic Biblical Quarterly* 82, no. 1 (2020): 64–83.

37. Quintilian, *Inst.* 6.2.33–34.

38. As Forbes ("Repentance and Conflict in the Parable of the Lost Son," 221) notes, the verb "let us celebrate" (v. 23) points to a communal celebration, and the banquet serves as an opportunity to reconcile the younger son with the entire village.

39. Ruben Zimmermann, *Puzzling the Parables of Jesus: Methods and Interpretation* (Minneapolis: Fortress, 2015), 53, is right when he argues that poetic *mimesis* helps not only imitate biblical parable material but also dares to speak of God in a new way using the images of the world.

40. Cf. Forbes, "Repentance and Conflict in the Parable of the Lost Son," 217.

41. Some scholars argue that the younger son does not show remorse, just overwhelming hunger; others claim that the son is acting out of purely selfish motives and not true repentance. See Forbes, "Repentance and Conflict in the Parable of the Lost Son," 218.

42. For a survey on the language of "return" and its association with Old Testament motifs, see John Drury, *Tradition and Design in Luke's Gospel: A Study in Early Christian Historiography* (London: Darton, Longman & Todd, 1976), 143–47.

43. Cf. Johnson, *The Gospel of Luke*, 237.

44. Hultgren, *The Parables of Jesus*, 77.

45. Park ("Revisiting the Parable of the Prodigal Son for Decolonization," 516) argues that the elder son degraded his younger brother to the level of human waste for associating with prostitutes (v. 30).

46. Forbes, "Repentance and Conflict in the Parable of the Lost Son," 222.

47. Forbes, "Repentance and Conflict in the Parable of the Lost Son," 223. Similarly, along this line, Park ("Revisiting the Parable of the Prodigal Son for Decolonization," 515) points out that the elder son's action caused an affront to the *paterfamilias* of the household, as it was viewed in the public eye as a serious familial disorder.

48. Forbes, "Repentance and Conflict in the Parable of the Lost Son," 215.

49. Cf. Gerd Theissen, *The Shadow of the Galilean: The Quest of the Historical Jesus in Narrative Form* (Minneapolis: Fortress, 2007), 124–28.

50. For studies on this parable, see Julie R. Perry, "God as an Unjust Judge? A Sermon on Luke 18:1–8," *Review & Expositor* 109, no. 2 (2012): 297–301; Barbara E. Reid, "A Godly Widow Persistently Pursuing Justice: Luke 18:1–8," *Biblical Research* 45 (2000): 25–33.

51. Hultgren, *The Parables of Jesus*, 253.

52. Most scholars agree that v. 8a about the Son of Man finding faith when he comes is a secondary addition made by Luke to the preceding verses. For other interpretations, see Joseph A. Fitzmyer, *The Gospel According to Luke X—XXIV: A New Translation with Introduction and Commentary*, Anchor Bible 28A (New York: Doubleday, 1983), 1176.

53. William R. Herzog II, *The Parables as Subversive Speech: Jesus as Pedagogue of the Oppressed* (Louisville, KY: Westminster/John Knox, 1994), 216–18; cf. John Mark Hicks, "The Parable of the Persistent Widow (Luke 18:1–8)," *Restoration Quarterly* 33, no. 4 (1999): 214; Donald Penny, "Persistence in Prayer: Luke 18:1–8," *Review and Expositor* 104 (2007): 737–44. It is debated what Jesus tells his audience in this parable. Some focus on the widow, others on the judge, and some others on both. Whether this parable is about prayer or justice has also been argued. For various views, see Reid, "A Godly Widow Persistently Pursuing Justice," 25–26. Stephen Curkpatrick, in "Dissonance in Luke 18:1–8," *Journal of Biblical Literature* 121, no. 1 (2002): 108–10, argues that in Luke 18:1–8, there are two parables: a parable about a widow's quest for justice from a reluctant judge (vv. 2–5) and another about an allegory of prayer, perseverance, and vindication of the elect (vv. 1–8).

54. Cf. Rom 12:12; 1 Thess 5:17; Hultgren, *The Parables of Jesus*, 253. This parable (18:1–8) is a twin parable of Luke 11:5–8. It portrays

a person in need going to another for assistance; that person goes with one degree of impertinence, and the one being visited becomes annoyed but does provide assistance. There is a linguistic similarity between 18:5 and 11:7, and in each case the parable has the theme of prayer.

55. According to Chron 19:6–7, Jehoshaphat instructs judges to take care in what they do, because they are judging, not on behalf of human beings, but on behalf of God, who judges with them. He explicitly admonishes them to let the fear of God be upon them and reminds them to act carefully because with God there is no injustice, no partiality, and no bribery.

56. Reid, "A Godly Widow Persistently Pursuing Justice," 29.

57. Hultgren, *The Parables of Jesus*, 253.

58. Hultgren, *The Parables of Jesus*, 253.

59. Hultgren, *The Parables of Jesus*, 254.

60. Reid, "A Godly Widow Persistently Pursuing Justice," 29. Interestingly, her complaint is against the very man who should have been her provider.

61. Hultgren, *The Parables of Jesus*, 254–55.

62. Cf. Deut 16:11, 14; 24:19–21; 26:12–13.

63. Johnson, *The Gospel According to Luke*, 269.

64. Gerhard Lohfink, *The Forty Parables of Jesus*, trans. Linda M. Maloney (Collegeville, MN: Liturgical Press Academic, 2021), 96.

65. Henry George Liddell and Robert Scott, *A Greek-English Lexicon: With a Revised Supplement* (Oxford: Clarendon Press, 1996), 1904.

66. Reid, "A Godly Widow Persistently Pursuing Justice," 29.

67. Johnson, *The Gospel of Luke*, 273.

68. Hultgren, *The Parables of Jesus*, 255.

69. See Aristotle, *Eth. nic.* 2.6.1107a6–8; Aristotle, *Eth. eud.* 2.3–3.7.1234b12. For a study on Aristotle's ethics, see Anthony Kenny, *The Aristotelian Ethics: A Study of the Relationship between the Eudemian and Nicomachean Ethics of Aristotle* (Oxford: Clarendon Press, 1978), 160–89.

70. Martinus C. de Boer, "Ten Thousand Talents? Matthew's Interpretation and Redaction of the Unforgiving Servant (Matt 18:23–35)," *Catholic Biblical Quarterly* 50, no. 2 (1988): 214–32.

71. R. T. France, *The Gospel of Matthew*, New International Commentary on the New Testament (Grand Rapids, MI: Eerdmans, 2007), 703, 706.

72. According to John Dominic Crossan, *In Parables: The Challenges of the Historical Jesus* (New York: Harper & Row, 1973), 105, this parable is Matthew's advice to a divided community: if they do not forgive their brothers and sisters, God will withdraw His forgiveness from them.

73. Hultgren, *The Parables of Jesus*, 22–23.

74. Hultgren, *The Parables of Jesus*, 23.

75. Crossan, *In Parables*, 107.

76. Putting one's fellow servant in prison for debt was forbidden by Jewish law from biblical to Talmudic times, but it was a custom spread by Greco-Roman law in the first century CE. See Hultgren, *The Parables of Jesus*, 27.

77. Plato, *Euthyphr.* 11E; 12A–D. See also Plato, *Apol.* 28B–29B, 35C–D.

78. Carlston, "Reminiscence and Redaction in Luke 15:11–32," 385.

79. Herzog, *Parables as Subversive Speech*, 216; Fitzmyer, *The Gospel According to Luke X—XXIV*, 1177.

80. Edward Sri, in *The Art of Living: The Cardinal Virtues and the Freedom to Love* (San Francisco: Ignatius Press, 2021), 65, catalogs them as "subvirtues" for each cardinal virtue.

Chapter 5

1. Edward Sri, *The Art of Living: The Cardinal Virtues and the Freedom to Love* (San Francisco: Ignatius Press, 2021), 64.

2. Cf. David K. Bryan, "Transformation of the Mustard Seed and Leaven in the Gospel of Luke," *Novum Testamentum* 58 (2016): 126.

3. Pheme Perkins, *Hearing the Parables of Jesus* (New York: Paulist Press, 1981), 4–5.

Glossary

allēgoria (allegory): mode of figurative speech in which a metaphor is sustained throughout a discourse, often to express a secret meaning.

auxēsis (amplification): used to set the facts before the eyes, expanding on a subject by means of repetition, enumeration, elaboration, etc. It often operates through sense perception to achieve vividness.

diēgēsis/narration (narrative): language descriptive of or exposition about things that have happened or as though they have happened. Narrative has six elements: person, action, place, time, manner, and cause.

dilogia/anaphora (repetition): a device that gives the effect of vividness and increases the emotional impact. It occurs when a word is repeated successively.

ekphrasis (descriptive speech): one of the exercises of the *progymnasmata* and a speech that brings the subject being described vividly before the eyes of the audience, or a vividly detailed account of a person, place, object, or experience that aims to bring the subject before the eyes of an audience.

enargeia/demonstratio (vividness): a generic term for visually powerful, vivid description that has the quality of bringing the subject before the eyes, or a technique by which an orator creates the illusion of sight through the use of a concrete, detailed description of a situation or action as though it were present.

huperbolē (hyperbole): an exaggerated or extravagant statement, used to express strong feeling or produce a strong impression, and not intended to be understood literally.

lexis/elocutio (style): rhetorical technique that serves and enhances vividness but requires clarity.

mimesis (imitation): a form of representation used to describe what an artist or poet does in creating his work by which the images of absent things are presented to the mind in such a way that they can be physically seen with the eyes.

parabolē (parable): a comparison, a simile, as in poetry or poetic prose, taken from a present or imagined object or event.

phantasia (imagination): a rhetorical weapon to get around the censor of the intellect and persuade the audience to adopt the speaker's point of view; in its most extreme and provocative expression to enslave the audience through an emotionally evocative and compelling visual representation of mental images that makes the listener into a participant or spectator of the scene described.

pithanotēs (verisimilitude): believability provided by a rhetor to help the audience imagine the scene described in order to experience vividness; the credibility of a narrative, making it persuasive and readily imaginable.

progymnasmata (preliminary exercises): the title of a series of rhetorical exercises that introduced students to the study of rhetoric. It is also the sequence of fourteen preliminary exercises of prose and composition at the core of Hellenistic and Roman rhetorical training.

rhētorikē (rhetoric): art of speaking or the art of effective expression, argument, and persuasion in speech, writing, and other media.

saphēneia (clarity): a characteristic of descriptive speech to enhance vividness that makes one almost see what is being spoken about. Clarity and style are intimately connected; together they are necessary for the hearer to imagine or see in the mind's eye something described.

similitude/comparatio (simile): an explicit comparison between the speaker's subject and a fact of natural life or of general human experience, introduced by "like" or "as."

suntomia (conciseness): ability of a narrative to maintain a focused point of view.

synkrisis (comparison): arguments by comparison of two entities of the same order to persuade the audience.

Bibliography

Primary Sources

Aelius Theon. *Progymnasmata*. Paris: Les Belles Lettres, 1997.
Aphthonii Sophistae Progymnasmata. Caen: Cavelier, 1666.
Aristotle. *The Complete Works of Aristotle: Revised Oxford Translation*. Edited by Jonathan Barnes. Bollingen Series 74. 2 vols. Princeton, NJ: Princeton University Press, 1995.
Aristotle, Longinus, Demetrius. *Poetics. Longinus: On the Sublime. Demetrius: On Style*. Translated by Stephen Halliwell, W. Hamilton Fyfe, Doreen C. Innes, W. Rhys Roberts. Revised by Donald A. Russell. Loeb Classical Library 199. Cambridge, MA: Harvard University Press, 1995.
Cicero. *On Invention. The Best Kind of Orator. Topics*. Translated by H. M. Hubbell. Loeb Classical Library 386. Cambridge, MA: Harvard University Press, 1949.
———. *On the Orator*: Book 3. *On Fate. Stoic Paradoxes. Divisions of Oratory*. Translated by H. Rackham. Loeb Classical Library 349. Cambridge, MA: Harvard University Press, 1942.
———. *The Verrine Orations*. Vol 2: *Against Verres*, Part 2, Books 3–5. Translated by L. H. G. Greenwood. Loeb Classical Library 293. Cambridge, MA: Harvard University Press, 1935.
Hermogenes. *Progymnasmata*. In *Progymnasmata: Greek Textbooks of Prose Composition and Rhetoric*, 73–86. Translated by George A. Kennedy. Leiden: Brill, 2003.
Josephus. *The Works of Josephus: Complete and Unabridged*. New Updated Edition. Translated by William Whiston, A. M. Peabody: Hendrickson Publishers, 2016.

Juvenal and Persius. Translated by G. G. Ramsay. Loeb Classical Library 91. Cambridge, MA: Harvard University Press, 1961.

Lucian. Vol. 3. Translated by A. H. Harmon. Loeb Classical Library 130. Cambridge, MA: Harvard University Press, 1921.

Nicolaus Sophista. *Nicolai Progymnasmata.* Edited by Josephus Felten. Rhetores Graeci XI. Leipzig: B. G. Teubner, 1913.

Petronius. Translation by Michael Heseltine. Loeb Classical Library 15. Cambridge, MA: Harvard University Press, 1930.

Philo. Volume 7. Edited by Jeffrey Henderson. Translated by F. H. Colson. Loeb Classical Library 320. Cambridge, MA: Harvard University Press, 2006.

Philo. Volume 10. Translated by F. H. Colson. Loeb Classical Library 379. Cambridge, MA: Harvard University Press, 1991.

Philostratus. Apollonius of Tyana. Vol. 1: *Life of Apollonius of Tyana, Books 1–4.* Edited and translated by Christopher P. Jones. Loeb Classical Library 16. Cambridge, MA: Harvard University Press, 2005.

Plato. *The Collected Dialogues of Plato with Introduction and Prefatory Notes.* Edited by Edith Hamilton and Huntington Cairns. Bollingen Series 71. Princeton, NJ: Princeton University Press, 1989.

Plutarch. *Lives.* Vol. 11: *Aaratus. Artaxerxes. Galba. Otho. General Index.* Translated by Bernadotte Perrin. Loeb Classical Library 103. Cambridge, MA: Harvard University Press, 1926.

———. *Moralia.* Translated by Frank Cole Babbitt et al. 16 vols. Loeb Classical Library. Cambridge: Harvard University Press, 1927–1976.

Quintilian. *Institutio oratoria.* Vols. 2–3. Translated by H. E. Butler. Loeb Classical Library 125 and 126. Cambridge, MA: Harvard University Press, 1959.

———. *The Orator's Education.* Vol. 4: Books 9–10. Edited and translated by Donald A. Russell. Loeb Classical Library 127. Cambridge, MA: Harvard University Press, 2002.

Secondary Sources

Annas, Julia. *The Morality of Happiness.* New York: Oxford University Press, 1993.

Bailey, K. E. *Finding the Lost: Cultural Keys to Luke 15.* St. Louis: Concordia, 1992.

Bibliography

———. *Poet and Peasant.* Grand Rapids, MI: Eerdmans, 1983.

Black, C. Clifton. "Mark as Historian of God's Kingdom." *Catholic Biblical Quarterly* 71 (2009): 64–83.

Boys-Stones, George. *Platonist Philosophy 80 BC to AD 250: An Introduction and Collection of Sources in Tradition.* Cambridge: Cambridge University Press, 2018.

Braun, Adam F. "Reframing the Parable of the Pounds in Lukan Narrative and Economic Context: Luke 19:11-28." *Currents in Theology and Mission* 39, no. 6 (2012): 442–48.

Brower, Kent. "Mark 9:1: Seeing the Kingdom in Power." *Journal for the Study of the New Testament* 6 (1980): 17–41.

Brown, Schuyler. "'The Secret of the Kingdom of God' (Mark 4:11)." *Journal of Biblical Literature* 92 (1973): 60–74.

Bryan, David K. "Transformation of the Mustard Seed and Leaven in the Gospel of Luke." *Novum Testamentum* 58 (2016): 115–34.

Bumgardner, Pat. "Luke 15:11-32." *Union Seminary Quarterly Review* 55, no. 3 (2001): 43–49.

Cadoux, A. T. *The Parables of Jesus: Their Art and Use.* New York: Macmillan, 1931.

Carlston, Charles E. "Reminiscence and Redaction in Luke 15:11-32." *Journal of Biblical Literature* 94, no. 3 (1975): 368–90.

Carroll, John. "Sons, Hired Hands, and Slaves: Luke 15:11-32." *Perspectives in Religious Studies* 46, no. 2 (2019): 137–39.

Carter, Rich. "Buried under Excellent Soil: Matthew 25:14-30." *Lutheran Mission Matters* 27, no. 1 (2019): 147–55.

Carter, Warren, and John Paul Heil. *Matthew's Parables: Audience-Oriented Perspectives.* CBQMS 30. Washington, DC: Catholic Biblical Association of America, 1998.

Cheong, C. S. A. *A Dialogic Reading of* The Steward *Parable (Luke 16:1-9).* Studies in Biblical Literature 28. New York: Peter Lay, 2001.

Clüver, Claus. "Quotation, Enargeia, and the Functions of Ekphrasis." In *Pictures into Words*, edited by Valerie Robillard and Els Jongeneel, 35–52. Amsterdam: VU University Press, 1998,

Cohen, Shaye J. D., Robert Goldenberg, and Hayim Lapin, eds. *The Oxford Annotated Mishnah*, 3 vols. Oxford: Oxford University Press, 2022.

Crossan, John Dominic. "Aphorism in Discourse and Narrative." *Semeia* 43 (1988): 121–40.

———. *In Parables: The Challenges of the Historical Jesus*. New York: Harper & Row, 1973.

Curkpatrick, Stephen. "Dissonance in Luke 18:1–8." *Journal of Biblical Literature* 121, no. 1 (2002): 107–21.

Curzer, Howard J. *Aristotle and the Virtues*. Oxford: Oxford University Press, 2012.

Dalman, Gustaf. *Arbeit und Sitte in Palästina*. 7 vols. Gütersloh, Germany: Verlag C. Bertlsmann et al., 1928–41.

De Boer, Martinus C. "Ten Thousand Talents? Matthew's Interpretation and Redaction of the Unforgiving Servant (Matt 18:23–35)." *Catholic Biblical Quarterly* 50, no. 2 (1988): 214–32.

Derrett, J. D. M. "Fresh Light on St. Luke 16: The Parable of the Unjust Steward." *New Testament Studies* 7 (1960–1961): 198–219.

De Silva, David. "The Parable of the Prudent Steward and Its Lucan Context." *Criswell Theological Review* 6 (1993): 255–68.

Devettere, Raymond J. *Introduction to Virtue Ethics: Insights of the Ancient Greeks*. Washington, DC: Georgetown University Press, 2002.

Dillon, John M. *The Middle Platonists: 80 B.C. to A.D. 220*. Ithaca, NY: Cornell University Press, 1996.

Dodd, C. H. *The Parables of the Kingdom*. Rev. ed. New York: Charles Scribner's Sons, 1961.

Donahue, John R. *The Gospel in Parable: Metaphor, Narrative and Theology in the Synoptic Gospels*. Philadelphia: Fortress, 1988.

Donahue, John R., and Daniel J. Harrington. *The Gospel of Mark*. Edited by Daniel J. Harrington. Sacra Pagina 2. Collegeville, MN: Liturgical Press, 2002.

Doran, Robert. "The Parable of the Talents/Pounds: Apocalyptic Warning or Economic Critique?" *Biblica* 100, no. 4 (2019): 527–42.

Dowling, Elizabeth. "Hearing the Voice of Earth in the Lukan Parable of the Pounds." *Colloquium* 48, no. 1 (2016): 35–46.

Drury, John. *The Parables in the Gospels: History and Allegory*. New York: Crossroad, 1985.

———. *Tradition and Design in Luke's Gospel: A Study in Early Christian Historiography*. London: Darton, Longman & Todd, 1976.

Enniss, P. C. "The Forgiving Child: Luke 15:11–32." *Journal for Preachers* 25, no. 2 (2003): 37–41.

Filas, Francis L. *The Parables of Jesus: A Popular Explanation*. New York: MacMillan, 1959.

Bibliography

Fitzmyer, Joseph A. *The Gospel According to Luke X—XXIV: A New Translation with Introduction and Commentary.* Anchor Bible 28A. New York: Doubleday, 1983.

———. "The Story of the Dishonest Manager (Lk 16:1–13)." *Theological Studies* 25 (1964): 23–42.

Forbes, Greg W. *The God of Old: The Role of the Lukan Parables in the Purpose of Luke's Gospel.* Sheffield: Sheffield Academic Press, 2000.

———. "Repentance and Conflict in the Parable of the Lost Son (Luke 15:11–32)." *Journal of the Evangelical Theological Society* 42, no. 2 (1999): 211–29.

Ford, Richard Q. *The Parables of Jesus: Recovering the Art of Listening.* Minneapolis: Fortress, 1997.

France, R. T. *The Gospel of Matthew.* The New International Commentary on the New Testament. Grand Rapids, MI: Eerdmans, 2007.

Funk, Robert W. *Language, Hermeneutic, and Word of God: The Problem of Language in the New Testament and Contemporary Theology.* New York: Harper & Row, 1966.

———. "The Looking-Glass Tree Is for the Birds: Ezekiel 17:22–24; Mark 4:30–32." *Interpretation* 27, no. 1 (1973): 3–9.

———. "The Parable as Metaphor." In *Language, Hermeneutic, and Word of God: The Problem of Language in the New Testament and Contemporary Theology,* 133–62. New York: Harper & Row, 1966.

———. *Parables and Presence: Forms of the New Testament Tradition.* Philadelphia: Fortress, 1982.

Garnsey, Peter. *Famine and Food Supply in the Graeco-Roman World.* Cambridge: Cambridge University Press, 1988.

Gavigan, James, and Brian McCarthy. The Navarre Bible: Saint Matthew's Gospel. Dublin: Four Courts Press, 1993.

Getty-Sullivan, Mary Ann. *Parables of the Kingdom: Jesus and the Use of Parables in the Synoptic Tradition.* Collegeville, MN: Liturgical Press, 2007.

Goodrich, John K. "Voluntary Debt Remission and the Parable of the Unjust Steward (Luke 16:1–13)." *Journal of Biblical Literature* 131, no. 3 (2012): 547–66.

Gowler, David B. "'At His Gate Lay a Poor Man': A Dialogic Reading of Luke 16:19–31." *Perspectives in Religious Studies* 32 (2005): 260–62.

———. *What Are They Saying About the Parables?* Mahwah, NJ: Paulist Press, 2000.

Gutzwiller, Richard. *The Parables of the Lord*. New York: Herder and Herder, 1964.
Harrill, J. Albert. "The Indentured Labor of the Prodigal Son (15:15)." *Journal of Biblical Literature* 115 (1996): 714–17.
Harrington, Daniel J. *The Gospel of Matthew*. Sacra Pagina 1. Collegeville, MN: Liturgical Press, 2007.
Hatcher, Karen M. "In Gold We Trust: The Parable of the Rich Man and Lazarus (Luke 16:19–31)." *Review & Expositor* 109, no. 2 (2012): 277–83.
Hedrick, Charles W. *Many Things in Parables: Jesus and His Modern Critics*. Louisville, KY: Westminster John Knox, 2004.
Hendrickx, Herman. *The Parables of Jesus: Studies in the Synoptic Gospels*. San Francisco: Harper & Row, 1983.
Henning, Meghan. *Educating Early Christians through the Rhetoric of Hell: "Weeping and Gnashing of Teeth" as* Paideaia *in Matthew and the Early Church*. WUNT 2. Reihe 382. Tübingen: Mohr Siebeck, 2014.
Herzog II, William R., *The Parables as Subversive Speech: Jesus as Pedagogue of the Oppressed*. Louisville, KY: Westminster John Knox, 1994.
Hicks, John Mark. "The Parable of the Persistent Widow (Luke 18:1–8)." *Restoration Quarterly* 33, no. 4 (1999): 209–23.
Horbury, Ezra. "Aristotelian Ethics and Luke 15:11–32 in Early Modern England." *Journal of Religious History* 41, no. 2 (2017): 181–96.
Hultgren, Arland J. *The Parables of Jesus: A Commentary*. Grand Rapids, MI: Eerdmans, 2000.
Jensen, M. H. *Herod Antipas in Galilee*. WUNT 2. Reihe 215. Tübingen: Mohr Siebeck, 2006.
Jeremias, Joachim. *Die Gleichnisse Jesu*. Göttingen: Vandnhoeck & Ruprecht, 1952.
———. *The Parables of Jesus*. 2nd rev. ed. Upper Saddle River, NJ: Prentice Hall, 1972.
Johnson, Luke Timothy. *The Gospel of Luke*. Edited by Daniel J. Harrington. Sacra Pagina 3. Collegeville, MN: Liturgical Press, 1991.
Jülicher, Adolf. *Die Gleichnisreden Jesu*. 2 vols. 1899. Reprint Darmstadt: Wissenschftliche Buchgesellschaft, 1963.
Kennedy, George A. *Classical Rhetoric: Its Christian and Secular Tradition from Ancient to Modern Times*. 2nd ed. Chapel Hill: University of North Carolina Press, 1999.

Bibliography

———. *Progymnasmata: Greek Textbooks of Prose and Rhetoric.* Leiden: Brill, 2003.

Kenny, Anthony. *The Aristotelian Ethics: A Study of the Relationship between the Eudemian and Nicomachean Ethics of Aristotle.* Oxford: Clarendon Press, 1978.

Kim, Yung Suk. "Justice Matters, But Which Justice? In the Case of Jesus' Parables." *Currents in Theology and Mission* 46, no. 3 (2019): 41–43.

Kingsbury, Jack D. "The Parables of Jesus in Current Research." *Dialog* 11 (1972): 101–7.

Kloppenborg Verbin, John S. "The Dishonored Master (Luke 16, 1–8a)." *Biblica* 70, no. 4 (1989): 474–95.

———. *Excavating Q: The History and Setting of the Sayings Gospel.* Edinburgh: T & T Clark, 2000.

Kuan-Hui Wang, Sunny. *Sense Perception and Testimony in the Gospel According to John.* WUNT 2. Reihe 435. Tübingen: Mohr Siebeck, 2017.

Lebacqz, Karen. "Justice, Economics, and the Uncomfortable Kingdom: Reflection on Matthew 20:1–16." *The Annual of the Society of Christian Ethics* (1983): 27–53.

Levine, Amy-Jill. *Short Stories by Jesus: The Enigmatic Parables of a Controversial Rabbi.* New York: HarperOne, 2004.

Liddell, Henry George, and Robert Scott. *A Greek-English Lexicon: With a Revised Supplement.* Oxford: Clarendon Press, 1996.

Lindars, Barnabas. "Two Parables in John." *New Testament Studies* 16, no. 4 (1970): 318–29.

Lischer, Richard. *Reading the Parables.* Interpretation: Resources for the Use of Scripture in the Church. Louisville, KY: Westminster John Knox, 2014.

Lohfink, Gerhard. *Die vierzig Gleichnisse Jesu.* Verlag Herder GmbH: Freiburg im Breisgau, 2020.

———. *The Forty Parables of Jesus.* Translated by Linda M. Maloney. Collegeville, MN: Liturgical Press Academic, 2021.

———. *Las Cuarenta Parábolas de Jesús.* Translated by Robert H. Bernet. Estella, Navarra: Verbo Divino, 2022.

Long, A. A., and D. N. Sedley. *The Hellenistic Philosophers.* Vol. 1, *Translations of the Principal Sources, with Philosophical Commentary.* Cambridge: Cambridge University Press, 2012 [1987].

Malina, Bruce J., and Richard L. Rohrbaugh. *Social-Science Commentary on the Synoptic Gospels*. Minneapolis: Fortress, 2003.

Mann, C. S. *Mark: A New Translation with Introduction and Commentary*. Garden City, NY: Doubleday, 1986.

Marulli, Luca. "'And How Much Do You Owe…? Take Your Bill, Sit Down Quickly, and Write…' (Luke 16:5–6)." *Tyndale Bulletin* 63, no. 2 (2012): 199–216.

Mays, James L., ed. *Harper's Bible Commentary*. San Francisco: Harper & Row, 1988.

McWhirter, Jocelyn. "Between Text and Sermon: Luke 16:19–31." *Interpretation: A Journal of Bible and Theology* 69, no. 4 (2015): 463–65.

Mescher, Marcus. *The Ethics of Encounter: Christian Neighbor Love as a Practice of Solidarity*. Maryknoll, NY: Orbis, 2020.

Metzger, Bruce M. *Exhaustive Concordance: Complete and Unabridged*. Nashville, TN: Thomas Nelson, 1991.

Miller, Robert J., ed. *The Complete Gospels: Annotated Scholars Version*. Santa Rosa, CA: Polebridge Press, 1994.

Naveros Córdova, Nélida. *Living in the Spirit: Paul and the Spirit of God*. Lanham, MD: Lexington Books/Fortress Academic, 2018.

———. *Philo of Alexandria's Ethical Discourse: Living in the Power of Piety*. Lanham, MD: Lexington Books/Fortress Academic, 2018.

———. "Q [Luke] 12:27: The Lilies of the Field and the Kingdom of God." *Catholic Biblical Quarterly* 82, no. 1 (2020): 64–83.

Ndekha, Louis W. "'I Am Not Strong to Dig and I Am Afraid to Beg': Social Status and Status Concern in the Parable of the Dishonest Steward (Lk 16:1–9)." *Hervormde Teologiese Studies* 77, no. 4 (2021): 1–9.

Neumann, Nils. *Hören und Sehen: Die Rhetorik der Anschaulichkeit in den Gottesthron-Szenen der Johannesoffenbarung*. Leipzig: Evangelische Verlagsanstalt, 2015.

Oder, Danila. *The Two Gospels of Mark: Performance and Text*. Rozzano, Milan: Domus, 2019.

O'Kane, Martin. "'The Bosom of Abraham' (Luke 16:22): Father Abraham in the Visual Imagination." *Biblical Interpretation* 15 (2007): 485–518.

Park, Rohun. "Revisiting the Parable of the Prodigal Son for Decolonization: Luke's Reconfiguration of *Oikos* in 15:11–32." *Biblical Interpretation* 17 (2009): 506–20.

Bibliography

Parsons, Mikeal C., and Michael Wade Martin. *Ancient Rhetoric and the New Testament: The Influence of Elementary Greek Composition.* Waco, TX: Baylor University Press, 2018.

Penny, Donald. "Persistence in Prayer: Luke 18:1–8." *Review and Expositor* 104 (2007): 737–44.

Perkins, Pheme. *Hearing the Parables of Jesus.* New York: Paulist Press, 1981.

Perrin, Norman. *Jesus and the Language of the Kingdom: Symbol and Metaphor in New Testament Interpretation.* Philadelphia: Fortress, 1976.

Perry, Julie R. "God as an Unjust Judge? A Sermon on Luke 18:1–8." *Review & Expositor* 109, no. 2 (2012): 297–301.

Pesch, R. "Zur Exegese Gottes durch Jesus von Nazaret: Eine Auslegung des Gleichnisses vom Vater und den beiden Söhnen (Lk 15, 11–32)." In *Jesus: Ort der Erfahrung Gottes,* edited by B. Casper, 179–89. Freiburg: Herder, 1976.

Porter, Phillip. "The Parable of the Talents (Matt 25:14–30): Preparing Jesus' Disciples to Lead the Worldwide Expansion of the Mission of Jesus." *Novum Testamentum* 63, no. 3 (2021): 159–76.

Powell, Mark Allan. *Fortress Introduction to the Gospels.* Minneapolis: Fortress, 1998.

Rabens, Volker. *The Holy Spirit and Ethics in Paul: Transformation and Empowering for Religious-Ethical Life.* WUNT 2. Reihe 283. 2nd ed. Tübingen: Mohr Siebeck, 2013.

Reed, Jonathan L. *Archaeology and the Galilean Jesus: A Re-examination of the Evidence.* Harrisburg, PA: Trinity Press International, 2000.

Reid, Barbara E. "A Godly Widow Persistently Pursuing Justice: Luke 18:1–8." *Biblical Research* 45 (2000): 25–33.

Ricœur, Paul. *Die Lebendige Metapher: Mit einem Vorwort zur deutschen Ausgabe.* Übergänge 12. 3rd ed. Munich: Fink, 2004.

Robinson, James M., Paul Hoffmann, and John S. Kloppenborg Verbin, eds. *The Critical Edition of Q: Synopsis Including the Gospel of Matthew and Luke, Mark, and Thomas with English, German, and French Translations of Q and Thomas.* Minneapolis: Fortress, 2000.

Schellenberg, Ryan S. "Which Master? Whose Steward? Metalepsis and Lordship in the Parable of the Prudent Steward (Lk. 16.1–13)." *Journal for the Study of the New Testament* 30 (2008): 263–88.

Schneemelcher, Wilhelm. *New Testament Apocrypha*. Vol. 1, *Gospels and Related Writings*. Rev. ed. Translated by R. McL. Wilson. Louisville, KY: Westminster John Knox, 1990.

Scholz, Bernhard F. *Sub Oculos Subiectio*': Quintilian on *Ekphrasis and Enargeia*. In *Pictures into Words*, edited by Valerie Robillard and Els Jongeneel, 73–99. Amsterdam: VU University Press, 1998.

Schottroff, Luise. *Die Gleichnisse Jesu*. 2nd ed. Gütersloh: Gütersloher verlagshaus, 2007.

———. *The Parables of Jesus*. Translated by L. M. Maloney. Minneapolis: Augsburg Fortress, 2006.

Schultz, Fritz. *Classical Roman Law*. Oxford: Clarendon Press, 1951.

Scott, Bernard Brandon. *Hear Then the Parable: A Commentary on the Parables of Jesus*. Minneapolis: Fortress, 1989.

Selby, Gary S. *Not with Wisdom of Words: Nonrational Persuasion in the New Testament*. Grand Rapids, MI: Eerdmans, 2016.

Sellew, Philip. "Interior Monologue as a Narrative Device in the Parables of Jesus." *Journal of Biblical Literature* 111 (1992): 239–53.

Snodgrass, Klyne R. *Stories with Intent: A Comprehensive Guide to the Parables of Jesus*. Grand Rapids, MI: Eerdmans, 2008.

Spitaler, Peter. "Welcoming a Child as a Metaphor for Welcoming God's Kingdom: A Close Reading of Mark 10.13–16." *Journal for the Study of the New Testament* 31, no. 4 (2009): 423–46.

Sri, Edward. *The Art of Living: The Cardinal Virtues and the Freedom to Love*. San Francisco: Ignatius Press, 2021.

Steffen, Daniel S. "La Justicia del Mayordomo Injusto (Lucas 16:1–13)." *Kairós* 58–59 (2016): 135–55.

Stern, David. "Jesus' Parables from the Perspective of Rabbinic Literature: The Example of the Wicked Husbandmen." In *Parable and Story in Judaism and Christianity*, edited by Clemens Thoma and Michael Wyschogrod, 42–80. Studies in Judaism and Christianity. Mahwah, NJ: Paulist Press, 1989.

Szesnat, Holger. "Bible Study on Economic Justice: Luke 19:11–28." *Pacific Journal of Theology* 56 (2016): 19–29.

Talbert, C. H. *Reading Luke*. New York: Crossroad, 1982.

Theissen, Gerd. *The Shadow of the Galilean: The Quest of the Historical Jesus in Narrative Form*. Minneapolis: Fortress, 2007.

Thiessen, Henry Clarence. "The Parable of the Nobleman and the Earthly Kingdom." *Bibliotheca Sacra* 91 (1934): 180–90.

Bibliography

Thoma, Clemens, and Michael Wyschogrod, eds. *Parable and Story in Judaism and Christianity.* Studies in Judaism and Christianity. Mahwah, NJ: Paulist Press, 1989.

Tobin, Thomas H. *The Creation of Man: Philo and the History of Interpretation.* Catholic Biblical Quarterly Monograph Series 14. Washington, DC: Catholic Biblical Association of America, 1983.

Tönsing, Gertrud. "Scolding the 'Wicked, Lazy' Servant; Is the Master God? A Redaction-Critical Study of Matthew 25:14–30 and Luke 19:11–27." *Neotestamentica* 53, no. 1 (2019): 123–47.

Via, Dan. *The Parables: Their Literary and Existential Dimension.* Philadelphia: Fortress, 1967.

Webb, Ruth. *Ekphrasis, Imagination and Persuasion in Ancient Rhetorical Theory and Practice.* Burlington, VT: Ashgate, 2009.

———. "The *Progymnasmata* as Practice." In *Education in Greek and Roman Antiquity*, edited by Yun Lee Too, 289–316. Leiden: Brill, 2001.

Whitaker, Robyn J. *Ekphrasis, Vision, and Persuasion in the Book of Revelation.* WUNT 2. Reihe 410. Tübingen: Mohr Siebeck, 2015.

Young, Brad H. *Jesus and His Jewish Parables: Rediscovering the Roots of Jesus' Teaching.* Mahwah, NJ: Paulist Press, 1989.

Zerwick, Max, and Mary Grosvenor. *A Grammatical Analysis of the Greek New Testament: Unabridged Revised Edition in One Volume.* Rome: Biblical Institute Press, 1981.

Zimmermann, Ruben. *Kompendium der Gleichnisse Jesu.* Gütersloh: Gütersloher Verlagshaus, 2007.

———. *Puzzling the Parables of Jesus: Methods and Interpretation.* Minneapolis: Fortress, 2015.

Milton Keynes UK
Ingram Content Group UK Ltd.
UKHW021049021124
450589UK00013B/1093